DATE DUE

		WITHDRAWN FROM B'ham-Sou. College Lib.	
		WITHDRAWN FROM B'ham-Sou. College Lib.	
			Printed in USA

In the Web of Politics

In the Web of Politics

Three Decades of the U.S. Federal Executive

JOEL D. ABERBACH
BERT A. ROCKMAN

BROOKINGS INSTITUTION PRESS
Washington, D.C.

Copyright © 2000
THE BROOKINGS INSTITUTION
1775 Massachusetts Avenue, N.W.
Washington, D.C. 20036
www.brookings.edu

Library of Congress Cataloging-in-Publication Data
Aberbach, Joel D.
  In the web of politics : three decades of the U.S. federal executive /
Joel D. Aberbach and Bert A. Rockman.
    p. cm.
Includes bibliographical references and index.
  ISBN 0-8157-0061-X (alk. paper)—ISBN 0-8157-0062-8 (pbk. : alk. paper)
  1. Government executives—United States.   2. Bureaucracy—United
States.   3. Administrative agencies—United States—Management.
4. United States—Politics and government.   I. Title: Three decades of the
U.S. Federal Executive.   II. Title: Three decades of the United States
Federal Executive.   III. Rockman, Bert A.   IV. Title.
  JK723.E9 A6 2000   99-050508
  352.3'0973—dc21   CIP

9 8 7 6 5 4 3 2 1

Typeset in Minion

Composition by R. Lynn Rivenbark
Macon, Georgia

Printed by R. R. Donnelley and Sons
Harrisonburg, Virginia

To Joan, Ian, Amy, Matthew, and Rachel

J. D. A.

To Susan and Robin

B. A. R.

Foreword

AS THE U.S. FEDERAL government has grown and become a more important presence in people's lives, those who administer its major programs have become increasingly controversial. The federal bureaucracy, particularly its top career executives, has been widely criticized—even vilified—especially when agencies enforce unpopular laws. Because of the stakes involved, presidents have scrambled to gain control of the bureaucracy. These attempts have altered the face of government: Richard Nixon's "responsiveness program" ultimately contributed to significant changes in federal personnel policies. Most important, though, such efforts have led to charges that the bureaucracy is being politicized, with consequent ill effects on the quality and morale of the senior career service.

Joel D. Aberbach and Bert A. Rockman examine the controversy surrounding the federal bureaucracy for the past three decades. The authors draw on interviews that they conducted with top political executives and career civil servants in 1970, 1986–88, and 1991–92, as well as on documentary and other evidence to analyze three themes that have dominated much of the public debate about administration in the United States. They ask whether there has in fact been a decline in quality and morale among federal executives. They examine bureaucratic responsiveness to political authority, focusing on the effectiveness of efforts to increase political control of the bureaucracy during this period. And they analyze the recent movement to "reinvent" American government, examining its prospects and problems and its underlying political significance.

Surprisingly, the authors find that the quality and the morale of top federal executives have held up remarkably well in the face of intense criticism. They also find that the bureaucracy has changed substantially over time in response to changes in presidential administration, indicating that the federal executive is much more politically responsive than many critics believe. Finally, the authors conclude that many of the bureaucratic problems that the reinvention movement claims to be able to solve by administrative means are in fact functions of decisions made by political leaders.

Without downplaying the many problems that exist in American public administration, Aberbach and Rockman argue that much of the debate about government administration has less to do with the bureaucracy per se than with the role of government and its policies. Top federal executives, and the bureaucracy more widely, are caught in the web of politics. Administrative reforms will not unravel that web, since the alleged bureaucratic problems are in fact rooted in the political system.

The authors gratefully acknowledge financial support for this project from the Dillon Fund. Fellowships from the Swedish Collegium for Advanced Study in the Social Sciences in 1997 gave them time to work on the manuscript together. Their work has also benefited from support provided by the Academic Senate and the Center for American Politics and Public Policy at the University of California, Los Angeles. Further support was provided by the National Science Foundation to the University of Michigan, the University of Pittsburgh, and the University of California, Los Angeles.

Aberbach and Rockman express special thanks to those at Brookings who helped make possible their long-distance collaboration. In particular, they are grateful to Thomas E. Mann, former director of the Governmental Studies program, who also carefully read and critiqued the original manuscript; and to Judge Robert Katzmann, then with Governmental Studies and now on the U.S. Second Circuit Court of Appeals. They also thank Susan Stewart and Judy Light for their assistance.

A large number of able research assistants helped with interviews, coding, and data analysis. They are listed here as a small token of appreciation: Vivian Chackerian-Bournasian, Robert Copeland, Wendy Hunter, Bill Koppell, Kerry Manning, John Medearis, Dan Mezger, Klinton Miyao, Paul Mullen, Elizabeth Tech, Nick Valentino, and Anthony Zito.

Valerie Norville edited the manuscript, Anita Coryell proofread the pages, and Deborah Patton prepared the index.

The views expressed in this book are solely those of the authors and should not be ascribed to the trustees, officers, or other staff members of the Brookings Institution.

MICHAEL H. ARMACOST
President

January 2000
Washington, D.C.

Contents

CHAPTER ONE

Reforming the Bureaucracy

MOST PEOPLE THINK of bureaucracy as a downright dull subject. Yet for thirty years the American federal executive has been awash in political controversy. From George Wallace's attacks on "pointy headed bureaucrats," to Richard Nixon's "responsiveness program," to the efforts of Al Gore and Bill Clinton to "reinvent government," the people who administer the American state have stood uncomfortably in the spotlight.

Time and again, the American federal executive has been caught in the web of politics. This book covers the turmoil and controversy swirling around the bureaucracy since 1970, when the Nixon administration was trying to tighten its control of the executive branch. Drawing on interview data, documentary evidence, and analysis of the politics of the period, we aim to understand the reasons for the controversy about administration and what can (and can't) be done about it.

We focus on three major themes of the era. The first is often called the "quiet crisis" of American administration: a hypothesized decline in the quality and morale of federal executives. The second, which we call the "noisy crisis," refers to the large question of bureaucrats' responsiveness to political authority. Administrators are important people in the policy process. Presidents and members of Congress want to control what goes on in the bureaucracy because that has much to do with who gets what from government. Political leaders also find it convenient to blame bureaucrats when things go wrong. As a result, administrators of federal agencies often find themselves in the thick of the political debate, whether they like it or not. When this natural controversy is exacerbated by intense disagreements about what government ought to do and who ought to decide what it should do, great conflicts involving administration are likely to follow.

The third theme is the movement to "reinvent" American government. At least overtly, the reinventors reject the notion that there is a problem with the people in the federal government. They do, however, believe government is broken and needs fixing, and they argue that one way to do this is to introduce a variety of private sector techniques into public administration, such as making federal agencies more responsive to the preferences of what they call customers—that is, individuals and groups directly affected by public agencies. They also argue that government should "cut back to basics." In the end, the vital questions of what government should do and to whom it should respond are central to the debate about administration.

We examine these themes and their linkages in some detail as we progress through the book. We look in detail at why these issues arise and at their validity. And we consider changes that might make the federal government's administration work better. But our underlying argument is that much of the debate about the administration of government is really a debate about what government ought to do. Bureaucrats are convenient targets in contemporary political battles, but in the end it is up to elected leaders to reach agreement on what they want done and how they want policy carried out. If they can do that, our evidence suggests that American federal executives will carry out the authorities' political will (assuming they are given adequate support and realistic policies to implement). Without such agreement, the federal executive will be caught in a web of controversy that is essentially political rather than administrative.

Reform in Perspective

Reports and commissions come and go detailing the purportedly grim state of some aspect or other of the U.S. federal executive and its organization.[1] Different diagnoses are issued. Reform efforts big and small are made. A few, such as the 1978 Civil Service Reform Act, have lasting effects. In the 1960s, the emphasis of reform proposals was on representativeness, responsiveness to new participants, and systems thinking.[2] In the 1990s, the emphasis was on efficiency, markets, and even on transforming citizens into "customers."[3] At each point, the bureaucracy was thought to be resistant to new tidings.

Trying to make government work better is a long-standing feature of American public life. Some of this may well have to do with the democratic culture that infuses American politics and the popularized Jeffersonian belief that any system needs to be shaken up from time to time. The presumption is that a system undisturbed for long may prove to be uncontrollable. This long-standing populist impulse is reflected today in citizens' general attitudes about the bureaucracy and in their views of career politicians.

In the first decades of the twentieth century, the Progressive movement attempted to bring two disparate forces together: direct popular democracy and proficient government. Proficiency in government, the Progressives believed, required honesty, legality, and selection to service by merit. It required, above all, eliminating the influence of political parties and party patronage in staffing public administration. Eliminating the corrupting influences of political parties was also seen as the way to restore the vitality of American democracy. Professionalism in public administration and direct popular participation in making policy choices were the two capstones of the Progressive movement. The underlying assumption was that policymaking and administration were distinctly different activities, an assumption known as the politics-administration dichotomy.[4]

Upon examination, however, this stark dichotomy fails to hold up. Politics and policy cannot be held in a watertight compartment separated from the administrative sector. It is true, of course, that politicians and civil servants tend to engage policymaking in different ways. Politicians tend to think in broader brush strokes and bureaucrats in terms of specifics, seeking technically appropriate solutions to more precisely defined problems.[5] However, neither the role of the bureaucracy nor the views of administrative officials can be kept free from the political debate or from political machinations, as the Progressives had hoped they could be.

In our view, reformers will not get very far if they define administrative problems only as apolitical matters. What underlies a management or personnel reform crafted in response to government's problems are more fundamental issues: Who exercises power? How much discretion and judgment should administrators have? Who is legally responsible for government actions? And to whom in a system of separated and often divided powers should bureaucratic agents respond? Bureaucracy is very much about power; it is thus eminently political. It is therefore not surprising that the U.S. federal executive is controversial, since the government it serves has been steeped in controversy. Norton Long argued many years ago that administrative activity was energized by power, and that power was the product of the clarity of signals sent from political principals to administrative agents.[6] Other observers have noted that administration is itself a form of power.[7] The fact is that administration is a crucial mechanism for achieving policy intentions or for thwarting them. Political leaders, consequently, often fear the ability of administrators to circumvent their will.

Because bureaucracy is enmeshed in politics, so too are administrative reform efforts. While we do not dismiss the value of reform, we cast a skeptical eye at the panaceas many reforms promise. In the long term, reforms always have unforeseen consequences. Reformers are kept in business by tending to the consequences of previous reforms.[8] This is because reform solutions tend to be driven by the problem of the day, which is not the problem of every day. However they are rationalized over the short run, reform proposals typically reflect self-interested behavior on the part of supporting interests. Riding the hobbyhorse of administrative reform is often useful to some set of political actors for stoking their political ambitions, gaining advantages in political power, and furthering their policy goals. This also means that other political actors will find any particular set of reforms that disadvantage their interests worth resisting.

If the issue is not just the bureaucracy, but the politics in which it is embedded, then it is relevant to ask not only how the U.S. federal executive system is changing, but also how American politics is changing. It is necessary, among other things, to note the ways in which the federal executive adapts to such changes in the political system as well as what forces in the political environment are working to change the nature of government—its operations, scope, and activities.

The changing political context in which the federal executive functions and the alteration in the fundamental problems it and government in general face are central to our book. Thus we examine the environment of the federal executive over time as well as the composition and nature of the federal executives themselves. The raw ingredients of this investigation are the characteristics, perceptions, views, and beliefs of America's top federal civil servants and subcabinet-level political appointees in the agencies. We are primarily concerned with domestic policy across three Republican presidential administrations from 1970 through the early 1990s. The data were gleaned from extensive face-to-face interviews with these officials during the second year of the first Nixon administration (1970), at the midpoint of the second Reagan administration (1986–87), and toward the end of the Bush administration (1991–92). We supplement these data with other sources of evidence, particularly in chapter 7 on reinventing government where we make extensive use of documents and of various surveys of government officials.

Numerous issues affect the bureaucracy as a whole, including recent emphases on customer satisfaction, downsizing, and employee morale and training. It is, however, at the top levels of the bureaucracy where leadership is demanded and where attention to issues of representativeness, quality, morale, responsiveness, and adaptability is especially crucial. What happens throughout the administrative system is strongly affected by top leadership. Signals and cues are important in organizations. Clarity in them does not ensure that they will be followed, but a lack of clarity or the presence of contradiction ensures that there will be many interpretations about what policy is.

Politics, policy, and expertise meet uneasily at the top of the bureaucracy. A presidential administration's ambitions (and its political appointees) join there with a senior career civil service that is not invested in these ambitions. Presidential administrations demand responsiveness from career officials, but career officials must balance neutrality with helpfulness. The tensions between political direction and skepticism bred from experience are notable at the top levels of any administrative system. Because of the institutional features of the American system of government, these tensions are particularly strong at the top of the federal bureaucracy. Not everything important to the functioning of the federal bureaucracy, of course, occurs at the top levels, but most everything ultimately reverberates from the top. Therefore, we have chosen to focus our attention on the top layers of the bureaucracy—the politically appointed officials of presidential administrations and the senior career executives.

History tends to have little standing in Washington, and some may dismiss this work as merely history—perhaps, as history goes in Washington, even ancient history. While in one sense, this is indeed history, the issues the data help us address are very much alive and relevant now. The discussion about altering the traditional contours of the administrative state in the United States and elsewhere continues today.[9] Some of this discussion has even been translated into action, though to date more outside of the United States than in.[10]

Why the Quest for Administrative Reform?

Why have so many and varied attempts been made to reform the federal bureaucracy? Why has so much attention been focused on it and on those who fill high positions within it? Why has so much energy been expended in the last thirty years on getting the management of the federal executive "right"?

The rush toward reform of the bureaucracy over the past three decades reflects a combination of factors. We believe these factors can be boiled down to five broad considerations. One is the growth in the complexity of government. A second factor is the increasing level of populistic democratization in public life. A third has to do with the growth of "management science," which is always on the prowl for something "new and better." The displacement of older political coalitions by newer ones is a fourth consideration. Who controls the administrative apparatus of government was always important, especially in the heyday of party patronage and political machines. Although political machines are no longer what they once were, the bureaucracy remains a vital resource for politicians. In fact, the bureaucracy is probably far more important now, even though it can no longer supply legions of party campaigners. Its importance as a resource for political leadership is bound up in the growing complexity of government but also in a fifth reason behind the rush to reform—namely, a perceived bureaucratic resistance to change.

Governmental Complexity

The New Deal regime of Franklin Roosevelt created an alphabet soup of regulatory agencies designed to soften the negative externalities associated with the unrestrained play of free markets. This accelerated a process that had been going on for some time.[11] Rapid expansions of industrialization and commerce brought regulatory responses from government. While the growth of the regulatory state began earlier, it found a justificatory theory in the positive state doctrines of the New Deal.

New problems emerged, especially as scientific advances showed that nearly every aspect of living was in some way dangerous to the health or well-being of the citizenry. From pesticides to automobiles that either would not work (lemon laws), or were dangerous if they did (the ill-fated Corvair), or spewed noxious by-products, a range of problems was placed on the public agenda for solution. The solution was typically to write a law, establish an agency, and set the agency to do its regulatory work. But the work of the agencies would often prove contentious, whether the agencies were coming to terms with the negative by-products of an increasingly complex economy or with problems that stemmed from patterns of social behavior and discrimination. If all of these activities were controversial, there is no doubt that the regulation of social behavior was especially so. The civil rights revolution of the mid-1960s, for example, spawned laws leading to many regulations that were unpopular with large segments of the population. Activist courts also promoted regulations, with little visible public demand driving them other than the zealous support of advocacy groups.[12]

Government was becoming more complex and, inevitably, more intrusive. Not all of this was a product of Democratic hands. At its outset, Richard Nixon's presidency invigorated older regulatory agencies and espoused new regulatory causes such as environmentalism. Most regulatory crusades are popular when they begin, except with those who know they will be adversely affected. Only later do broader segments of the population become aware of the costs they will incur. That typically is when regulations become unpopular or at least controversial.

The important thing to point out is that it is the bureaucracy that carries the burden of enforcing regulations, popular or not.[13] It may be, of course, that bureaucrats are inclined to carry out unpopular regulations as strictly as popular ones. That, naturally enough, would lead to their being targets of hostility or ridicule. Politicians can then have it both ways: produce regulations to satisfy some constituencies, and then rail against their enforcement to other constituencies.

The American citizenry seems, at the very least, ambivalent about the regulatory state. It is not uncommon for the public to desire public goods that may be most easily produced through regulation, such as cleaner air and water, better public health, or equal treatment. It also is not uncommon for the public to complain when generally desirable outcomes require specific do's and don'ts. Some regulations are relatively popular because they seem to involve costs for only a few concentrated interests, while purportedly achieving a larger public good. If successfully articulated in public propaganda campaigns, however, the intense opposition of the concentrated interests may sour the regulatory climate over time. Regulations will be especially controversial, though, when broader publics find themselves adversely affected—for example, on issues such as school busing or centralized inspections for automobile emissions. In such cases, authority itself becomes controversial, and the bureaucracy is seen as insensitive to public concern. This, we believe, is one reason there has been such attention to administrative reform in the contemporary era. Yet while distrust of government grew along with the growth of the regulatory state,[14] administration per se is only a small part of the problem. Rather, the fundamental causes lie in deceptive or illegal practices by leaders such as Presidents

Johnson and Nixon and in disagreements about what government should be doing.

More Democracy

Along with other institutions during the 1970s, bureaucracies democratized their procedures. Some of this was achieved by statutory law and some by court edicts. For the most part, as William Gormley has shown, the 1970s saw the expansion of procedural rights and participatory claims throughout the bureaucracy.[15] Gormley, in fact, regards the 1970s as a decade of inspired governmental reforms. These reforms, he argues, increased the accountability of bureaucratic agencies through such mechanisms as impact statements. They also purportedly increased the representativeness of agencies' staffs and their responsiveness to citizen (which may also be read as interest group) claims. The possibility, of course, is that all of these efforts at reform created other, maybe even larger, problems. One thing the reforms began to do was to tie agencies up in an avalanche of paperwork and internal regulations to meet new criteria of accountability and procedural responsiveness.

The democratization of government, the increasingly active role of Congress and the courts in governing agency behavior, a tremendous growth in the number of advocacy groups,[16] and the declining level of citizen confidence in government are possible contributors to an erosion of bureaucratic legitimacy. Increasingly assertive publics have little reason to defer to authorities whom they distrust. The idea that the problems of governing could be blamed on bumbling bureaucrats and an oppressive bureaucracy is now widespread. In a culture of democratic populism, the federal (and any other) bureaucracy becomes an easy target for the perceived ailments of government, which are often characterized by the catch phrase "fraud, waste, and abuse." Accordingly, the citizenry believes that the answer to broad-scale policy problems, such as balancing the budget, lies not in trade-offs between cutting popular expenditures or raising taxes, but in eliminating fraud, waste, and abuse.[17]

While none of these factors alone provide the definitive reason for a growing quest for reform of the bureaucracy, all of them together have contributed substantially to perceptions of a ponderously inefficient and unresponsive bureaucracy—inefficient and unresponsive in part, ironically, because of the accumulation of demands that were themselves the product of reform.

Organizational Engineering

The development of management science and industrial engineering as a response to large-scale organizational management promotes the belief that there is always a better way to do things. Organizational and procedural rearrangements can be designed and implemented amidst a sea of otherwise uncontrollable factors, though their consequences are not always foreseeable. Nevertheless, an understandable tendency (particularly in a world where humankind has mastered many of its problems through industrial organization) is to look for engineering solutions to problems, even to problems that have few definitive answers. If no one believed in the efficacy of management science, business schools and schools of public administration would lose their raison d'être.

Techniques for organizational engineering come and go with remarkable rapidity. New techniques come into fashion and old ones go out, much like the outfits modeled in Paris, Milan, and New York. Today it is New Public Management (NPM); yesterday it was Program, Planning, Budgeting, Systems (PPBS). John Kingdon's description of how policies are made is applicable to the streams of management reform and why some are chosen at any given point.[18] A set of promoters of a technique come together with a set of "buyers" at key moments, joining problems and solutions in ways that satisfy their immediate needs. Key buyers are presidential administrations, most of which feel the need to look proficient at managing the government.

While our language here is skeptical about the reasons presidential administrations buy into management techniques and other organizational prescriptions, we are willing to grant that some presidents (Carter certainly) may themselves have great faith in "management science." But if presidents have higher motives, they also clearly have political ones. Aside from the benefits that accrue to them for touting how they will make government work more efficiently and effectively, presidential administrations clearly have an interest in strengthening their political leverage and advancing their policy goals. The bureaucracy can be central to facilitating or impeding these objectives. Understandably, presidents want the bureaucracy to work well—for them.[19] This point is elaborated shortly, but, in the meantime, it is worth observing that Ronald Reagan, the recent president who for good or ill probably had the largest impact on the bureaucracy, used mostly blunt instruments—targeting people, budgets, and programs. He had little reason to hide his schemes behind the facade of management science. His administration, nonetheless, was helped by the Civil Service Reform Act bequeathed by Carter, which allowed the Reaganites to manipulate the personnel system to accord with the strong policy preferences they and their leader held.

To some extent, there is a contagion effect in bureaucratic reform. Something that seems to work somewhere (the private sector, a different level of government, another government) is likely to lead to its adoption somewhere else.[20] These days, the contagion is international, and reforms of a similar nature have spread extensively around the globe, suggesting that the industrialized democracies are coping with similar problems.[21] These reforms are reflected in the National Performance Review in the United States, but they have been in some ways more extensively implemented elsewhere, under the general rubric of New Public Management. A Norwegian observer describes the main emphases of NPM as "market orientation, efficiency, flexibility, merit pay, [and] consumer orientation."[22] This should sound familiar.

Displacement of Political Coalitions

One powerful motive for bureaucratic reform is to ensure the responsiveness of the system and its executives to the reigning political coalition. The fact that the American system divides authority across political institutions invites a struggle for responsiveness. "Responsive competence" is language that came into fashion during the Reagan administration to replace the ideal of "neutral competence."[23] The idea of responsiveness, however, was not intended by the Reagan administration to mean responsiveness to those in Congress or even to the courts. The intent was for the bureaucracy to be exclusively responsive to the White House and its key appointees.

All presidential administrations, to a greater or lesser degree, believe that the civil service they inherit reflects the biases of the previous administration, particularly when that previous administration, as is usually the case, was of the opposite party. The longer the previous party was in power, the greater the level of suspicion. Even the moderate Eisenhower administration was initially convinced that its predecessor left office after ensconcing many of its patronage appointments into the career service.[24] The Nixon administration grew increasingly attentive to what it perceived to be a disloyalty problem, largely because the career service was, in Nixon's view, more committed to the programs of the previous Kennedy-Johnson administrations than it was to the Nixon priorities. Whatever the truth of that perception, Nixon's priorities were to have his political interests served, even when these violated lawful procedure.[25]

The stronger an administration's policy objectives and the more these contrast with those of the status quo, the more attention that administration is likely to give to the bureaucracy. A Bush appointee, for example, contrasted the situation of the Bush administration, coming to office after eight years of its own party (the Republicans) holding executive power, with that of the Reagan administration, which not only succeeded a Democratic administration but also was largely at war with the policy legacy of earlier Democratic administrations:

> If you are really there to make a change in a fairly dramatic way, I think the civil servants will rate you bad. There is an important value in government stability and sameness. But, on the other hand, when the political will is to make the change, you need certain kinds of people who will not be rated as high by civil servants. . . . In 1989 we wanted stability, and marginal adjustment, and competence. In 1981, we said, hey, let's make changes.[26]

More generally, presidential administrations sometimes find administrative reform a tool they can use to uproot past structures, behaviors, and personnel. The extent to which administration is perceived to be an important policy resource means that presidents will also seek to make it more responsive to them, sometimes by blunt instruments, sometimes by circumvention, and sometimes by offering reform as an instrument of political control. And sometimes all three will be employed at the same time.

The Dead Hand Theory

Related to the aforementioned motivation for seeking administrative reform is the belief that bureaucrats resist change and are responsible to no one. Political leaders come to office with the desire that the bureaucracy do their will or undo the will of their predecessors. Yet the bureaucracy is grounded in notions of stability, continuity, and regularity, without which a nation of laws becomes one merely of capricious power holders. In a properly functioning system of law, bureaucrats will not chase after every stick they are told to fetch by some putative superior. By definition, bureaucracy will not be immediately transformed to suit the tastes of the day, mainly because that is not and never was its role. Nevertheless, bureaucracies do change, a matter on which we will produce ample evidence. And in changing, they tend to reflect changing political tastes and preferences.

But this change will never be speedy enough to satisfy those in political authority. Where bureaucrats perceive stability, politicians often see a lack of responsiveness. Politicians deal in a world of kaleidoscopic claims and wants, bureaucrats in a world where policy has been institutionalized. The bigger the changes the politicians want, the deader the hand that bureaucrats will be perceived to have.

This is not so much because bureaucrats necessarily oppose new political agendas; rather, in the benign version of the dead hand theory, bureaucrats tend to coast along on the prevailing inertia, feel comfortable with it, know what can be done under it, and therefore cast a skeptical eye toward novelty. Richard Rose described this phenomenon among British civil servants as "directionless consensus."[27] From this standpoint, bureaucrats protect the status quo mainly because, in essence, it is already being done.[28]

Looked at from this perspective, the bureaucracy is not the enemy of any given administration or of any particular set of public demands. Instead it indiscriminately resists all of them, save those that do not threaten the status quo. Robert Putnam's description of the Italian bureaucracy of the 1970s emphasizes a sclerotic civil service suspicious of political interference and of civil society alike.[29] Presumably, the problem here is deeper than merely changing faces in high positions. Rather, in this analysis, the solution is to change the culture, which is what Margaret Thatcher attempted to do in Great Britain through deep structural reforms of the civil service and the public sector. Efforts to change the culture of public management have become more pervasive, especially but not exclusively, throughout the Anglo democracies, and have been initiated, at least as often as not, by left of center governments.

Similarly, the 1978 Civil Service Reform Act advocated by President Carter was designed to enhance the responsiveness of the higher civil service by allowing individuals to be transferred to other jobs, ostensibly to broaden their perspectives or to make better use of their talents. More likely, the idea was to provide incentives for recalcitrant or difficult individuals to leave the civil service. Carter no doubt figured that this would help his own administration, but in the end it proved to be a valuable tool for his successor.

The Clinton administration's National Performance Review is the American version of New Public Management, and it too seeks to change the culture of public management. Its emphasis is less tied to people than the Carter administration's reform had been. In fact, its claim is that good people have been harnessed to bad systems.[30] As do NPM reforms in other countries, it seeks to alter the administrative culture by rearranging structural incentives through use of performance reviews that focus on goal attainment and similar modes of achievement tracking.

Multiple Motives

This is the story so far: First, bureaucracy has become a contentious institution for many reasons. Government's complexity and the unpopularity of some of its policies create resentment against government and its operating arm, the bureaucracy. Citizens have been primed by politicians and commentators to target their resentments toward the bureaucracy. Not that citizens required much priming. Bureaucracy and bureaucrats are not popular anywhere, despite the fact that citizens are often quite fond of the programs being administered. Second, presidents, for a variety of reasons, have tinkered with the bureaucracy. At a minimum, presidents want to appear to be proficient governors. Almost all want to exercise greater control over policy as well. In the mold of a mystery, we now have both motives and actors. All that is missing is the supplier of the weapon—namely, the idea mongers.

What particular ideas come into play? As we noted earlier, much results from fashion, and increasingly a great deal results from contagion, as ideas spread around the globe. Yet the ideas do have to fit, or at least appear to fit, a definable problem. And the nature of these problems differs dramatically over time. When Lyndon Johnson instituted PPBS in the mid-1960s, the problem was how to use the budget process for policy rationality; the solution was to rearrange budget lines to fit policy concepts. The problem thirty years later was how to cut costs and make the bureaucracy more responsive to consumer demands in an era of scarce resources—or, perhaps less charitably, how to allow the political leadership to steer the ship of state and allow the nation to remain competitive in a tough global economy while giving much responsibility but few resources to those below decks.[31] The two main threads to contemporary reform proposals emphasize increasing bureaucratic responsiveness to the consumers of government services and increasing managerialism in a public sector that has become more austere.

Reforms stem from a multiplicity of motives, often indiscriminately overshoot their targets, and sometimes reflect contradictions that result from political deal cutting. This does not mean they are all to be abhorred or that they fail to do some good—or more properly, do someone some good. But none of them are bloodless. All of them change the balance of interests and values. Indeed, one of the problems inherent to reform is that any reform changes the goods and bads likely to emanate from the administrative apparatus. None can eliminate all the bads, nor produce only goods. From this standpoint, we turn to a discussion of the major value conflicts built into reform.

Conflicting Values in Reform

It may be an iron law of social tinkering that producing a favorable outcome of one kind produces a corresponding ill of another. The literature on administration is filled with complexities of this sort. Writing in the 1970s, for example, Herbert Kaufman noted that bureaucratic red tape was the product of other social goods, such as holding bureaucracies accountable or producing policy goods requiring regulation.[32] Accountability, in fact, is a legal concept, requiring that delegated authority ultimately be grounded in the authority citizens give to the officials they elect. Many people hate bureaucracy because they dislike filling out the reports that accountability requires. In its function as a legalistic and impersonal source of authority—to spin that more positively, a grounded and regularized source of authority—the bureaucracy produces lots of paperwork to ensure regularity and compliance with the rules.

The problem of getting bureaucracy right is that not everything can be gotten right, at least simultaneously. The logic of accountability, as we have described it, is to ensure that agencies perform in regularized ways and in accordance with the law. But if we push accountability, we increase red tape and inflexibility and decrease responsiveness and, most likely, efficiency as well. A government of laws, as Americans often like to think theirs is, is a government thick with safeguards against the arbitrary or capricious use of power. Many of those safeguards also prevent administrators from responding in commonsense ways that might be regarded as responsive or adaptive.

A great deal depends upon how laws are written. The tighter they are, the more constrained the administrator and therefore the less discretionary judgment the administrator can employ.[33] Alternatively, the looser the legal framework, the more discretion administrators have. The more blanks there are under general framing or enabling laws, the more administrators will have to fill them in. Some people think this gives great power to administrative agencies and essentially removes them from lawful guidance.[34] One fear is that agencies may fall in bed with powerful interests or clienteles and decide matters in their interests rather than the broader public interest. Another fear is that, without sufficient legal guidance, bureaucrats will make decisions based on their preferences rather than public preferences (assuming the latter to be discernible). Yet a different fear is that when bureaucrats are given too much discretion by virtue of being given too little guidance, they may actually shirk responsibility, concerned that they will be second-guessed ex post by politicians or even the courts.[35]

At the heart of much of the debate about bureaucracy is the impossibility of simultaneously optimizing all of the values that Americans think may be appropriate for a properly functioning administrative system in a democracy. Indeed, some analysts go even further to suggest that the basic problem is that it is not possible to define what a properly functioning bureaucracy might be.[36] James Q. Wilson notes in this regard that it may be possible to judge public organizations whose product is a tangible service more clearly than those whose product is intangible.[37] Judgments concerning the latter will more likely be based on policy preferences and values. Some activities—diplomacy, for example—defy standardized criteria.

More emphasis on accountability is likely to mean less on responsiveness, adaptability, or flexibility, and vice versa. Red tape is the by-product of a system of law and documented behavior. Many bureaucrats themselves dislike bureaucracy, so defined, as much as citizens do because it ties them up in knots and reduces their ability to make discretionary judgments. As we note in chapter 2, a tendency, indeed a strategy, of presidential administrations since the Nixon era has been for central monitoring agencies, especially the Office of Management and Budget (OMB), an arm of the presidency, to tie up program agencies with reports and justifications of their behavior. Congress and the courts also have added to the paperwork burden of agencies. One of the ideas behind the National Performance Review, chaired by Vice President Al Gore, is to diminish that paperwork burden and place more discretionary responsibility in the agencies. All of this, of course, is wedded to politics. Republicans wanted to tie the bureaucracy into knots so that it would be less able to regulate society, whereas Democrats wanted to reduce the paperwork burden on the bureaucracy so that it would be more able to regulate society.

Increasing responsiveness may well clash with the laws and rules bureaucrats have inherited. Responding to a present principal may be at odds with existing law. Carried to its extreme, political meddling with the legalized routines of bureaucracy constitutes abuse of executive authority. The Nixon administration took the logic of executive authority to an extreme. The notion that the law ought to be ignored while the bureaucracy should be made responsible exclusively to the president was a major part of the Watergate crisis.

The American system makes responsiveness, as well as accountability, problematic at the outset. The system is complex, marked by a division of powers and often exacerbated by different political coalitions in control of different, yet coequal, governing institutions. Whose writ is to be followed? In parliamentary systems, the bureaucracy, at least in theory, is the agent of the prevailing government. In the language of principal-agent relations, the principal is the government (cabinet or relevant cabinet minister) and the agent is the bureaucracy. Complications may arise, especially in multiparty coalition governments, but on the whole, the idea is simple: one principal, one agent. The American system of government, however, introduces multiple principals for the same agent. Where does accountability lie in such a system? And where does responsiveness lie?

The lines of accountability are wired in very complicated ways, and sometimes rest for a time on decisions made by courts. Responsiveness is even more problematic. Who should be responded to? When government is divided by party (and sometimes even when not), the bureaucracy is cross-pressured between conflicting demands of the politicians in the executive and those in the legislature, not to mention the interest groups that are part of an agency's constituency. A senior career official in the Department of Housing and Urban Development noted the consequences of this inter-branch rivalry for his agency:

> I don't know whether this reflects too many years of divided government or whether it is just a general trend, but there seems to have been a pattern of executive defiance of congressional will. When that continues, Congress responds by starting to write into law things that were previously left to administration to do by regulations. As a result, our agency is not trusted, and we have a constant series of more and more layers of congressional rule making in the administration.[38]

As this comment illustrates, both the political executive and the Congress pressure the bureaucracy to be responsive to them and accountable only to their writs. In a system of shared powers, divided institutionally, the American bureaucracy is uniquely cross-pressured and perhaps, consequently, is uniquely distrusted. Should it then be so surprising that it operates under the constraints it does, with the demands of both Congress and the presidential administration often formalized in complex procedural requirements?

In many respects, managerial adaptability and flexibility and the pursuit of efficiency may be at odds with both accountability and responsiveness. Managerial autonomy and maximizing discretion—letting the managers manage, in the parlance of the present—may enhance organizational effectiveness and efficiency (though these two concepts may also come into conflict). Managerial flexibility as a means to efficiency is a key aspect both to New Public Management and the Clinton administration's National Performance Review. Discretion inherently means less emphasis on red tape and less need to respond immediately to demands, though obviously any bureaucrat looking to accumulate political support for future needs will be cautious about offending anyone.

The idea of providing managers with latitude may allow organizations more flexibility to fulfill their missions. It may also permit managers to proceed more efficiently. Yet it is important not to conflate these two ideas. Effectiveness refers to goal achievement, which often enhances the legitimacy of the agency. Achieving performance goals or satisfying customers are two ways in which effectiveness is often expressed. Efficiency, however, refers to the most expeditious use of resources. In the private realm an efficient organization produces large returns on investment. This is often achieved by *not* serving the customer. It is very unlikely that this is a winning strategy for public organizations operating within a highly political (that is, demand-sensitive) context.

Creating an adaptive, flexible, and possibly more effective or efficient public organization requires that the reins of control should be loosened. Does this mean that public agencies will not be accountable? It certainly seems to mean that such organizations will operate within more casual political constraints than previously, certainly since the early 1970s. The degree to which bureaucrats are given latitude is likely to be a result of consensus about the policies they implement, the degree of trust across political institutions, and hence the degree of trust between politicians and bureaucrats.

Finally, the question of who should staff the higher level civil service (a matter we discuss in chapter 3) has important implications for reform. The best and brightest is one common answer. Those willing to fulfill the goals of the president is another.[39] Yet why staff a public service with highly qualified individuals if they will not be given some latitude in figuring out how to do things and in advising their superiors as to their options? A high-quality civil service implies that people are selected on the basis of their capacity for judgment. In a fully rule-driven system, in contrast, judgment is not very important. But the idea of getting the best and the brightest implies that they will have to make a range of difficult judgments that rest on appropriate combinations of technical knowledge, political sensitivity, and management and leadership skill. Such a reliance on the best and the brightest, however, may come at the price of a high degree of accountability and democratic responsiveness. To what extent do we want our administrative machinery in the hands of a mandarinate? How elite, in other words, do we want our civil service to be? Do we want them to be in touch or above being touched?

In reality, all administrative and civil service systems operate in ways that allow these disparate values to coexist to some degree. But there is no doubt that these compromises have different equilibrium points, and the points arrived at reflect the extent to which there is relative consensus about policy and relative clarity about sources of authority. The constraints on U.S. bureaucracy, which have been growing since 1970, reflect the absence of both policy consensus and clear authority. If the bureaucracy has become a point of growing contention, it is precisely because American politics have become more contentious.[40] This is a formulation we elaborate more extensively in chapter 2 as we trace the nature of U.S. politics and the role of the bureaucracy in it from the time we began our study in 1970 to the present.

Three Themes of Administrative Reform

As we mentioned at the outset, this book is organized around three themes about contemporary administration. The first involves people. Is there a serious problem in the quality of the U.S. public service? A blue-ribbon National Commission on the Public Service, headed by the former chair of the Federal Reserve Board, Paul Volcker, thought so. It described the problem as "'a quiet crisis' in government."[41]

The second theme involves responsiveness. To what extent is there a problem of bureaucratic unresponsiveness to political authorities? To whom should the bureaucracy be responsive? And how responsive should it be? Since politicians have publicly hammered bureaucrats for purportedly being unresponsive to their (politicians') definitions of the public good, we label this "the noisy crisis."

The third theme is a more difficult one to characterize. It is about reinventing government. In the United States, reinvention is embodied in the National Performance Review and in the broader concept of New Public Management. Unlike our first two themes, reinvention emphasizes multiple factors. These include, among others, changing organizational cultures, developing "customer"-oriented agencies, running government in a more businesslike and efficient manner, creating more flexible responses and adaptive structures, and evaluating organizational and individual performance. To what extent can government adopt the features of new managerialism without eroding the distinction between public sector activity and private sector activity and, therefore, between public sector goods and private sector goods? What difference would it make if the distinction were eroded?[42] To what extent is the role of citizen different from that of customer, and the role of government different from that of a firm? Reinvention raises these questions and many more.

Theme 1: The Quiet Crisis

Government service in the United States has rarely been a highly prestigious calling.[43] American society appears to value achievements in the private sector more. Appointment to public service, especially at local and state levels, traditionally was patronage driven. Not only did the professionalization of the American bureaucracy develop late, the bureaucracy itself was a late bloomer. Major developments in the role and expansion of the bureaucracy really began to take shape in the 1930s, as the positive state emerged more fully to combat the Great Depression and, not unimportantly, to solidify the New Deal coalition with new programs. Yet the American polity had, as the French observer Alexis de Tocqueville noted as far back as the 1830s, a vibrantly active civic life. Tocqueville inferred from the popular culture that Americans did not want their leaders or their institutions to stray very far from them.[44] The decentralized structure of government, American resistance to a remote elite, and its own late development each in part explain why the U.S. bureaucracy could not create a mystique of indispensability as the institution responsible for the country's development or its maintenance in times of political crisis.

That the U.S. bureaucracy has lacked the aura surrounding the long-standing bureaucracies of countries such as France and Japan or of others in Europe does not necessarily mean that its top-level civil servants are any less motivated to serve government. One should not confuse the external prestige of an institution with the commitments and qualities of those who serve it, nor with its influence on society. There is a frequent misidentification of the two—a misidentification so casual that it has seeped unwittingly into our assumptions about those who populate the civil service.

Whatever deficiencies of prestige may accompany federal service, civil servants often derive their satisfaction from the belief that they are doing important public good. Claimed one top-level civil servant, "It is very satisfy-ing to be in a working environment where the Secretary . . . and his top polit-ical leadership all want to accomplish something, as opposed to dismantling or to stand pat."[45] Asserted another, "The only thing that keeps us still here . . . is that we do have a hell of a dedication to the mission of whatever it is that we are doing, and we seem to be willing to try to cope with all of these frustrations. We do it because we believe so deeply in these bigger things."[46]

Theme 2: The Noisy Crisis

In contrast to what the Volcker Commission on the public service in the United States called the "quiet crisis," we have dubbed the concerns often expressed by presidential administrations that the bureaucracy is too often unresponsive to their directions the "noisy crisis." Few presidents have been reticent about claiming that the bureaucracy, unless brought to heel, would not respond to their direction. Nixon was perhaps the least reticent.[47] Judging by events of his presidency, he was apparently also the least discreet in expressing and acting upon his feelings. But Nixon was hardly alone among presidents in many of his feelings, even if he expressed and acted upon them in a unique fashion.

As we indicated earlier, it is quite natural for political leaders to feel that the bureaucracy either reflects some other leadership's legacy or is just self-interestedly unresponsive. The Reaganites clearly felt that they were on a mission to gain control of the bureaucracy so that it would do the adminis-tration's bidding. They were interested in deinstitutionalizing the past and institutionalizing the future with their own imprint. One high political appointee in the Office of Personnel Management (OPM) during the Rea-gan administration claimed that the administration's influence in the selec-tion of high-level career officials (members of the Senior Executive Service) was politically strategic:

> The executive resources boards that choose senior [career] execu-tives are appointed by the agency head. They are a majority politi-cal appointees, not career appointees. Those people would have had a particular agenda in selecting the senior executives coming into the SES. I guarantee you that. . . . That was one of our big agendas in the Reagan administration. Here was an opportunity to leave a lasting imprint on the career civil service, and I would be . . . very surprised if the majority of agencies didn't pick up that bias in an eight year period of the Reagan administration.[48]

It may be the case—and it certainly is perceived to be the case—that the themes of people and responsiveness are related in important ways. First, where greater power is placed in the hands of appointees who have been selected principally for their zealousness on behalf of the president in power, and where control over agency and civil service behavior is centralized as part of a strategy of political control, career officials find their discretion diminished, the challenges of their jobs lessened, and their ability to manage reduced. It seems reasonable enough (which does not necessarily make it true) that able people would find this diminution of latitude frustrating and would thus exit the federal service.

Second, the noisy crisis story may impinge on the quiet crisis story through the counteractions that reverberate throughout the political system when one institutional actor seeks to make the bureaucracy more responsive to it alone. There is plenty of recent history to attest to the fact that under such circumstances micromanagement will rise and career executives will find themselves squeezed in a pincer movement of political forces seeking to counteract each other. This too will add immeasurably to the frustrations facing creative career executives in the federal government. Presumably, such limitations would drive the most able from their jobs. But this needs to be taken as a hypothesis, not a certified fact.

Third, the two themes may be connected if public perception of a responsiveness problem leads to public recriminations against the bureaucracy that in turn might lower civil servants' morale. One way presidential administrations deal with the problem of responsiveness, as they perceive it, is to fulminate against the bureaucracy as a major source of the country's governing problems, or at least a manifestation of them. A senior career official noted, for example, that he felt that both Presidents Reagan and Carter taught "the general voting population . . . that government is a bad thing" and produced "the sense that the profession [I had] chosen to go into [the public service] was somehow a disreputable one."[49] A drumbeat of accusations against the bureaucracy would not be likely to lift the spirits of bureaucrats and might be perceived as hastening the flow from the civil service of the best and the brightest. All of these concerns in some fashion came into play in the Volcker Commission report.

To what extent is a presidential administration entitled to a responsive bureaucracy? That is not an easy question to answer. What we can do is to assess the extent to which the political complexion of bureaucracies change and the extent to which efforts to control the behavior of bureaucrats appear to have been successful.

Theme 3: Reinventing Government

Underlying the third theme, reinvention of government, is the perception that government is a cumbersome, highly inefficient operation. We already noted that the reinvention theme is common to many countries, not just the United States. This leads us to believe that there are similar forces acting upon governments to reduce their classic bureaucratic features (character-ized by myriad rules). Along with a reduction in bureaucracy's rule-driven character, New Public Management aims to change administrative culture by focusing on organizational results, individual performance, market incentives (even privatization), and on bringing outsiders into government. Practices from the private sector have been extolled as appropriate models for government. Results-oriented management is at the heart of it. This new culture of government could be described in similar terms from one gov-ernment to another. One public official in the United Kingdom who is involved with these reforms drew this picture:

> What will the Civil Service of the future look like? . . . Numbers will fall to new lows. . . . There will be a minimum framework of prescribed rules concentrated on "ethical" standards and effective accountability. Operational management will be delegated to Departments and Agencies. Departments will be restructured with . . . smaller staffs concentrating on policy making, strategic management, and target setting and monitoring contracts or agreements for service provision supplied by a mix of public and private sector providers. . . . There will be a greater emphasis on leadership and on management and professional skills in picking and developing managers. . . .[50]

The National Performance Review in the United States sums up the change in culture it wishes to promote in the title of its report, *From Red Tape to Results* (1993). With only minor flourishes, it reads much like the quote from the British official above. The report speaks of a crisis of gov-ernment and characterizes it as one of industrial-era structures in an infor-mation age.[51] A U.S. career executive, speaking like one of those "good people trapped in bad systems" that the report talks about,[52] concurs with this conception of the problem of government: "I think the private sector is much more self-conscious about their management challenge than the fed-eral government. They are much more concerned about how they are going to adapt to these changing times and keep on top and keep competitive, while we sit and continue to do that stuff that we were doing in the 1940s and wonder why we are not respected." [53]

The reinvention phenomenon promises many improvements in government, particularly in the areas of greater efficiency, managerial responsibility, and "customer" responsiveness. It emphasizes the marketplace and the notion that there is no inherently inviolable function to be performed by the public sector per se.[54] These managerial enthusiasms raise a number of important issues. One is whether a responsive government can also be an efficient one, and vice versa. Another vital issue has to do with the definition of the public sector itself and why there is one. Our purpose is to locate each of these three themes in broader assumptions about how government should work, in many respects about how society should work, and about what the role of government should be.

The Plan of the Book

In chapter 2 we discuss the political context of the years encompassed by our interviews (1970–92) and the subsequent years of the Clinton administration. Our focus is on the changing context as that affects the federal executive. We then discuss the nature of our study and elaborate it in sufficient detail for the reader to understand our data base, our samples, and the occasional shorthand necessary to discuss our findings.

Chapter 3 elaborates the people issue, particularly why Americans should care who staffs the upper reaches of the bureaucracy, where top federal executives come from, what their qualifications are, whether they are the best and brightest, and what that might mean. In chapter 4, issues of representativeness, quality, career patterns, and the morale of senior U.S. federal executives are explored empirically.

Chapter 5 focuses on the issue of responsiveness—what it is and why it is important. It looks at how institutions and political and policy divisions may affect perceptions of responsiveness. The issue of responsiveness connects to those of neutral competence and accountability. These are all admirable values in the abstract, but ones that necessarily require trade-offs. The responsiveness issue also raises the stability-sclerosis problem. Everyone wants a bureaucracy with some stability, yet no one wants sclerosis. Responsiveness provides the focus for discussing what we want the bureaucracy to be. A fundamental question from the standpoint of the relationship of administration to its political environment is whether career administrators adapt to political change. An equally fundamental, though not empirically answerable question, is, how much should they adapt?

We follow up this discussion in chapter 6 with empirical analysis centered on the question of whether the U.S. senior career executive reflects political change in its environment. We examine the involvement of both senior career civil servants and political executives with other actors in the U.S. system and also their perceived influence over policymaking. To what extent, moreover, do presidential administrations appear to be successful in molding the federal executive? And to what extent do they, in turn, reconcile themselves to the career bureaucracy? In the end, how do civil servants think they should respond to policies they deeply question?

Chapter 7 examines the movement to reinvent government. What is behind this new wave? Is it only about *how* government does things or also about *what* things government should do? The reinvention push is a powerful one, and its emergence in so many places, despite differences in specifics, leads us to think that the factors pushing it are not intrinsic to any one country's system of government or its bureaucracy. To what extent do the managerialist ideas behind reinvention ignore the constitutional authority of Congress and also the courts? To what extent do they present problems for accountability? And of perhaps greatest importance, how does the marketplace motif of the reinvention strategy deal with values of fairness, equity, and community? Such values are an essential part of public functions and encompass the rights and obligations of citizenship.

We conclude in chapter 8 by summarizing our key findings and drawing from them an empirical assessment of change and stability in the federal executive during a highly eventful period. We try to assess the quality of the nation's federal executive, especially its much maligned senior civil servants. We also assess the extent to which the U.S. federal executive responds to the changing political forces in its environment. But more speculative questions remain, and these, perhaps, cannot be answered in strictly empirical terms. They have less to do with the bureaucracy that exists than the bureaucracy that is desired—indeed, even the kind of government that is desirable, what it should do and what it ought not do. Such larger matters underlie the issues of bureaucratic reform.

Our book examines the nature of the U.S. federal executive within the larger context of shifts in the nature of political power and public responsibility. For now, power has shifted away from the state sector nearly everywhere and increasingly has gravitated to private sector institutions and to important agents in financial investment markets. The business of the state has come to be more businesslike because, as Donald Kettl observed, "organizations everywhere shared the . . . need to squeeze more services from a shrinking revenue stream."[55] Such concerns, of course, are bound to affect not merely how government does things but what it does because big cost savings are achieved by altering the programs of government, not its processes. Administrative reform movements imply otherwise, but the reality is that administrative reform is often the refuge of those seeking to change policy agendas by other means. When we shift agendas for policy change from the political process directly to the administrative machinery, we place expectations on the administrative process that are beyond its scope.

CHAPTER TWO

Three Decades of
the Federal Executive

SINCE 1970, WHEN we began our study of the federal executive, presidents and members of Congress have made major efforts to get the federal bureaucracy to be more responsive to their needs. The first part of this chapter looks at this historical context. The second part discusses the nature of our study: what we did and how we did it. Some of the more finely grained details can be found in the appendix.

The Growing Importance of the Federal Bureaucracy

It is hard to pinpoint when the modern administrative state emerged in Washington, but by the standards of other developed democracies it was a latecomer. Authority pushed toward the center in the United States only with great difficulty, spurred by a devastating civil war, rapid industrialization, massive nation building, and then extraordinary economic and military challenges. State building at the federal level came late. A familiar explanation is that, unlike in the rest of the developed world, democratization preceded bureaucratization in America. The federal government's presence in the lives of most people was rather minimal. It was far off, with few responsibilities in the lives of its citizens. Government's presence was felt most significantly at the state and local levels, the latter particularly with respect to public investments.[1] The devolution revolution, now in fashion, marks a limited return to the condition that has characterized much of U.S.

history, namely state and local governments as the locus of much of the action and innovation.

The modern U.S. federal executive establishment did not arise instantaneously, of course. Its development reflected an accretion of demands from society that Washington do something about some problem or other, and it also reflected politicians' warming to the idea of federal responses to society's problems. The modern federal bureaucracy was the inevitable concomitant of public acceptance of a state with growing responsibilities at the center. Administrative capabilities grew along with these responsibilities, and the central government's growing capability in turn was widely viewed as a basic component of nation building.[2]

The New Deal Consensus and Institutional Harmony

Franklin Roosevelt's New Deal administration, launched in response to the Great Depression, is often considered a demarcation point in the creation of a more active federal government, one that was to be engaged in greater economic interventionism through business regulation, intervention in labor markets, and social welfare. How continuous or discontinuous the New Deal was from what preceded it is a matter of debate. But there is no doubt that bureaucratic growth and presidential activism were on the upswing. New Deal politics created a coalition to sustain and support governmental activism. The New Deal regime and its descendant, the Great Society administration of Lyndon Johnson, had in common both a zest for federal involvement in social and regulatory policies and large Democratic majorities in Congress to support these policies. In retrospect, these administrations seem to have been the alpha and omega of enthusiasm for federal interventionist policies and equally the beginning and end of a relatively politically quiescent environment for the federal bureaucracy.

This relative quiescence was not due to any lack of opposition to the New Deal programs and their descendants. But many of these programs became popular and acquired stakeholders. Moreover, World War II tightened the regulatory grip of government on society. For a long time to come, the dominant political mood was that "new needs" demanded new or enlarged programs. Except during unusual periods of large Democratic majorities and unified government or of bipartisan or cross-partisan consensus, such programs were not necessarily enacted, but proposals for them were typically on policy agendas. To quite a considerable degree, the character of the bureaucracy was built during the New Deal period and infused with the values of the New Deal—values that remain at the core of the New Deal's heirs, today's liberal Democrats.

The New Deal coalition and its ideas outlasted the New Deal itself. The burden of proof for nearly two generations was generally on why government should not do something rather than on why it should. This has obviously changed—largely a consequence of altered circumstances (public sector financial problems and pressures from increased international competition), altered political coalitions, and changes in the relative influence of interests (the weakening of the New Deal coalition and of labor, and the strengthened hand of business), the role of the bureaucracy in implementing unpopular policies (social regulation), and the triumph of conservative ideas organized around neoliberal economics trumpeting the superiority of markets. The burden of proof now is on why government should do something when markets could presumably do it better, assuming anything ought to be done at all.

Yet the New Deal legacy on the federal executive remains. With substantial party majorities in favor of government action during the New Deal, much of the U.S. federal bureaucracy came into being endowed with reformist purpose, a condition that would be strongly reinforced by the Johnson administration. Consequently, not only is America exceptional because democracy preceded state building but also because the defining period of U.S. state building is associated with the politics and policies of the left-center. And the U.S. federal bureaucracy is often associated, certainly in its most controversial guises, with the reformist impulses of the New Deal rather than with the maintenance of a conservative ancien régime, which elsewhere is the more prevalent image of the bureaucracy as a predemocratic remnant within democratic systems.

Our point is that all bureaucratic systems are infused with a set of values stemming from their creation. Those that preceded democracy have tended to reflect relatively more conservative values and traditionally have become the symbol of resistance to changes promoted by the democratic left. The U.S. bureaucracy, having come to bloom during the New Deal to serve a controversial policy agenda, became the bugbear of American conservatives. The federal bureaucracy, of course, is polymorphic, not monolithic; its various parts came into existence at different times supported by very different patrons. Still, the most controversial issues in U.S. political history dealing with the proper role of the public sector and of the federal government are bound up with American imagery of the bureaucracy as friend or foe. So long as there remained a New Deal consensus, frayed as it became, and so long as there was unified government with a Democratic president and Congress, fragile as it might have been, the bureaucracy was less controversial than it later became when neither condition held. Once divided government became the norm and the programs the government administered became even more controversial, the federal bureaucracy became a lightning rod for politicians. Presidents sought to tighten their control of it, and so did Congress.[3]

The Federal Executive at the Center of the Political Storm

We were fortunate to begin our study of the federal executive on the cusp of dramatic change. Only four years later, the incumbent president, Richard Nixon, would resign under threat of impeachment, based in part on a charge of presidential abuse of executive authority. Thus our story begins here.

The Nixon Presidency

Richard Nixon is regarded as the first truly partisan Republican president since the onset of the New Deal. Although Dwight Eisenhower broke a twenty-year skein of Democratic incumbency in the White House, "Ike" was not a professional politician, a source of his popularity, and he preferred instead, as had other generals such as Charles de Gaulle, to affect a posture of being above partisan conflict.[4] Nixon came to office, following eight years of Democratic presidencies, with a paper-thin plurality, less a resounding choice of voters to move in a clear direction than a beneficiary of a loss of confidence in the incumbent administration. Were it not for the candidacy of George Wallace, the segregationist ex-governor of Alabama, Nixon likely would have waltzed into the White House with a big margin rather than the narrow one by which he won election in 1968. Lacking a clear policy gyroscope, especially in its first year and a half, the Nixon presidency contained both liberal and very conservative elements designed to appeal to diverse constituencies, although no one would have thought Nixon a Democrat.

One early goal of the Nixon administration was to change selected government organizations. A prime example was the transformation of the Bureau of the Budget (BoB) in 1970 from a civil service–dominated presidential agency into the Office of Management and Budget (OMB). The new

OMB was supposed to make management of the federal executive a priority equivalent to that of managing the budget. While that shift was never effectively accomplished, the Nixon administration eventually used OMB to monitor activities in the executive branch more proficiently than they had been and to draw the executive branch and OMB itself more closely under the presidential wing. OMB was to become more of a tool for a sitting president and less of an institution available for the presidency, which BoB had been.[5] What had been a rather intimate organization grew and was layered over with a new set of presidential appointees.

Despite Herculean efforts to impose more central clearance and control later on, the Nixon presidency in its early days paid relatively little attention to the workings of the executive branch, especially on the domestic side. This was to a degree a consequence of diversions elsewhere and significantly a consequence of its hydra-headed domestic policy. The early Nixon administration focused its attention overseas. It attempted to find what it deemed an acceptable resolution to the Vietnam conflict (or at least America's role in it). The climate for domestic policy had not yet turned against the interventionist policies of the federal government in a variety of areas. In fact, new constituencies such as environmental groups had successfully galvanized extensive public support to press for additional regulatory programs. The Nixon administration responded to the claims of such groups and to popular sentiment with programs that expanded the regulatory arm of the state and, as a consequence, the bureaucracy. At the same time, the administration embarked on policies to gain the loyalty of the Wallace constituency of 1968. This required clamping down on government efforts to support school busing or to litigate school desegregation cases in the South. The Nixon administration's strategy on race was dualistic. It brought a substantial number of blacks into government at the subcabinet level (about 15 percent of the administration's appointees in domestic agencies in 1970 were black), and it allowed the enforcement of affirmative action and of contract and employment set asides. Nevertheless, the administration actively discouraged the civil rights offices of crucial agencies, especially in the Department of Health, Education, and Welfare (HEW) and the Justice Department, from aggressively pursuing compliance with court edicts that were unpopular in the South and among whites generally. With this dualistic domestic policy agenda and the diversion abroad, the administration for a time failed to convey an overarching direction to the bureaucracy. It also failed to generate what it regarded as effective controls over the bureaucracy, a condition about which Nixon bitterly complained, as noted in the proceedings of the Senate committee to investigate the Watergate scandal.

The tensions in the Nixon agenda were resolved by a turn to the right, which became more pronounced over time. As Richard Nathan, a former OMB appointee of the administration noted, "Nixon's domestic program . . . [and] its tone and emphasis changed as political conditions changed."[6] Ultimately, this change affected the Nixon administration's relations with the bureaucracy and also dramatically distanced its relations with the cabinet.[7] The Nixon White House staff ballooned to record numbers, and the administration developed a shadow bureaucracy of its own, answerable only to the president. Distrust between the White House and elements of the bureaucracy (especially in social service agencies such as HEW) grew as a function of the policy tensions between them. Indeed, tension between the White House and its own appointees in the agencies accelerated as the administration came to believe that its appointees had been captured by preexisting programs and clienteles.

By its second year the Nixon administration was evolving a strategy to gain control over a bureaucracy that it believed was committed to Great Society programs and allied with Democrats in Congress and with groups hostile to Nixon's presidency. But the more deeply the White House staff was drawn into agency operations, the more overloaded it became. Thus it could not effectively gain control. By the beginning of its second term the administration began penetrating the agencies with White House loyalists and naming cabinet secretaries with little political standing of their own. This strategy coincided with a hardening of the administration's earlier shift to the right in its policy agenda.[8] The administration also became much more aggressive about vetting its appointees, and it maximized efforts to ensure loyalty in the departments and agencies.

Beyond this, the Nixon administration maneuvered around congressional opposition to its management and policy proposals. For example, it created a set of super cabinet secretaries. The super-secretaries were originally recommended by the Ash Council (appointed by Nixon and headed by Roy Ash, an industrialist later to become Nixon's OMB director) as part of a larger effort to streamline the cabinet departments. The Ash Council recommendations had been submitted to Congress, from which they failed to surface. The administration acted on them anyway. The administration also defied Congress by impounding funds appropriated for a variety of programs, and it used regulation writing in a "creative" manner to interpret statutes as it saw fit. Operating through executive action, the Nixon administration sought, with little subtlety, to circumvent legislative constraint.

The Nixon administration was hardly the first U.S. presidency to use administrative means as a substitute for legislative action or to avoid the effects of legislative action, but it did so aggressively and with contempt for other political institutions. Its efforts to govern in this manner brought the term "the administrative presidency" into use. The isolation of the Nixon administration from the rest of the government continued apace as the Watergate scandal deepened. Most of the methods the Nixon presidency employed to strengthen its hand vis-à-vis the bureaucracy could not be sustained in the face of the developing scandal. In fact, in the ruins of the Nixon administration, a congressional move to assert greater control over policy operations and thus over the bureaucracy itself became increasingly prominent.[9]

There have been other great dust-ups between presidential administrations and their opponents in American history. But this time an administration went on the attack against the bureaucracy it inherited and yet had done little at the outset to influence. Nixon's initial indifference to the bureaucracy was transformed into a monumental effort to control it when he believed his policy choices, as well as some of his more questionable tactics, were being resisted. Given the growth of governmental activity, the bureaucracy was now the mechanism through which programs could be changed, initiatives stymied, and policy operationalized. The bureaucracy, in other words, was a battleground made important by the growth of government itself and the maze of regulations this growth engendered. The efforts of the Nixon presidency to maximize bureaucratic responsiveness left their mark, despite Nixon's fall from grace. Others looked at what the Nixon presidency sought to do and paid attention to how it might be done more effectively.

The Carter Presidency

After Nixon's resignation in August 1974, the unelected vice president, Gerald Ford, became president. Ford initially sought to bring peace to Washington and pronounced himself a president who would play by the rules. After the 1974 congressional elections, in which Democrats sizably reinforced their majorities in both chambers, there was little Ford could do on the domestic front other than to veto legislation (although many of those vetoes were overridden). The 1976 campaign for the presidency put Ford under great pressure from candidates outside the Washington establishment. Ronald Reagan, a decidedly nonestablishment figure, contested Ford for the Republican presidential nomination, and Jimmy Carter, the Democrats' nominee, also stressed his role as an outsider. Ford symbolized the Washington establishment, having served in the House of Representatives for over a quarter of a century and having been the Republican floor leader for several years before he was anointed to replace Spiro Agnew as vice president in 1973. During Ford's brief presidency, few major initiatives were undertaken to transform the bureaucracy, though there were a number of efforts to improve policy coordination across departments and between the White House and the departments.[10]

One aspect of Jimmy Carter's campaign as an outsider in 1976 was a commitment to reform the civil service and to reorganize government.[11] Carter devoted more energy to fiddling with the organizational design of government than most, if not all, presidents. Perhaps this was a natural exercise for a politician who was an engineer and who tended to think in terms of managerial and policy rationality rather than interests and ideologies.

The centerpiece of Carter's governmental reform efforts, however, was the proposal providing the basis for the Civil Service Reform Act of 1978 (CSRA). CSRA was an omnibus bill. It contained a wide variety of provisions, including mechanisms for the dismissal of federal employees. Indeed, the image of the indolent bureaucrat was a critical element to political salesmanship of the bill. The act also contained provisions for protecting whistle-blowers, paying bonuses for excellent performance, creating agencies to oversee the personnel system and to foster research on it, and limiting veterans' preference to allow for more women in the federal work force. But from the standpoint of the senior career service and the political appointees with whom these officials rub elbows, the critical feature of the legislation was the creation of the Senior Executive Service (SES).

As with most new institutions, the SES was designed to serve multiple purposes. Put differently, it was the product of contradictory intentions. As Mark Huddleston noted:

> The framers of the SES brought to the table fundamentally conflicting ideas about what an American higher civil service ought to look like—ideas that had, at turns, shaped a series of unsuccessful reform efforts for the preceding thirty years. For some, the SES was to be the reincarnation of the aborted Senior Civil Service, an elite, European-style corps of generalist civilian executives. For others, it was a second chance at a Federal Executive Service, a system that

would help elected officials and their appointees get a firmer political grip on the vast federal bureaucracy. Still others saw the SES primarily as a vehicle for bringing the supposed rigor of private sector management techniques to the federal government or as a backdoor way to increase the pay and perquisites of civil servants.[12]

One of the key provisions of the SES changed the basic job classification system from rank in the job to rank in the person. Rank in the job means that status and salary are invested in a given position, whereas rank in the person means that these investments are in the person. The idea of rank in the person was to create a more flexible cadre of top civil servants who could be shifted from one position to another. A shift to rank in the person, of course, would also provide greater flexibility to a presidential administration wanting to move civil servants it perceived as troublesome from more to less vital jobs, since this could now be done without the individual losing pay or status. Richard Nixon's blustery tirade to George Shultz, immortalized on tape, about sending a civil servant of whom he disapproved off to Guam became a somewhat more realistic scenario as a consequence of the SES.[13]

Another key provision of CSRA was that it allowed for noncareer (that is, political) appointments to the SES of up to 10 percent across the system and up to 25 percent within a given department or agency.[14] The Senior Executive Service was divided into two groups of approximately equal size. One is known as the SES reserve list. In principle, highly technical and specialist jobs that needed to be divorced from political influence were to be on the reserve list and made off-limits to noncareer appointees. The second SES list is known as the general list. These positions are supposed to be less technical and specialized in nature and therefore available to noncareer appointees.

Taken together, these two sets of provisions—the job portability of SES career personnel and the ability of presidential administrations to make strategic political appointments to the SES—enabled administrations with the will and wits to use them to gain greater control over sectors of the bureaucracy critical to their interests.

Another provision that can enhance control from the top is merit pay, which rests upon performance appraisal. In the absence of clear criteria and a systemwide consensus as to what constitutes good performance and therefore merits additional compensation, there is much room for political manipulation of this provision. And there appears to have been such manipulation, particularly during the Reagan presidency.[15] When it comes to the number and amounts of bonuses, however, congressional restrictions have had the most influence on the operation of the system.[16]

Whatever President Carter's intent in pushing CSRA and the SES, the net effect was to increase managerial flexibility and to provide political leaders of the executive branch better tools with which to sculpt the senior civil service, especially in agencies deemed critical to achieving policy objectives. The Carter administration was less inclined to push the use of these tools than its successor was, in part because its lack of ideological single-mindedness was associated with more flexible and complex goals. And it is not easy to direct the bureaucracy in the absence of clarity and stability from the top. The Reagan administration did not suffer from such problems, however. It not only knew where it was going but came close to perfecting the administrative presidency techniques that the Nixon administration developed. It could be said that the CSRA was Carter's gift to Reagan.

Another unintended gift Carter provided to the Reagan administration stemmed from Carter's desire to streamline government and reduce paperwork. Carter's wish to reduce the amount of paperwork the federal government imposed on external actors led to the Paperwork Reduction Act of 1979. The OMB's Office of Internal Regulatory Affairs (OIRA) was set up to monitor the act. During the Reagan administration OIRA created numerous impediments for agencies issuing regulations. It decreased the external paper flow by increasing regulations on the federal bureaucracy itself.

The Reagan Presidency

Few if any presidential administrations come to Washington with as clear a game plan as the Reagan administration had. The administration's top leadership, most of all Reagan himself, knew what it wanted: a smaller government, lower marginal taxes on income, more money for defense and crime prevention, and less for everything else (although it could not always control everything else). The Reagan administration wanted to put in place an administrative presidency that could operate in ways that would little involve its little-involved principal. This led to a two-pronged strategy requiring, on the one hand, selective centralization, especially concentrating a lot of authority in OMB, and, on the other, delegating authority to faithful followers in the agencies. Well-developed internal regulatory processes were key to central monitoring. These included such internal regulatory activities as OMB's micromanagement of agencies and ex ante restrictions such as cost-benefit analyses of proposed external regulations. Unlike the Nixon administration, however, the Reagan administration at the outset paid a great deal of attention to recruitment within the agencies, particularly at the subcabinet level.

The strategy of the Nixon White House at the outset of its second term was to penetrate the agencies with loyalists who would be the eyes and ears of the White House. The Reagan administration employed this strategy in a much more extensive way at the outset of its first term, often choosing committed subcabinet officials before it appointed its cabinet secretaries. Putting this strategy in action was made easier for the Reagan presidency due to a number of factors, many having to do with its unique ideological character. The Reagan administration had a supercharged agenda, a clarity of message, and a willingness to try to make changes so extensive that its people talked about the "Reagan revolution." It vetted its appointees with unusual thoroughness and indoctrinated them in the administration's mission, though most of its appointees hardly needed further indoctrination. It knew what it wanted from the start, and it selected individuals who were bent on reversing existing policy, especially in regulatory areas.[17] The Reagan administration also used other tactics of both a personnel and program nature to get control of the apparatus of government. It reduced administrative personnel in agencies through reductions in force (RIFs), cut off liberal or Democrat-oriented constituencies through defunding (often through contract reviews or by moving programs from the federal level outward to the states via block grants), and required central clearance in the form of internal regulatory requirements before agencies could issue new regulations. In sum, the Reagan administration centralized the personnel reviewing process and centralized tactics for throwing off balance the normal routines of agencies whose programs it wished to downgrade or eliminate. But by centralizing personnel selection so effectively,[18] it could confidently decentralize operations to a greater degree.

Much of what the Reagan administration could accomplish in the administrative realm—and it did accomplish much—it was able to do as a consequence of past legacies. The transformation of BoB into OMB under Nixon and the enlarged regulatory capabilities given OMB under the Carter administration (particularly through OIRA) helped the Reagan administration gain programmatic compliance with its policy objectives by essentially gumming up the machinery of state. Further, effective use of the SES provisions of the 1978 CSRA helped the Reagan administration infiltrate those agencies it most wanted to change. While other administrations, especially Nixon's, may have had the will to exert presidential control over the bureaucracy, the Reagan administration not only had more will but also had greater means to effect its will. It came into office with a well-honed script, which it followed closely and which put it in a position to "hit the ground running."[19]

We revisited our study of the federal executive in 1986–87, deep into the Reagan presidency. At this point, the administration had lost some of its zest for transforming the bureaucracy.[20] Once the initial cast of characters departs, it becomes increasingly difficult to sustain a game plan. By 1986–87, the Reagan presidency had in any case achieved a good bit of what it set out to do. After enjoying a robust legislative success during its first year, the Reagan administration was much more limited in what it could do legislatively. Nonetheless, it already had substantially shifted the equilibrium point of public policy. It successfully used the administrative presidency strategy to further its goals and to put in place the people it wanted.[21]

At the same time, concern arose in some quarters that the Reagan administration had so successfully molded top administrative personnel to its tastes that it was contributing to a politicization of the federal bureaucracy, to the demoralization of the career service, to a deterioration of quality in government, and to an erosion of its institutional capability. Many of these concerns motivated the formation of the Volcker Commission, discussed in chapter 1, and influenced the content of its report. There was certainly significant anxiety regarding the standing of the civil service on the part of those concerned with the institutions of government. There was also concern within the federal work force. Some of this was the product of the Reagan administration's rhetorical targeting of government as a source of unending evil. Much of it also had to do with the tendencies of the administration to think it had the answers and needed only administrative compliance from a downgraded and dominated civil service.

There is no doubt that the landscape of government had changed by the midpoint of the second Reagan administration (1986–87). Its horizons, for one thing, were much narrower. The fundamental task of government was no longer to find new worlds to conquer but to find ways to strip away much of what it had been doing. In this regard, the Reagan presidency was fundamentally successful. Long after the New Deal coalition had dissolved, the policy legacy of the New Deal and its successor, the Great Society, was also dissolving. A bureaucracy that had been organized around agendas Democrats favored was being reshaped. The Reagan presidency may not have finalized a revolution, but it clearly left its imprint on government and on the bureaucracy.

The Bush Presidency

Unlike Ronald Reagan, whom George Bush served as vice president, Bush was an experienced federal executive. As his party's nominee for president in 1988, Bush opted for modest product differentiation from Reagan. He also made symbolic gestures early on in his administration when symbols have maximum impact. One was to address members of the Senior Executive Service on January 26, 1989, at Constitution Hall in his first presidential speech outside the White House. Bush thus showed in a public forum that he understood how government worked and that he respected the role and performance of career executives.

The theme of Bush's presidency—at least in its first year or so—was that it was a gentler, kinder version of the Reagan administration. This style applied also to management of the federal executive and relations with the career service, where the notable hostilities of the Reagan years abated. Despite these modifications, the Bush administration continued the practice of the administrative presidency in centralizing White House vetting of appointments (although cabinet members chose most of the subcabinet appointees and pragmatism marked both the process and many of the appointments). Still, like the Reagan administration, the Bush administration had an active strategy for "governing without Congress." It used "signing statements" to announce its intention not to enforce parts of statutes that it objected to or to interpret statutes in ways that fit administration goals.[22] Although less thorough than the Reagan administration in its exercise of central control of administrative regulations, the Bush administration likewise persisted in controlling such regulations to advance its interests. However, Bush largely avoided denigrating the career service, the bureaucracy generally, or even the government. Bush was, as David Mervin described him, a guardian president with little agenda of his own.[23]

Bush's principal problems, as he and his inner White House staff saw them, came from Congress, particularly the Democratic majority. Despite the Bush administration's softer, gentler stance in the agencies, the inner circle of White House advisers took a hard-boiled approach to Congress, frequently acting as though Congress was an obstacle on the administration's path toward doing what it knew had to be done. Boyden Gray, the counsel to the president, John Sununu, the chief of staff, and Richard Darman, the director of OMB, pressed a presidency-centric view. After the budget deal in autumn 1990, which Bush consummated only with the support of congressional Democrats, the Bush presidency was in trouble with its own party for reneging on promises that were deemed crucial to Republican chances to build a congressional majority. Once the Gulf War was won, conflict between the Bush White House and the congressional majority intensified.

Despite an emphasis on the prerogatives of the presidency, the Bush administration differed in emphasis from the Reagan administration. The Bush White House focused less on ideological vetting and far less on articulating a policy vision (and thus was criticized for being a bit short on "the vision thing") and more on asserting presidential prerogative whenever it deemed appropriate. This assertion of prerogative included the persistent tack that the president rather than Congress was the authoritative interpreter of congressional action. Vis-à-vis the agencies, however, the Bush presidency was a time of relative quiet. We came back to Washington toward the (unexpected) end of the Bush administration, 1991–92, to study the federal executive for a third time.

The Clinton Presidency

Like the Bush administration that preceded it, the Clinton administration seemed to lack a clear strategic direction. Its early personnel process sent confusing signals, with many clashes between the transition team and cabinet appointees over who should be in the subcabinet. To some extent, this was the consequence of a presidency sliding between "New Democrat" and "New Deal" coalitions and policies. The Clinton administration was committed, however, to diversity in its political appointments to the executive branch.[24] In noting this commitment, one of us asserted earlier, "In [Clinton's] appointments strategy, policy goals were not the key, the mosaic was the key" and added sardonically, "A demographically perfect group that doesn't quite know where it is headed is apt to be as lost as any other."[25] Clinton was quite successful in generating a demographically diverse and perhaps politically diverse administration, despite the fact that he had difficulty filling positions. This difficulty was partly a function of the drawn-out process of vetting before nomination and of diversity considerations. But it also was due to delays in approving nominees imposed by key senators who either objected to particular candidates or hoped to bargain for other concessions from the administration.[26]

The contrast between the Clinton administration's recruitment strategy and that of the Reagan administration could not be starker. The Reagan

White House sought a team whose direction was unmistakable, and diversity was of little concern to it from a demographic perspective and of no concern politically. The Reagan presidency knew where it wanted to be, unlike either the Bush administration, which could not decide how much kinder or gentler it wished to be, or the Clinton administration, which was unable to decide exactly in what proportions it wished to be "new" or "old" Democrat. Diversity, consequently, became an end in itself in the Clinton administration, and it was rather successful in achieving this end.

Unlike some previous administrations, the Clinton administration did not exhibit a clear view of the civil service. As discussed earlier, the Nixon administration, after initial indifference, came to believe that the civil service was essentially a foe wedded to its own (largely Democratic) agenda rather than to the interests and policy goals of the administration. The Reagan White House, building on lessons it learned from the Nixon experience, came to the executive branch wars with a clear battle plan, and it had a firmly held view that the civil service was part of the problem. Its concern was how to overcome the inertial resistance of government, which was wedded to an unfavorable status quo as the Reaganites saw it. The Bush administration mostly wanted to maintain the status quo bequeathed by the Reagan administration. The Clinton administration, in contrast, wanted to spring into action, but could articulate neither where nor how to do so. Moreover, while the Bush administration had little desire to be venturesome in policy, it was an administration with a fairly keen sense of governmental organization. The Clinton administration was different. It debated policy options endlessly, a favorite activity of its president, but was less apt to think organizationally, except for the National Performance Review, and that was mainly the responsibility of the vice president.

In any event, the Clinton administration seemed to accept that administrative problems—or perhaps even larger ones—were not necessarily the product either of unable or unresponsive civil servants. Instead, bad results were seen as the product of a bad system of organization. This argument was summed up in the National Performance Review, chaired by Vice President Al Gore, which was publicly released toward the end of 1993. For the most part, this review was the vice president's project. It was not clear how committed the Clinton administration was to it, however, since this was an administration not particularly notable for persistence or commitment. Furthermore, it appeared to have no clear-cut agenda in whose service it wished to deploy the bureaucracy.

It is difficult, if not impossible, to discern motivation behind organizational reform, but it seems the Nixon and Reagan administrations put their efforts into organizational activities that would help them better achieve their goals or at least enhance their power. The motives were less clear in either the Carter reform proposals or the reinvention project of the Clinton administration. In these two cases, the political benefits of reform appeared less driven toward enhancing control over the bureaucracy (though that inevitably would be a by-product, at least to some extent) and more toward sending up a flare to indicate that the administration was doing something to make government work better and, above all, cost less. Especially in the case of the Clinton administration, there was political logic in creating such an image of a Democratic administration: it could thereby neutralize the advantage Republicans had enjoyed in painting the Democrats as the party of big, bloated, and presumably wasteful and inefficient government.

There were certainly many reasons (more fully delineated in chapter 7) for the particular character of the management reforms proposed in the National Performance Review, perhaps foremost the budgetary pressures on government. The Clinton administration, as described in chapter 1, was operating within a context of public management reform to which the U.S. federal government was a relative latecomer. It was also operating in a context in which the values of the market had (probably temporarily) come to be seen as the ultimate arbiter of how public-sector organizations should behave. As with most proposed management reforms, we noted in chapter 1, there is naturally a mix of constraints and motives, not the least being that some of the sponsors genuinely believe the reforms will make government work better. However, it is also true that pushing "good management" makes the most of the narrowed entrepreneurial opportunities available to presidents at a time when policy expenditures and programs are greatly constrained. Ultimately, all such reform packages inevitably represent a mixture of the administratively desirable, the politically feasible, and political self-promotion.

Certainly, the National Performance Review is now front and center in the thinking about the federal executive. It has shifted attention from people to systems. While we did not interview federal executives during the Clinton administration, we followed closely the reinvention of government syndrome in the United States and elsewhere. Consequently, we examine reinvention as the latest, though we are sure not the last, initiative for producing better government.

Our empirical data come from surveys of officials at the critical inter-sections where top-level career and politically appointed executives meet. Reinvention, in contrast, focuses on organizations and assumptions about behavior for which neither its proponents nor its detractors as yet have much data, nor even agree on how its key concepts should be measured. There are many elusive and inconsistent elements to the reinvention syndrome (see discussion in chapter 7). For the most part, however, the re-invention effort is important in that it takes us from the realm of how lawyers and politicians are likely to think to how economists and business managers might think. Such a shift has important implications for politics and our system of government, which we discuss more fully in chapter 8.

What We Did and How We Did It

We interviewed representative samples of senior civil servants and presidential appointees in federal agencies in the Washington metropolitan area at three points (1970, 1986–87, and 1991–92). All were drawn from agencies of the federal executive primarily concerned with domestic policy. Political executives were at levels ranging from division or program chief to the assistant secretary level (and on rare occasions slightly beyond). Civil servants were drawn from the top supergrade career officials in their administrative units in 1970 and from similar positions in the SES in 1986–87 and 1991–92. These civil servants reported to political executives. In 1986–87 and 1991–92 we also interviewed supplementary samples of SES executives serving in slightly lower-level positions. They reported to other civil servants. In total, we interviewed 126 federal executives in 1970, 199 in 1986–87, and 151 in 1991–92. (See the appendix for more details on the nature and size of the samples.)

We began in 1970, the second year of the Nixon administration—a period, as we noted, that in retrospect also began a transformation of American politics and the policy agenda. When we completed this initial project, we did not expect to relive it more than a decade and a half later. However, the political and policy transformation that was beginning to take place under Nixon had come to fruition during the administration of Ronald Reagan. The bureaucracy was an important part of this story, as both the Nixon and the Reagan administrations sought to gain control over policy by gaining greater control of the bureaucracy. Things had changed significantly by 1986. We wanted to know, among other things, how the bureaucracy was adapting to this changed reality. And we wanted to know what political and career officials now thought were the problems of government and how the environment for operating in government was now perceived. Moreover, shortly before the Reagan revolution came to Washington, a landmark reform of the civil service (the CSRA) had been promoted by the Carter administration and enacted by the Congress in 1978. Thus in 1986–87 we revisited the scene, seeking to find out what influence the CSRA, particularly its SES provisions, had on the federal executive. It was now also clear that public sector privation was very much in vogue. Contraction was the theme, as contrasted with the still heady days of public sector expansion (soon to be ended) that we encountered during the second year of the Nixon administration. Finally, we returned again about five years later (1991–92) during the Bush administration, a consolidating period after the Reagan revolution.

Our interview data allow us to look at people in similar positions in the federal executive at three slices in time. In each case, Republican presidents and Democratic Congresses were in office (except for 1986, when the Republicans still held the Senate). We have, in other words, three discrete pictures of the U.S. federal executive. Because these pictures are discrete, the evidence drawn from our surveys is often elucidated by reference to events occurring in the broader political and governmental contexts. When there is evidence of change, we explore when the changes occurred, why they occurred, and their implications. Our method is to draw plausible inferences from a web of evidence and to narrow the path of causality.

In all instances, we acquired extensive background and career information on our respondents both before and during the interview. We asked questions in each phase of the study about how these officials saw their jobs and the environment in which they worked. We probed their roles, their policy views, and their political identities. In addition, we tapped into their understandings of how government and influence worked in Washington, the sets of actors with whom they were in contact, and the changes they believed were occurring in the environment of governance. Our interviews were conducted face to face in a structured yet conversational manner. The interviews combined open-ended questions, questions with precoded answers, and sets of lists from which the respondents could choose from among precoded alternatives. Our interviews averaged a little over an hour and virtually all were conducted in the respondents' offices. All of the interview and background data were coded to provide quantitative indicators, and nearly all of the interviews were recorded on tape with the permission of the respondents.

On the whole, high-level administrative officials are a cooperative group. We averaged a nearly 90 percent interview success rate across the three periods. The interview success rates for senior civil servants generally run better than 90 percent while those for the political appointees are a little above 80 percent for each period. Additional sample information can be found in table A-1 of the appendix.

When we began in 1970, we interviewed civil servants at the top of their organizational hierarchies. By the time we returned to do interviews in 1986–87, the SES had been created, with rank now residing in the person rather than the job. Consequently, as noted above, in both 1986–87 and 1991–92, we took two samples of SES civil servants from the general list: those who met the criterion established in 1970 and who thus reported to a political appointee, and SES career officials who reported to other career officials. We have separated them throughout the study with the designations of Career I (CSI) and Career II (CSII), respectively.

Armed with these interview, career, and background data, we can answer some key questions about reputed problems of the federal executive. Definitiveness is always elusive, to be sure. But we believe that our data respond to assertions about the problems of the federal executive presented in chapter 1. While these asserted problems of declining quality in the senior career service and a lack of responsiveness of the career service seem persuasive at first blush, the evidence suggests otherwise. Although our data cannot put all of these concerns to rest, they do speak directly to the issues raised about declining quality, demoralization, and the purported lack of responsiveness of the federal executive. At the very least we hope to elevate the level of evidentiary grounding upon which claims regarding the federal executive have been made.

Data on the nature and effects of reinvention are more indirect and are drawn mainly from the existing literature. The literature on reinvention in the United States is just now emerging, so the existing evidence is hardly definitive. One obstacle to evaluating reinvention is that it is multipronged and not always consistent across its facets, so that it is difficult to define precisely. But the reinvention syndrome is far too important to ignore, so we seek to understand why it has come into play, globally as well as in the United States, and what its implications are for U.S. governing processes. However worthy or unworthy its actual applications may be, like many administrative reform nostrums it is trying to solve fundamentally political problems by focusing on administration. As reinvention continues, there will no doubt be more to say. Some of the results are becoming clearer from the experiences of pioneers of the reinvention movement, particularly in Australia and New Zealand. One thing is already clear: political support for reinvention initiatives is inconstant in places where New Public Management has been in effect longer than it has in the United States.[27] While the road to administrative reform is both much traveled and much ballyhooed, such reform is often a cover for deeper problems that go well beyond the need to manage the machinery of government better.

CHAPTER THREE

Representation, Democratic Norms, and Quality

WHAT KINDS OF people serve in high positions in the bureaucracy? For years scholars have been interested in this question, but there are reasons beyond academic curiosity why this is regarded as an important matter. One has to do with notions of representation. A bureaucracy that is representative of the population may be—or may be seen as being—more sensitive to citizens' needs and more legitimate in their eyes.[1] A second reason rests on a notion that the norms of officials are central to the proper operation of the bureaucracy in a democratic system. Officials who are devoted to democratic values, in this view, will behave in a manner that will help preserve democratic government. A third reason why many care about who is in the bureaucracy has to do with quality of performance. Putting this argument in the simplest terms, if the best people serve the nation (leaving aside for the moment the difficult problem of defining what "best" means), they are more likely to produce outcomes that are beneficial to the nation than people who are of lesser quality.

These deceptively simple statements mask many complex issues about those who serve the federal government. We cannot cover them in depth, but we will lay out the basic arguments in this chapter and then focus in the next chapter on a few vital issues in the contemporary debate.

Representation

The argument that a bureaucracy that mirrors a nation's people will be more sensitive to their needs and seem more legitimate to them is at least plausible. Samuel Krislov and David Rosenbloom, the authors of a leading book on the subject, make even greater claims: "It is not the power of public bureaucracies per se, but their unrepresentative power, that constitutes the greatest threat to democratic government. If this power cannot be constrained by legislatures and political executives, it can nevertheless be made to operate democratically by making it representative of the public."[2]

Representation in the bureaucracy, as Krislov and Rosenbloom note, can have many meanings (or aspects, as they call them). The simplest is the one we most associate with the concept, which is representation by personnel. Even here there can be many types of representativeness. A bureaucracy could be representative of the social composition of the populace—surely the most common meaning of the term. But the personnel working for the state could also reflect the partisan or attitudinal profile of the population, or for that matter reflect any other attribute people might think important. There are problems with all of these forms of representation by personnel, and we return to these shortly.

A second meaning in the Krislov and Rosenbloom scheme is what they call representation by organization. The notion here is that interests in the nation can be represented in the government through the organizational structures and missions of government agencies. In other words, the Agriculture Department can represent agricultural interests, the Labor Department can represent labor, and so on.

Criticisms of this form of representation are legion both in the academic literature and in the popular media. First of all, government agencies tend to be set up to reflect groups that are organized. Interests that lack organizational structures in society or whose resources are limited may be shortchanged by such an arrangement. Second, a major criticism of the personnel in government departments is that they too often represent the interests of their clienteles at the expense of others. They are criticized for their narrow views of the world. In fact, reform proposals often call for rotation of personnel between administrative units so as to diminish their parochialism—that is, the tendency of individuals to reflect the interests their administrative units serve. To some, the countervailing influence of self-designated public interest groups (sometimes referred to as PIGs) is another way that the narrow representation of interests in public organizations can be checked.[3] However, the membership of public interest groups tends to be decidedly middle class, so there is no guarantee that these groups will represent the underrepresented.[4] Finally, government itself can help organize the unorganized, as in the War on Poverty programs of the Great Society, but the groups created thereby are unusually vulnerable to their political opponents when they take controversial stances.

A third meaning of representative bureaucracy identified by Krislov and Rosenbloom is representation through citizen participation. As they note, this is closely related to representation by administrative organization but is more direct.[5] Most of the problems with representation by administrative organization are found here too. In particular, the most typical form of citizen participation, representation through advisory groups and committees, tends to duplicate the problems of zealousness, narrow vision, and the unrepresentativeness of activists that are found when representation of interests takes place directly through government organizations.

Leaving aside the problems and prospects of the other two types of representation, most emphasis has been on demographic or social class representativeness. Some even have argued that the bureaucracy is the most legitimate U.S. governmental institution because it is the most representative of the nation's people.[6] Donald Kingsley, who coined the term "representative bureaucracy,"[7]

> put forth notions of the advantages that a broadly recruited, open, nonelitist civil service had over restrictive, taut, narrowly based bureaucracies. In contrast to the British bureaucracy, this service, drawn from all elements in society, could be expected to be motivated by much the same forces and attitudes as others are. It would be more in harmony with its environment, responsive to changes and nuances in opinion, as well as more effective in disseminating and in securing compliance.[8]

There are numerous counterarguments to this thesis. One concerns the socialization within organizations that occurs when people serve in them for a long time, as is typical of service in bureaucracies. As individuals learn the mission and routines of their organizations and as they work over time with others who are similarly inculcated with the values of their organizations, they are likely to behave more in accordance with organizational expectations than with the values that come from their groups of origin. Robert Putnam quotes Allen Barton as concluding that "value-socialization is not parental, or even based on early political experience, but apparently takes place from working in a given field or institutional setting."[9]

A second counterargument is that socialization in organizational norms is supplemented by the demands of the role one plays within it. Robert Putnam notes that "study after study has found that much of the variation in outlook within the elite is related to role differences."[10] One of the more famous aphorisms of organization theory is "where you stand depends on where you sit." Service over a long period plus the demands of the role one plays usually overwhelm the influences of one's background. This should especially be the case for ambitious individuals who attain decisionmaking roles because they were most likely to adopt the organization's ethos and to otherwise do what was necessary to rise to the top.

Third, and closely related to the first two points, there is little evidence of an impact of social background on the work-related attitudes and behavior of those in the bureaucracy, especially those who reach the top. Putnam's summary is direct and to the point: "At the elite level the correlations between social background and policy preferences are remarkably weak and unpredictable."[11]

Our own previous survey work on top-level bureaucrats in Western democracies confirms this conclusion. We found, for example, that the correlation between paternal partisanship and the respondent's own political ideology was quite robust for elected politicians (.44) but only a meager .09 for top-level bureaucrats. And we also found that in at least two of the countries, including the United States, "a civil servant's ideological stance is much more closely related to the department in which he works than to his sociopolitical origins."[12]

An issue like this can probably never be permanently settled. There are findings that suggest some areas in which particularly salient characteristics of an individual may matter a great deal in the bureaucratic setting. Krislov and Rosenbloom, for example, cite some studies indicating the importance of religion and ethnicity for bureaucratic attitudes on matters of administration and policy in societies where there are serious religious and ethnic divisions relevant to the issues at hand.[13] Other studies, in addition, have reported similar results.[14] Overall, though, demographic or social class representativeness is apparently a weak reed on which to hang hopes for a truly representative bureaucracy.

Finally, when looking at the representational qualities of a bureaucracy, it is important to distinguish the entire organization from those at the top who have the major influence over how policy is interpreted and implemented.

One can imagine a bureaucracy that mirrors society when one considers all of its employees, but whose leaders are less representative of that society. In point of fact, this is close to an accurate description of the U.S. bureaucracy. Data from as far back as the 1960s indicate that a profile of federal employees, taking into account religious preference, age, race, and party identification, looks much like a profile of the working public in the United States, except for the greater prevalence of nonwhites in the federal work force.[15] However, if one looks at the leadership of the same federal bureaucracy, the picture is quite different.

Putnam concludes that the phenomenon just described is so universal that it goes beyond a mere empirical regularity and has the status of a "law" of social relations. He labels the phenomenon "the law of increasing disproportion." It applies, he says, to every political system and can be stated as follows: "No matter how we measure political and social status, the higher the level of political authority, the greater the representation for high-status groups."[16] We'll see some evidence in the next chapter that this law can be amended a bit, at least with regard to sex as a social status category (and Putnam's discussion of Scandinavia in the same study leads him to a similar conclusion), but educational levels in particular seem safe from even the slightest amendment of this law.

The reasons those at the top of bureaucracies are more highly educated than society at large are hardly mysterious. Apart from the formal requirements placed on eligibility for the top jobs (a factor that guarantees increasing disproportion as one goes to the top of most bureaucratic hierarchies), it takes conceptual and technical skills of the type one develops or enhances through higher education to do most of the executive jobs with even a minimum level of competence. For this reason, even the most revolutionary governments eventually succumb to this law's dictates.[17]

In short, the most representative bureaucracies in the modern world—representative when one looks at a profile of all their employees—have a very different appearance at the top. One can debate the relative impact of this difference, but at a minimum it does cast a pall over notions underlying ideas about the genuine representativeness of what may appear on the surface to be a fairly representative bureaucracy. After all, if the people in the top positions are unrepresentative, then the overall composition of the bureaucracy does not much matter (even if one thinks that social origins determine attitudes and behavior). There may still be many advantages to having a representative profile in the bureaucracy as a whole—increased legitimacy, for example, or exposure by those who eventually reach the top to people from many social backgrounds—but the people at the top still will not be "representative" in the way those who write about the advantages of representation through the composition of personnel would like.

Norms

Stepping away from demography, there are many other concerns about those who serve the nation as public employees. Of particular interest to those who consider the problems of bureaucracy in a democratic setting is the debate centering on control of bureaucratic power. Like the representative bureaucracy issue, there is much that could be said about it. Indeed, one of us has written a book on the subject. But our goal here is simply to outline the core of the issue.

The classic debate on the subject is the one between Carl Friedrich and Herman Finer. It can be summed up rather easily, although the implications are subtle and difficult to deal with. Friedrich argues that the main checks on bureaucratic power come from bureaucrats' own values and from anticipation of public reactions to their decisions. In essence, he argues that lay politicians are not equipped to oversee the complex decisions (which define public policy) that high-level officials are called upon to make in the modern state. Bureaucrats have expertise and knowledge that politicians cannot hope to match. The keys to control are the bureaucrats' own standards of professional conduct (an "inner check") and their anticipation of the adverse consequences that can come from an aroused public opinion (which would lead to legislative interference in policy implementation).[18]

Herman Finer strongly counters Friedrich's position:

Moral responsibility is likely to operate in direct proportion to the strictness and efficiency of political responsibility, and to fall away into all sorts of perversions when the latter is weakly enforced. While professional standards, duty to the public, and pursuit of technological efficiency are factors in sound administrative operation, they are but ingredients and not continuously motivating factors, of sound policy, and they require public and political control and direction.[19]

In brief, inner checks may be useful, but external controls are still necessary.

Obviously this is a complex issue, and Francis Rourke is surely correct when he argues that the differences spelled out in the Friedrich-Finer debate are differences of emphasis. Even in Friedrich, the internal checks that come from the norms and values of bureaucrats are effective in part because the threat of external sanctions is there in the form of legislative reactions to an aroused public opinion. As Rourke so aptly puts it, the two forms of controls (internal and external) should "be regarded as complementing rather than substituting for one another."[20]

The American tradition, we should note, seems rather clearly to favor Finer. In one of the most famous of the *Federalist Papers* (number 51), James Madison argues strongly against the position that the values of the governors are a sufficient check on their use of power. He stresses that if people were "angels," no government would be necessary. And if angels were our governors, we would have little to worry about no matter what the structures of governance. However, since ours was to be a government of "men over men" (women being governmental nonpeople in Madison's era), the "necessity of auxiliary precautions" was imperative.[21] These auxiliary precautions were organized as a complex system of controls featuring institutional separation and incentives for each institution to check the others. If good people happened to staff the institutions, so much the better. But, as in the Finer argument, it would be foolish to rely on this alone.

Much of the concern about bureaucratic norms and values is manifested in controversies about bureaucratic responsiveness to political authorities, which we articulate in chapter 5. As we noted in the preceding chapters, politicians can be extremely suspicious of the "permanent government"—the career civil servants in the agencies. They often suspect them of resisting policy directions and initiatives that the politicians want to pursue. And they fear that the bureaucrats, motivated by their own values and attachments to the clienteles of their agencies, do not see the world in the proper way and therefore cannot be counted on to administer programs in a manner that politicians will find acceptable.

These fears take two related forms. One is that civil servants will actively resist and perhaps even sabotage legitimate (or sometimes illegitimate) directives given them by political superiors. The second is that the civil servants' personal views on issues, when they are contrary to those of politicians, will render them incapable of carrying out, in a sufficiently enthusiastic or effective manner, the policy directives given them. We examine both the overt willingness of civil servants to defy directives and selected elements of their political views in chapter 6.

Finally, when it comes to general values, previous research suggests that bureaucrats in Western democracies are neither the guarantors of political freedom nor threats to democratic government. The top civil servants we studied in the 1970s, for example, tended to be very accepting of the systems in which they operated (showing little inclination for change). And they were almost as supportive of pluralist freedoms as the politicians in their systems were. They were not, in short, people whose presence in government made one fear for the future.[22]

Quality

Public servants are an open target for derision in the United States. This is not a new phenomenon, but the debate about "bureaucrats" has flared with special intensity since the Nixon administration. Attacks on the quality and performance of the bureaucracy, although particularly common on the right, have not been confined to Republicans or a few renegade Democrats such as George Wallace. The National Commission on the Public Service, chaired by Paul Volcker and known as the Volcker Commission, was even-handed in castigating the presidential campaigns of Democrat Jimmy Carter in 1976 and Republican Ronald Reagan in 1980 for their attacks on the public service.[23]

The Volcker Commission grew out of a 1986 conference of government and business leaders. According to the conference conveners, the federal public service had been so dangerously eroded that a "quiet crisis" existed and that it was necessary to take action to reverse the deterioration.[24] The Volcker Commission continued this theme, subtitling its 1989 report "Rebuilding the Public Service." The commission was concerned about an "erosion in the quality of America's public service" and said that "it is evident that the public service is neither as attractive as it once was nor as effective in meeting perceived needs."[25] In the words of Paul Volcker, writing a few years later (1995) in *The Key Reporter*, a publication of Phi Beta Kappa:

> The Commission was dedicated to dealing with the evident problem of falling respect and morale, the thinning out of the "best and brightest," and the disheartening lack of interest (in the public service) by new graduates of our best institutions. In these circumstances, it's hardly surprising that there is so much cynicism about government itself. Performance in many areas is less than that to which we are entitled. But few people make the connection between those results and our failure to nourish a committed professional and effective career service.[26]

Most people would argue that the state should be served by high-quality individuals. Some might counter that the private sector is more important than the public since it produces most of the wealth in the society, and therefore the private sector ought to attract the finest personnel available. But overall the Volcker Commission's assumption that America's "best and brightest" should be represented at the top of the federal government is not a very controversial proposition.

The difficulty comes in defining what one means by the best people. There are, in fact, a variety of ways to think about who the best people might be. One is to think of the best people as those who are the brightest, as the Volcker Commission did. This reflects a widely held assumption that "best and brightest" are synonymous.

However, there are other ways to think about what might represent quality in the individuals who serve the state. For example, one might put an emphasis on the ability to work in teams or on the ability to bargain with other actors in the policy process. The latter two abilities could be emphasized above raw intellect, although few would want negotiators or team members who lacked intelligence to serve in responsible positions in government organizations.

Even the Volcker Commission's Task Force on Recruitment and Retention, which clearly shared the overall commission emphasis on the "best and brightest" definition of quality, noted that "quality is an illusive term" and that it "will always be difficult to measure."[27] It cited a General Accounting Office assessment that one needs information on employee knowledge, skills, and ability, as well as data on individuals' attitudes, values, and motivations and on the match of an individual's capacities and the requirements of the job in order to assess employee quality. Such data, not surprisingly, were unavailable for analysis.

Research commissioned by the task force therefore fell back on more easily obtained data—data that the commission clearly found an acceptable indicator of what is meant by "best and brightest." The research report appended to the Task Force on Recruitment and Retention's statement was titled "The 'Best and Brightest': Can the Public Service Compete?" The report analyzed the results of a survey of members of four major collegiate academic honor societies (Phi Beta Kappa, Beta Gamma Sigma, Sigma Xi, and Pi Alpha Alpha). Respondents, the research report noted with pride, had a mean grade point average of 3.72 (on a four-point scale), and more than half had completed graduate school.[28] We think it fair to say that academic accomplishment of a prestigious sort is clearly at the heart of the commission's definition of best and brightest, and we will use that definition when we test the commission's own claims about a decline in quality of the federal executive. But it is important to bear in mind that academic achievement is only one indicator of quality.

There are other aspects of quality that have concerned those who write about organizational personnel.[29] Again, assuming a certain level of general intelligence is present, do Americans want organizations to be led by people who have particular technical skills, who are trained as specialists in a substantive field or in a support area such as accounting or personnel administration, or do they want generalists who bring a wide scope of learning and conceptual ability to an organization? These are vintage personnel system questions for which there is no optimal answer.

The top rung of the American bureaucracy has long been populated by specialists who have risen through the ranks of the agencies. These people are experts in the areas they administer. Specialists in agriculture are found in the Agriculture Department, health specialists in the relevant parts of the Department of Health and Human Services, and so on. For years, reformers have attempted to change the system to give more emphasis to generalists and, in particular, to encourage rotation of agency executives so as to break the strong ties that often build up between specialists in the agencies and their counterparts in groups and firms in the nongovernmental sector. One of the goals of the rank-in-the-person system established through the Senior Executive Service (see chapter 2) was to encourage rotation of executives across agencies and thereby to promote a wider vision, which was perceived as the strength of a generalist system.

Many, however, are critical of the archetypical generalist system, which, until recently at least, was found in Great Britain. Civil servants in the British administrative class were chosen by an examination system that favored humanist graduates of the elite British universities (Oxford and Cambridge). Martin Trow emphasizes the downside of this system in a description of the "British brilliance" looked for in candidates who succeed in reaching the top of the civil service:

> For a very long time the British have put a high premium on a certain kind of brilliance, the capacity to speak with style on a variety of subjects. It is in part the cult of the amateur and in part the cult of the "first class mind." . . . The inordinate admiration for this

kind of brilliance distracts many Englishmen from the awareness that brilliance is almost independent of knowledge. On the contrary, to educated Englishmen, brilliant talk appears to be wisdom. And consistently the British see wisdom as a good cheap substitute for knowledge.[30]

While this quotation obviously exaggerates the flaws of the generalist system for effect, there is no denying that both specialists and generalists bring assets and liabilities to top administrative posts. The strength of the specialists is that they have deep knowledge of technical issues and can fathom the pros and cons of any decision within their expertise that is put before them. This is no small advantage in settings in which complex technical issues are the common currency of decision. The strength of the generalists is said to be broad vision and the likelihood that they will make decisions that look to the wider interest rather than the interest of a particular profession or clientele. Both sets of people can be of high quality. The problem is to choose individuals (or, better put, combinations of individuals) who have the right package of qualities to make public organizations function well.

In sum, there are complex and little-understood trade-offs here. In the end, we want people in the public service who can produce quality work and who adhere to norms of democratic accountability—either because they have internalized them or because they are sanctioned if they violate them. However, this is a murky area. It is hard to say exactly what combination of qualities will produce the best outcome. We know that values count, but we don't know how much as compared with external sanctions. We know that many politicians care deeply about the views of those at the top of the public service who work for them, but we need to know much more about whether, how much, and under what circumstances civil servants' views affect how policy is developed and carried out.

One assumption that almost everyone makes is that the higher the position an executive holds in an organization (whether in the public or the private sector), the more important it is that he or she approximate the "best and brightest" standard in intellectual terms. Whether specialist or generalist, whether team player or not, such a person should have the ability to comprehend the issues and analyze them effectively.

However, even the best and brightest administrative personnel—no matter how we choose to define best and brightest—cannot ensure good outcomes in a democratic political system. Other problems aside, such as human error and organizational design flaws, administrators in a democratic system are there to advise elected (and politically appointed) policymakers and to carry out their wishes. They must work with the policy directives and resources they are given. Often they must do things they do not believe are wise and spend public funds in ways they do not think are efficient or effective. Factors such as these make it all the more difficult to evaluate the connection between the qualities of personnel and the quality of the product in the public sector.

Some Tests to Come

We do not try to address all the issues raised by the discussion above, though we recognize their import. Rather, we concentrate on a few questions that have been at the center of recent public discussion about the leaders of the American federal bureaucracy. One can doubt some of the assumptions underlying this debate, for example that the best and brightest can be identified by their educational accomplishments, or that one ought to be concerned if a particular set of individuals is not found at the top of the federal bureaucracy or if the numbers in that set are declining, or that the morale of those at the top is an important source of good performance. These assumptions, as we noted, are subject to question. But propositions based on them are important enough and sufficiently widely accepted by those who are concerned about the U.S. public service that it is essential to see what the reality is.

CHAPTER FOUR

Who Are the Federal Executives? A Longitudinal Analysis

THE ARGUMENT OF the Volcker Commission that a "quiet crisis" exists in the federal bureaucracy is widely accepted, particularly the notion that there has been, to use Chairman Paul Volcker's words, "a thinning out" in the quality of federal personnel.[1] In a 1996 book on civil service reform, for example, its authors declare: "Currently, the federal service does not attract and keep the smartest, most broadly educated citizens."[2]

More recently another view has come into focus. This view is reflected in the 1993 "reinvention" initiative of Vice President Al Gore and the Clinton administration. Gore chaired the National Performance Review (NPR), whose report emphasized failed systems as the cause of the federal government's problems while praising the quality of government personnel. An oft-quoted part of the report's introduction says, "The federal government is filled with good people trapped in bad systems: budget systems, personnel systems, procurement systems, financial management systems, information systems. When we blame the people and impose more controls, we make the systems worse." In its conclusions, the report emphasized, "Over time, it will become increasingly obvious that people are not the problem."[3]

We cannot know precisely what role people or systems play in making government function well, although clearly people and systems may combine in ways that improve or worsen government. But people are a critical building block regardless of where one places the main emphasis. It is not likely, for example, that the "reinventors" would suggest that less able people could work well in a system that was more properly designed. This chapter, therefore, focuses on people.

In particular, we focus here on the demographic and social characteristics of those at the top of the U.S. federal executive, analyzing data relevant to the questions of representation and quality of personnel raised in chapter 3. Who occupies the top administrative positions in the executive branch? What are their social backgrounds, educational attainments, and levels of experience? How do they compare with the public at large? Has the composition of the federal executive changed? How do top-level federal executives compare with top executives in the private sector? What does the evidence indicate about the purported decline in the federal service? How have the reforms of 1978 affected federal executives, particularly in terms of rotation across agencies? Has the morale of federal executives suffered the decline the Volcker Commission feared? What are the prospects for attracting and retaining top-flight people in the federal executive?

Diversity

The federal government, like most large organizations in American society, aims to increase the diversity of its work force. Recall from chapter 3 that the federal government's overall work force has been quite representative of the population at large for many years. Women and minorities, however, were most commonly in lower-level jobs. Over the years the government has worked to increase the number of women and minorities in the federal service, particularly at its top levels. In fact, the hiring of women and minorities has outpaced white male recruitment since the mid-1970s. Now there are even some who fear that through this emphasis on diversity "employee quality will be compromised."[4] We will get to the question of quality shortly, but for the moment we focus on diversity itself.

Table 4-1 presents data on the racial and ethnic composition of our samples of top career administrators and political appointees. The table, which minimizes detail on ethnicity for ease of presentation, shows a slow process of change at the upper levels of the career service and a much more volatile pattern for political appointees. Each presidential administration, of course, has great leeway to change the composition of the corps of

Table 4-1. *Racial/Ethnic Composition of Federal Executives, by Year*[a]

Percent

Race/Ethnicity	1970		1986–87			1991–92		
	PE	CSI	PE	CSI	CSII	PE	CSI	CSII
White	84	97	95	94	93	82	89	94
African American	15	3	2	4	7	7	8	2
Hispanic	0	0	2	0	0	9	2	4
Other	2	0	2	2	0	2	2	0
N	(61)	(65)	(62)	(68)	(69)	(45)	(53)	(53)

a. Because of rounding, percentages do not always sum to 100.

PE = political executives (political appointees).

CSI = career civil servants who occupy the top rungs in their administrative units and report to political appointees. Members of this group were called supergrade career civil servants in 1970; in 1986–87 and 1991–92 they were drawn from career civil servants in the Senior Executive Service (established in 1979).

CSII = career Senior Executive Service members who report to other civil servants, not political appointees.

appointed executives. And one can see quite a bit of variation between the administrations we studied. Nixon's administration had a sizable number of African American political appointees, mainly in agencies headed by relatively liberal secretaries, who were free to select their own subcabinet subordinates under the system used in the early part of the administration. Reagan's appointees were nearly all white. By contrast, the Bush administration had a significant percentage of minority appointees, including a meaningful representation of appointees from the Hispanic population, which made up about 9 percent of the U.S. population by 1990.[5]

To a significant degree, the composition of those at the top of the career civil service at any given time is a reflection of choices made at the point of recruitment twenty to twenty-five years before. Most civil servants work their way up a career hierarchy, starting at entry-level positions. Furthermore, the pace of change at the top—especially in terms of ascriptive characteristics of the service—will often be slow, even where an effort is made to promote members of groups deemed to be underrepresented. This may well explain the fact that racial and ethnic minority representation at the top of the civil service, while generally growing, is still quite modest. The changes over the more than twenty years of our interview studies are noticeable, especially among the Career I group, but they are hardly revolutionary.

Figure 4-1. *Female Federal Executives, by Year*[a]
Percent

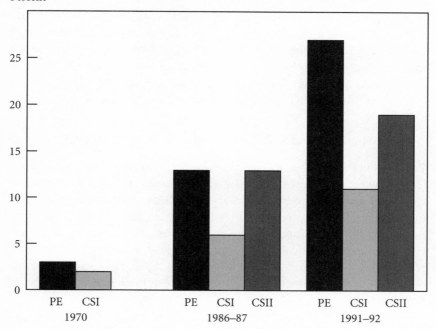

a. Entries are the percentage of each sample that are female. Executive categories are explained in table 4-1, note a.

Where the changes are both consistent and closer to revolutionary is in the percentage of women in the administrative elite. Figure 4-1 shows a marked rise of women in all categories. The increase is particularly rapid among appointees, a clear function of the relative ease with which the composition of the appointee ranks can be changed. Where 3 percent of our sample of Nixon administration appointees were women, the comparable percentage was 27 in the Bush administration, a ninefold increase. The figures are less startling for the career categories, as the previous discussion would lead one to expect, but still quite consistent and indicative of significant change. In the Career I category, those top civil servants who report to political executives (and in that respect the highest level), the percentage female went from 2 percent in the Nixon administration to 11 percent under Bush. In the Career II category the figure reached 19 percent in the

Bush administration. Women who previously would either have dropped out of the executive work force or hit the "glass ceiling" are clearly emerging as a significant component of the top administrative elite. In our earlier work, *Bureaucrats and Politicians in Western Democracies,* we observed that "the female half of the population is virtually excluded at the outset from . . . the administrative elite."[6] This is no longer the case. And, we should note, women are every bit as educated—in fact slightly more educated—than their male counterparts in administrative roles.

Social Status and Educational Accomplishments

We noted in the previous chapter that elites tend to come from more privileged backgrounds and to have superior educational attainments when compared with most others. Now we want to document the extent to which this is true for American administrative elites, to see how (if at all) their backgrounds and attainments have changed, and, in the area of education where the available data allow the appropriate analysis, to compare top government administrators with their "peers" in American society—that is, those outside government who are comparable to them in age and occupational status.

As table 4-2 indicates, top federal executives tend to come from upper status families. Their fathers were typically men with managerial or professional jobs. Indeed, the modal category in the table is "high professional or managerial," indicating occupations such as company director, senior manager, physician, university teacher, or engineer. There is no drop-off in this category over more than twenty years of interviews. If anything, there is actually a small increase, although one should not make much of small changes in these data. There are also signs of modest changes in the direction of greater representation of individuals whose fathers had lower-status occupations (manual workers), a balancing that would appeal to those who believe that the top ranks should be more representative of the public than they have been in the past. But the overall picture is one of an administrative elite drawn from the higher reaches of American society.

The educational attainments of the U.S. administrative elite continued to be every bit as impressive in 1992 as they were a generation earlier in 1970. In fact, the evidence in the second half of table 4-3 indicates an increase in the already high level of educational achievement. Across the three sample periods, all of the top civil servants and almost all of the political appointees had at least some college education. Indeed, most graduated

Table 4-2. *Occupational Status of Federal Executives' Fathers, by Year*[a]

Percent

Father's occupational status[b]	1970		1986–87			1991–92		
	PE	CSI	PE	CSI	CSII	PE	CSI	CSII
High management or professional	49	39	45	37	36	55	49	39
Low management or professional	27	30	19	12	13	18	10	18
Skilled nonmanual	11	11	10	12	12	10	16	10
Lower nonmanual	7	7	9	9	12	8	6	10
Skilled manual	4	7	10	19	10	5	2	10
Semiskilled or unskilled	2	7	7	10	16	5	16	14
N	(45)	(57)	(58)	(67)	(67)	(40)	(49)	(51)

a. Executive categories are explained in table 4-1, note a. Because of rounding, percentages do not always sum to 100.

b. The coding scheme was used in our earlier work, *Bureaucrats and Politicians in Western Democracies,* and came originally from David Butler and Donald Stokes, *Political Change in Britain* (St. Martin's Press, 1969).

from college. But the typical federal executive went beyond undergraduate study. An average of 72 percent of the political appointees had at least some postgraduate training, and the comparable figures for career civil servants are 87 percent in the Career I category and 91 percent in the Career II category. In short, the men and women who are top administrators in the American government—particularly top career administrators—have more schooling than most occupational groups in the country, including their peers in the wider society who are high-level professionals and executives.

The degree to which the educational attainments of administrative elites differ from those of the rest of American society is apparent from an examination of the first part of table 4-3. There we list the educational levels of the general adult population and then of three progressively more rarefied sections of the population who increasingly resemble top federal administrators in their ages and occupational status. These data provide standards for comparing top federal administrators to the rest of the population. The first entry presents the educational attainments of random samples of adults in the American population taken at three points comparable to the dates of our elite surveys. The second restricts the samples to those who are thirty-five to seventy years old, the age range encompassing most

Table 4-3. *Educational Attainments of Adult Population and Federal Executives, by Year*[a]

Percent

Sample and level of education	1970	1986	1992
Adult population			
Total sample			
Primary	9	3	2
Secondary	66	54	50
Some college	15	23	25
College graduate	8	11	13
Postgraduate[b]	3	10	11
N	(1,573)	(2,176)	(2,329)
Ages 35–70			
Primary	11	4	2
Secondary	67	51	48
Some college	11	22	22
College graduate	7	10	14
Postgraduate	4	13	14
N	(895)	(1,142)	(1,282)
Ages 35–70, management/professional			
Primary	3	0	1
Secondary	47	25	22
Some college	23	23	22
College graduate	18	22	26
Postgraduate	10	30	30
N	(230)	(533)	(591)
Ages 35–70, high management/professional			
Primary	2	0	0
Secondary	25	25	26
Some college	21	27	17
College graduate	19	20	24
Postgraduate	33	29	33
N	(48)	(167)	(204)

Federal executives[c]

	1970		1986–87			1991–92		
	PE	CSI	PE	CSI	CSII	PE	CSI	CSII
Primary	0	0	0	0	0	0	0	0
Secondary	3	0	0	0	0	2	0	0
Some college	2	6	10	0	0	4	0	2
College graduate	26	15	11	12	12	24	8	6
Postgraduate	69	79	79	88	88	69	93	93
N	(61)	(65)	(62)	(68)	(69)	(45)	(53)	(53)

Source: Mass data are drawn from the 1970, 1986, and 1992 U.S. Election Studies archived by the Interuniversity Consortium for Political and Social Research.

a. Because of rounding, percentages do not always sum to 100.

b. Persons who did postgraduate work are included in this category, whether or not they received a degree.

c. Executive categories are explained in table 4-1, note a.

members of the American administrative elite. The third is restricted to those in this age range who have managerial or professional occupations. And the last is a subset who hold higher-level managerial and professional jobs—the subset of the population that is as close to a sample of the private sector "peers" of the top federal administrators in our study as one can obtain from national survey data.

What these data show first is an increasing level of educational achievement in the adult national population. Whereas in 1970 about 26 percent of the national population reported at least some college education, almost 50 percent indicated the same level of achievement in 1992. The percentage with at least some postgraduate education rose from 3 to 11 over the same period. These figures are greater, of course, for people aged thirty-five to seventy who have managerial and professional occupations, increasing from 51 percent who had at least some college in 1970 to 78 percent in 1992, and from 10 percent who reported postgraduate training in the earlier year to 30 percent in 1992. And the figures are even more impressive (and also more stable) for those in higher managerial or professional occupations. Here over 70 percent had at least some college education in all three years, and the percentage with postgraduate training was at or above 30 percent in every year also.

These data say much about the increasing levels of educational attainment of the population at large and about the impressive educational credentials possessed by the "peers" of top federal executives, but they say even more about the executives themselves. Top federal executives are far and away the most educated group in this table (we are talking here about schooling, of course, and not more subtle notions about education or even educational quality). They not only outshine the population at large in this respect; they have a decided edge over those occupying roughly comparable positions in the private sector. And that edge for career civil servants has increased over the period of our study.[7] In 1970 the ratio of those in the Career I civil servants category who had at least some postgraduate education to those in the peer sample of high managers and professional was 2.4 to 1. In 1992 it was up to 2.8 to 1. The top of the federal administrative establishment is hardly wanting when it comes to the most obvious measure of educational achievement—how much schooling executives have had.

It is possible, however, that though the executives have more schooling, they have gotten it at less prestigious institutions. Where once they were the "best and brightest" from the most prestigious institutions, now they are perhaps something significantly less than that. We cannot, of course, know whether they are the best and brightest by any measure available to us or, for that matter, to anyone else. What constitutes the best and brightest is controversial, as we pointed out in chapter 3. Even the executives' university grades or SAT scores, if we had them, would not get to the intangibles that phrase implies, nor tap its multiple meanings. But we can see what institutions the senior executives attended and whether the mix has changed much—a reasonable, though incomplete, indicator of who would be among the best and brightest by the standards the Volcker Commission implied.[8]

Table 4-4 presents data on the types of undergraduate and graduate institutions top federal executives attended. These data show that the percentage of Career I federal executives who attended Ivy League or other prestigious private institutions declined from 26 percent in 1970 to 18 percent in 1991–92, a noticeable change but hardly evidence of a "quiet crisis." Political appointees actually show a larger and more surprising change, from 37 percent of President Nixon's appointees who attended prestigious private institutions down to 20 percent of the Bush appointees, who served a notoriously nonpopulist administration. The figures for graduate institutions attended are similar for political executives, down from 51 percent who attended graduate school at prestigious private institutions in the 1970 sample to 35 percent in 1991–92. Career executives show a slight drop-off in the Career I category who attended prestigious private institutions, from 32 percent in 1970 to 26 percent in 1991–92, with Career II executives going from 38 percent in 1986–87 to 25 percent in 1991–92.

These data show a generally consistent, though not precipitous, trend away from the prestigious private universities as sources of personnel for the top positions among career executives and a more pronounced but still not very drastic trend in the same direction for political appointees. It is important, however, to put these figures in perspective.

First, both appointed executives and career civil servants are at least as likely to have attended prestigious private institutions as are members of Congress.[9]

Second, while government administrators at the levels we sampled tend less often than corporate elites to be graduates of prestigious private institutions, data from a study done in the 1970s comparing the highest level government officials (such as cabinet secretaries) and top private sector executives indicated that their differences in this regard were not great.[10]

Table 4-4. *Type of Undergraduate and Graduate Institutions Attended by Federal Executives, by Year*[a]

Percent

Educational institution	1970		1986–87			1991–92		
	PE	CSI	PE	CSI	CSII	PE	CSI	CSII
Undergraduate								
Harvard-Yale-Princeton	13	3	8	4	1	7	4	2
Other Ivy League	4	5	2	2	3	2	6	2
Other prestigious								
private institutions[b]	20	18	18	15	16	11	8	15
Major state universities[c]	11	11	7	7	16	5	9	15
D.C. area institutions	7	10	3	12	4	5	13	14
Other institutions	46	54	63	60	59	71	60	52
N	(56)	(63)	(62)	(68)	(69)	(44)	(53)	(52)
Graduate								
Harvard-Yale-Princeton	15	8	8	7	12	13	8	4
Other Ivy League	12	10	6	7	8	3	8	4
Other prestigious								
private institutions[b]	24	14	16	12	18	19	10	17
Major state universities[c]	7	10	12	15	15	7	8	13
D.C. area institutions	12	19	8	23	12	10	20	23
Other institutions	30	40	50	37	36	48	45	40
N	(41)	(52)	(50)	(60)	(61)	(31)	(49)	(48)

Sources: James Cass and Max Birnbaum, *A Comparative Guide to American Colleges*, vols. 3 (1969), 13 (1987), and 15 (1991), (Harper & Row) and Kenneth D. Roose and Charles J. Anderson, *A Rating of Graduate Programs*, (American Council on Education, 1970).

a. Executive categories are explained in table 4-1, note a. Because of rounding, percentages do not always sum to 100. Includes only respondents for whom we have data on undergraduate or graduate school attended.

b. This category includes non–Ivy League private institutions that are either "highly competitive" in undergraduate entrance *or* rated among the top ten institutions in the United States in at least three graduate programs.

c. This category includes public institutions that are rated among the top ten institutions in the United States in at least three graduate programs.

And, as we discuss later in this chapter, contemporary federal agency heads continue to compare quite favorably in this regard with top private sector executives.

Third, career federal executives in the domestic agencies often have specialized training suited to the departments in which they serve—a characteristic of the highly specialized American bureaucracy. Their expertise, in other words, is substantive. And in many federal departments there is little chance that this expertise can be secured at the prestigious private universities. Agronomy, for example, is generally taught at the agricultural colleges of state universities and not at private universities.

Finally, we should reiterate that there is a significant value judgment involved in assuming that attendance at prestigious universities is a sufficient indicator that a person is among the "best and brightest." This is obviously questionable if these universities do not offer the field a person has studied, but in addition, opportunities to attend such institutions, especially in the years when the federal executives in our samples went to school, were often limited by factors other than talent and intelligence.

Overall then, there is a noticeable though hardly drastic decline in the proportion of career executives who attended prestigious private universities and a more marked decline in the proportion of political appointees who attended these schools. Given the large proportion of federal executives of all types who had graduate training, the similarity of the schools attended by the highest level public and private sector executives, and the many caveats one would attach to using attendance at the prestigious private universities as an indicator for the "best and brightest," one should probably not be overly concerned about these statistics. But if one were inclined to use these data as a source of worry about the quality of federal executives, the place to focus one's concerns would be on political appointees and not career executives.

A Closer Look

We have not collected longitudinal data to compare top public and private sector executives (except to a limited extent on their undergraduate schools), but we can compare these executives in the early 1990s. *Forbes*, a major business magazine, now annually publishes biographical data on the largest U.S. corporations' top executives, including level of education and institution attended. We can use these data to compare top corporate with top federal executives.

There is one huge difference between the executives in the public and private sectors that we should emphasize at the outset. While the public-sector executives in our 1991–92 study typically earned about $100,000 per year,[11] private sector executives in the 1991 *Forbes* listing averaged $1,617,859 in compensation.[12] This is one well-known fact that is definitely well-

Table 4-5. *Educational Attainments of Top Corporate and Federal Executives, 1991–92*[a]

Percent

Level of education	Top corporate executives (1991)	PE (1991–92)	CSI (1991–92)	CSII (1991–92)	Federal agency heads (1992)
Did not attend college	*	2	0	0	0
Some college	3	4	0	2	3
College graduate	46	24	8	6	19
Postgraduate	51	69	93	93	78
N	(766)	(45)	(53)	(53)	(37)
PhDs or equivalents	5	6	17	21	14
Professional degree[b]	35	36	49	32	54

* Negligible.

a. PE, CSI, and CSII federal executive categories are explained in table 4-1, note a. Other executive categories are explained in the text. Because of rounding, percentages do not always sum to 100.

b. These included LLBs, MBAs, MPAs, and MDs.

founded: top-level executives in the private sector don't just make more money than those in the public sector, they make 15 to 16 times as much, and that includes only what is easily gleaned from the public record.

But when one compares the two sets of executives in terms of level of education, one gets a different perspective. Table 4-5 presents data comparing the educational attainments of the *Forbes* top executives and executives from our 1991–92 sample. While there is a big difference between executives in the two sectors here also, the difference does not mirror that in earnings.

Indeed, table 4-5 shows that postgraduate education is much less common for top private sector executives than it is for their public sector peers. In particular, top career civil servants are about 80 percent more likely to have attended graduate school than top private sector executives. They are three to four times more likely to have PhDs. They are about as likely to have professional degrees. These gaps between education and earnings profiles might lead one to wonder about all the economics literature that extols the material returns from education or, as economists refer to them, "returns to education."

However, it is the case that top federal executives are less likely to have attended prestigious private universities as undergraduates. While about

Table 4-6. *Undergraduate and Graduate Institutions of Top Corporate and Federal Executives, 1991–92*[a]

Percent

Institution	Top corporate executives (1991)	PE (1991–92)	CSI (1991–92)	CSII (1991–92)	Federal agency heads (1992)
Undergraduate					
Harvard-Yale-Princeton	9	7	4	2	14
Other Ivy League	6	2	6	2	3
Other prestigious private institutions	21	11	8	15	25
Major state universities	10	5	9	15	11
D.C. area institutions	1	5	13	14	0
Other institutions	53	71	60	52	47
N	(758)	(44)	(53)	(52)	(36)
Graduate					
Harvard-Yale-Princeton	11	9	8	4	22
Other Ivy League	6	2	8	4	0
Other prestigious private institutions	11	13	9	15	14
Major state universities	8	4	8	12	5
D.C. area institutions	1	7	19	21	8
Other institutions	15	33	42	37	30
Did not attend graduate school	49	31	8	8	22
N	(768)	(45)	(53)	(52)	(37)

a. Includes only respondents for whom we have data on undergraduate and graduate school attended. Because of rounding, percentages do not always sum to 100. PE, CSI, and CSII federal executive categories are explained in table 4-1, note a; educational institution categories in table 4-4, notes b and c.

20 percent of both political and career executives in the federal government attended prestigious private institutions, the figure for top corporate executives is 36 percent. But even these figures are tempered somewhat by the fact that approximately the same percentage of corporate and federal executives attended prestigious private graduate institutions (table 4-6).[13]

While these findings seem impressive enough for the public sector personnel in a comparison of top public and private sector executives, one can argue that the comparison does not consider two populations of executives at the same level. Those from the *Forbes* data are the top executives of the largest U.S. public corporations, while the executives in our samples of political appointees and career civil servants are not the very top people in their organizations. A better comparison, from this perspective, would be with the heads of federal agencies: department secretaries, heads of independent agencies, the president's chief of staff, the director of the Office of Management and Budget, and similar positions.

The relevant data are readily available and presented in the far right columns of tables 4-5 and 4-6. Federal agency heads are 50 percent more likely to have gone to graduate school than top corporate executives (although less likely to have done so than top career civil servants). They are also three times as likely to have earned PhDs and much more likely (54 percent versus 35 percent) to hold professional degrees (table 4-5).

Looking at the type of undergraduate institution attended (table 4-6), it is the federal agency heads who are more likely to have attended prestigious private institutions (42 percent versus 36 percent for the top corporate executives). They are also more likely to have attended prestigious private institutions for graduate work.

Our main point, again, is not that these indicators establish definitively which sector has the highest quality people as executives, but simply that by some conventional measures of the "best and brightest" the public sector people stack up very well. And, based on the longitudinal data presented earlier, there is precious little evidence of a "quiet crisis" in the executive branch, at least in terms of its ability to attract and retain people with impressive credentials as its top executives.

Type of Education: The Dearth of Humanists

We alluded in the previous discussion to the specialized educational training received by American federal executives, particularly those who make the federal government a career. As table 4-7 indicates, career federal executives are most likely to have studied the social and natural sciences and least likely to have studied humanities. The social sciences are the modal field for political appointees, but law comes in a consistent second.

The figures vary a bit over the years, but what is particularly noteworthy about them is how they differ from the figures one finds in other Western nations.[14] The law dominates as the major field of study of top career civil servants in Roman law countries such as Germany, where legal training is essentially training for administrative roles.[15] The humanities is

Table 4-7. *Major Field of University Study of Federal Executives at Highest Educational Level Achieved, by Year*[a]

Percent

Field of study	1970		1986–87			1991–92		
	PE	CSI	PE	CSI	CSII	PE	CSI	CSII
Law	35	19	27	23	13	26	22	24
Humanities, including history	6	5	10	2	0	12	2	2
Social science	47	35	39	43	42	52	43	36
Natural science and technology	12	41	24	32	45	10	33	38
N	(49)	(63)	(51)	(60)	(64)	(42)	(49)	(50)

a. Executive categories are explained in table 4-1, note a. Excludes respondents without a university education or where the field of study was not ascertained.

by far the most common field of study for top British civil servants, where administrative generalists are valued for their ability to step into leadership positions in most any type of agency. The United States is the unusual nation, with its emphasis on nonlegal technical specialization for those who rise to the top of the civil service hierarchy in their departments. The creation of the rank-in-the-person Senior Executive Service (SES) in the Civil Service Reform Act of 1978 was designed to counteract the parochialism that technical specialization, combined with a pattern of service in a single agency, is believed to produce. We examine shortly whether there is now more rotation of senior career executives around the agencies than there was before passage of the act. But whatever changes there may be in the career patterns of senior executives, the data in table 4-7 make clear that the nature of civil servants' educational training has not changed much over the course of our study.

Careers in Government

Careers in government can be characterized in many ways. One of the most important concerns the permeability of recruitment channels:

At one extreme are what we may term *guild systems*, which require long apprenticeship within a single institution as a prerequisite for admission to the elite. At the other extreme are *entrepreneurial systems*, characterized by a high degree of lateral entry into the elite from outside careers and institutions. Guild systems ensure that elites will be more experienced and more fully socialized into the norms of the elite institution. On the other hand, entrepreneurial systems provide the elite with freshets of new ideas and with exposure to the skills and experiences of other social institutions. In short, guild systems maximize internal integration within the elite, whereas entrepreneurial systems maximize integration of the elite and other parts of society. Personnel turnover is likely to be higher in entrepreneurial systems than in guild systems, although in principle one could combine relatively high turnover at the top with long periods of prior apprenticeship.[16]

Table 4-8 presents data on the mean age and mean years of service in government, in the present agency, and in the present position of our respondents. The first and most obvious thing to notice is that the average executive, whether political appointee or civil servant, is about fifty years old, although political appointees are usually younger than top civil servants.[17] The variance around the mean age is also greater for political executives (note the standard deviations), a function of the fact that many more political appointees are in their thirties or late sixties than is the case for career executives, who are more tightly clustered around the mean.

The latter datum is one indicator of the fact that top career civil servants are part of a guild system, while political appointees are part of an entrepreneurial system. This becomes more apparent when one looks at the mean number of years that each group has served in the government. These figures are for total—that is, noncontinuous—service, and they show the large differences in government experience between political appointees and career executives. Most career executives entered the federal government in their twenties and have spent more than twenty years in its service. Political executives, on the other hand, have typically spent less than ten years in government service, with the majority of their employment outside the national government.[18]

This can be seen most clearly in table 4-9, which shows the percentage of political executives and top career civil servants who have spent 25 percent or more of their adult lives outside federal service. More than 75 percent of the political appointees in each of the three administrations we studied had spent at least one-fourth of their adult lives outside government

Table 4-8. *Mean Age and Tenure in Federal Government, by Year*[a]

Mean years

	1970		1986–87			1991–92		
	PE	CSI	PE	CSI	CSII	PE	CSI	CSII
Age	47.52	51.78	49.39	48.43	51.59	45.91	52.03	49.73
	(9.23)	(7.81)	(12.34)	(7.00)	(6.75)	(9.15)	(4.98)	(7.15)
Government service	9.13	21.66	7.04	20.25	20.27	9.14	22.54	21.35
	(11.59)	(10.93)	(6.22)	(6.72)	(7.40)	(8.54)	(7.48)	(6.12)
In present agency	8.05	17.91	5.02	16.10	18.15	3.76	19.40	19.35
	(11.54)	(12.01)	(5.04)	(7.98)	(7.81)	(4.44)	(8.87)	(7.03)
In present position	1.66	4.37	2.57	3.78	6.21	1.71	4.30	4.30
	(1.57)	(5.08)	(1.94)	(3.87)	(4.97)	(1.05)	(3.81)	(3.70)

a. Standard deviations are in parentheses. Executive categories are explained in table 4-1, note a. Data for 1986–87 include only line personnel for purposes of comparability. (Staff personnel are younger and have fewer years of government service.)

(and recall that many political executives are relatively young) compared with an average of slightly less than 35 percent of top career civil servants.[19]

Two facts are clear. Those who reach the top rungs of the civil service have usually spent the vast majority of their time working for the federal government. But they also tend to specialize within it. Some of this specialization is reflected in the data on education examined earlier, but it is most clearly demonstrated by table 4-8, which shows how long top civil servants have been employed by their present agencies (defined as a major organizational unit such as a department). If one takes the average years that civil servants in each category shown in the table have served in their present agencies as a percentage of their federal government service, they have averaged 85.7 percent of their time in their current agencies. Most top civil servants, in other words, have spent most of their careers in one agency. They have moved steadily up the ladder to top positions, with relatively little experience outside government or even away from the departments where they worked when we interviewed them.

Another way to look at the career specialization—or insularity, as some would say—of top career civil servants in the United States is to consider the percentage who have served in a department or agency other than the one where they now work. As figure 4-2 indicates, most top career civil servants

Table 4-9. *Adult Life Spent outside Government, by Year*[a]

Year and job status[b]	Percent who have spent 25% or more of adult life outside national government
1970	
PE	78
(N = 60)	
CSI	30
(N = 64)	
1986–87	
PE	86
(N = 53)	
CSI	37
(N = 68)	
CSII	41
(N = 69)	
1991–92	
PE	76
(N = 45)	
CSI	32
(N = 53)	
CSII	34
(N = 53)	

a. Adults are defined as age 25 and over.
b. Executive categories are defined in table 4-1, note a.

have served in only one agency. However, the figure also suggests the potential inherent in the Civil Service Reform Act of 1978 for influencing the pattern of service of top executives.

Focusing for now only on the top career executives, the proportion of those who have served in an agency other than the present one is similar in 1991–92 to what it was in 1970: between 22 and 24 percent. These figures exemplify the general tendency to promote from within those who have worked their way up the ladder within an agency. These individuals are extraordinarily well prepared in educational terms, as we documented earlier, and they have honed their specialized knowledge of the programs and functions of their agencies through years of service. What they may lack is the broader perspective that can come from service in agencies with different constituencies and missions.

Figure 4-2. *Career Mobility of Federal Executives, by Year*[a]

Percent

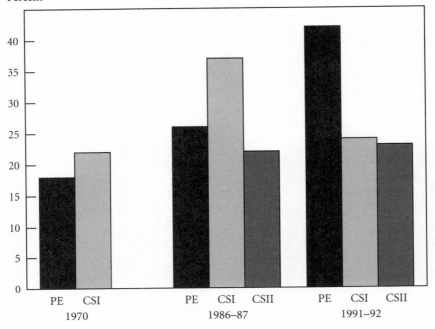

PE   CSI   PE   CSI   CSII   PE   CSI   CSII
   1970   1986–87   1991–92

a. Figure shows percent of each sample who have served in a department or agency other than their current one. Executive categories are explained in table 4-1, note a. Data for 1986–87 include only line personnel for purposes of comparability.

The single aberrant entry in figure 4-2 for top career civil servants is the 37 percent of Career I executives in 1986–87 who served in more than one department or agency. This is, we suspect, one manifestation of the Reagan administration's use of the flexibility of the 1978 Civil Service Reform Act (which created SES) to influence the composition and career patterns of the top civil service, particularly those career executives reporting to political appointees.[20] The Reagan administration wanted to shake up the agencies, and one way to do so was to put into top positions people who agreed with the Reagan political agenda or who, due to their varied experiences, would be less likely to identify strongly with an agency's mission. The Bush administration was much less zealous than the Reagan administration and therefore had less interest in moving civil servants to new agencies or in selecting SES executives within an agency who were sympathetic to its views.[21] The opportunity is now there, however, as it has always been in the more generalist-oriented British civil service, to more easily promote the interagency mobility of career executives.[22]

The data in figure 4-2 show a very different pattern for political appointees than for career civil servants. The percentage of political appointees who have served in a department other than the one employing them at the time of our surveys rose from 18 percent in 1970 to 26 percent in 1986–87 and then jumped to 42 percent in 1991–92. The large increase in 1991–92 is probably one manifestation of the Bush administration's desire to distinguish itself from its predecessor. Of the political appointees in our 1991–92 study, only 29 percent reported that the position they held before their present position was in the agency where they now worked, though almost half (47 percent) reported that they had worked for the executive branch of the federal government in some capacity right before their present appointments.[23] People who had held appointments in the Reagan administration, in other words, often received high-level appointments in the Bush administration, but they were most commonly placed in a different agency.[24]

In summary, our examination of career data for high-level U.S. civil servants shows that guildlike features still characterize the system. People who reach the top of the career bureaucracy generally enter federal service at a young age and work their way up. Although the norm is still service over a career in a single agency, it appears that a determined administration can now successfully increase mobility between agencies (or, more precisely, increase the probability that career people with experience in more than one agency will serve in top positions). The latter is said to promote broader perspectives among career executives by reducing the parochialism long service in a single agency can produce.

Over the course of our study, political appointees have continued to come from outside the government and to serve for relatively brief periods. But the average political appointee has served in government between seven and a half years (the mean figure for 1986–87) and a little over nine years (the mean in both 1970 and 1991–92), which should be enough to give an intelligent individual with a will to learn a pretty good grasp of how administrative agencies work.

Be that as it may, many who have examined the careers of top-level federal executives have stressed the fact that political appointees tend to stay a relatively short time in a given post.[25] Indeed, table 4-8 indicates that, in the years of our study, the average service for appointees in their current positions varied between 1.7 and 2.6 years. As Hugh Heclo correctly notes:

> This relative inexperience at the top does not mean that political
> executives are complete novices to government. . . . [However,] the
> single most obvious characteristic of Washington's political
> appointees is their transience. While most take up their appoint-
> ments with somewhat more government experience . . . than is
> usually assumed, political executives are not likely to be in one
> position for very long.[26]

Further, Heclo says: "Much more important than the experience or inexpe-
rience of political appointees as individuals is their transience as a group."[27]
This transience makes teamwork difficult, as political executives are unlikely
to know one another or to be bound by other unifying ties.

Consideration of our data and Heclo's arguments raises a series of
points about political appointees. First, while political executives have much
less experience in government than career executives, many have quite a bit,
and these experienced people should be effective in government roles more
quickly than their less experienced peers. The high standard deviations for
"mean years of government service" and "mean years in present agency" in
table 4-8 reflect the great spread about the mean in each of the periods studied. In other words, many executives have much experience and others have
little. Second, for those who have most of their experience in the same
agency (which was common for political appointees in the Nixon and
Reagan administrations), the experience handicap should be further
reduced. Third, while political appointees do tend to serve in a given post
for relatively short periods, this transience is most likely to handicap teamwork and the forming of unifying ties where an administration either lacks
clear goals or, if it does have them, fails to screen its appointees for adher-
ence to those goals. In other words, the impact of political executives' short
tenures is conditional, not absolute. Fourth, there is apparently a trade-off
between the advantages that come from service in more than one agency (a
broader perspective on government) and service in one agency (accumulation of substantive expertise).[28] In sum, each pattern has advantages and
disadvantages, and each is open to criticism.

Does It Run in the Family?

The Volcker Commission was quite concerned about what it saw as the
increasing difficulty of attracting outstanding people to the public service.

The commission cited a number of factors leading to a "trend" that would soon leave the United States with "a government of the mediocre, locked into careers of last resort or waiting for a chance to move on to other jobs."[29] One of these factors was a set of survey results indicating that only 13 percent of senior executives would recommend that young people start their careers in government and that less than half of senior civil servants would recommend a job in government to their own children.[30]

But these survey results represent a snapshot, not a trend. On the surface, the results are disturbing to those who believe that people in a desirable profession should overwhelmingly recommend a career in the same profession to their children. We do not have data on whether top federal executives have, over time, been more or less inclined to recommend jobs in government to their children, but we can examine whether those in high positions have decreasingly come from families active in politics or government service.

As table 4-10 indicates, there is absolutely no evidence of a decline in the percentage of political appointees or civil servants who come from families active in government or politics. Indeed, there are even some small though inconsistent signs of increase. Probably not too much should be made of these, since government was smaller when the top executives in 1970 were making their career choices than when those at the top in 1986–87 or 1991–92 made theirs. Perhaps the most interesting entry is the percentage of Bush administration appointees whose fathers were employed by government. Bush's appointees were as close to what Gaetano Mosca called "the political class" (a stratum of the population in which a tradition of participation in politics and government is passed from generation to generation) as any in our surveys. Another noteworthy fact is that the figure for top civil servants whose fathers were employed by government hovers steadily around 20 percent. To reiterate the main point, political appointees and high-level career civil servants were no less likely in 1991–92 than they were twenty years earlier to be people who went into the "family business" of public affairs.

Is the Job Still Attractive?

Any job has its negative features, and serving in a top position in the federal government can often be quite frustrating. The Volcker Commission was particularly concerned about what it saw as an erosion of morale in American government, with "too many of our most talented public

Table 4-10. *Family Background in Government and Politics, by Year*[a]

Percent

Family involvement in government and politics	1970		1986–87			1991–92		
	PE	CSI	PE	CSI	CSII	PE	CSI	CSII
Father employed by government	8	20	12	24	22	29	19	23
N	(54)	(61)	(60)	(68)	(69)	(45)	(53)	(53)
Mother employed by government	n.a.	n.a.	7	4	7	7	9	6
N			(60)	(68)	(69)	(45)	(53)	(53)
Father involved in politics	2	2	13	9	9	11	2	6
N	(54)	(61)	(60)	(68)	(69)	(45)	(53)	(53)
Mother involved in politics	n.a.	n.a.	5	0	1	4	2	0
N			(60)	(68)	(69)	(45)	(53)	(53)
Father in politics[c] and/or government	9	21	21	28	30	36	21	26
N	(54)	(61)	(62)	(68)	(69)	(45)	(53)	(53)
Mother in politics[c] and/or government	n.a.	n.a.	10	4	9	9	11	6
N			(62)	(68)	(69)	(45)	(53)	(53)

n.a. Not available.

a. Executive categories are explained in table 4-1, note a.

b. In 1970 the item used for this analysis read: "Have any members of your family or relatives been active in administration or in politics? (If yes), In what capacity?" In 1986 and 1991–92 the items read: "Have any members of your family or close relatives been involved in public administration or employed as a civil servant?" and, "Have any of your family or close relatives held political or party office?" (Items pertain to any level of geovernment.)

c. Entries are percentages of those employed or involved in either government or politics. Since some parents did both, the entries are not perfect sums of the relevant percentages listed above.

servants—those with the skills and dedication that are the hallmarks of an effective career service . . . ready to leave." The commission added, "Careers that were once seen as proud and lively are increasingly viewed as modest and dull—even demeaning." The president, Congress, and other officials at the highest level were urged to "articulate early and often the necessary and honorable role that public servants play in the democratic process."[31]

Figure 4-3. *Job Satisfaction of Federal Executives, by Year*[a]
Percent

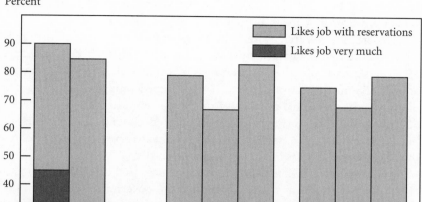

a. Executive categories are explained in table 4-1, note a.

The role of the top public servant in the United States is beset by many problems, which we examine in other parts of the book, but for the moment we look to see whether morale actually eroded over the period covered by our study. The simple answer is, not very much, but there are some signs of deterioration.

Figure 4-3 indicates that in 1970 most top federal executives liked their jobs and that a decided majority in 1986–87 and 1991–92 felt the same way. However, 1970 was a high point, and there was a noticeable (albeit modest) drop-off after that in the overall percentage of political appointees who were satisfied with their jobs and in the percentage of Career Service I executives who felt the same way. (Career Service II executives were the most satisfied of all the categories in the two periods for which we have data for them.) In addition, the percentage of political appointees whose answers indicated that they liked their jobs "very much" dropped from 45 percent in 1970 to 11 percent in 1991–92. The comparable figures for Career Service I civil servants went from 31 percent in 1970 to 13 percent in 1991–92.

Dissertation research by Kerry Manning of the University of Pittsburgh, who investigated data from the General Accounting Office (GAO) and Merit Systems Protection Board (MSPB) on morale and performance among SES members from 1979 to 1992, reached similar conclusions. He did find a dip in morale in 1983—from 83 percent satisfaction in 1980 to 56 percent satisfaction (the measure, as reported, contains no gradients)— but the level rose to 74 percent by 1986 (the next survey) and returned to the neighborhood of its initial level soon thereafter.

Manning attributes the drop in morale measured in 1983 to two factors: a reaction to the antibureaucratic and antigovernment climate of the early years of the Reagan administration and dissatisfaction with initial implementation of the CSRA, particularly the failure to provide promised bonus levels to members of the SES. He believes that morale increased in later years as relations between senior career administrators and Reagan appointees eased and as the initial disappointment with SES dissipated.[32] Be that as it may, the GAO and MSPB data reinforce our findings.[33]

To briefly summarize our findings, which present a more finely graded measure of morale than Manning employed, the data indicate a modest overall drop in morale and a more pronounced drop-off in the intensity of satisfaction. These are clearly warning signs, but it seems fair to say that they do not yet indicate that a crisis in morale, quiet or otherwise, is upon us.

What about the Future Generation of Executives?

Overall, our analysis indicates that the quality and experience level of top administrators have not declined. Indeed, contrary to the "quiet crisis" hypothesis, there are even signs of improvement.

One can make a strong argument that the quality indicators for top career executives in 1991–92, people who on average entered government service about 22 years earlier, should reflect a debilitating impact of the government bashing (particularly bureaucrat bashing) that began with George Wallace in the late 1960s and was reenergized in the mid-1970s by Carter and Reagan. Of course, it is possible that such factors did not have a significant impact on recruitment until the mid-1970s in the aftermath of the

Nixon administration. But even so, many of the best and brightest, at least according to the quiet crisis hypothesis, should have exited in the interim. Perhaps they did, and those who would have reached the top under other circumstances would be even better and more enthusiastic about government service than those in our samples.

Let us take a different tack for the moment, though, and see what is known about recent recruits into the federal service. Data on the recruits surely ought to reflect any quality problems that may exist as a result of the problems the public service has faced over the past two or three decades.

A study by Philip E. Crewson examined scores on the Armed Forces Qualifications Test (AFQT). This exam was given to a cross-section sample of 12,000 young men and women as part of the National Longitudinal Survey of Youth (NLSY) sponsored by the Department of Labor. According to Crewson, "The NLSY provides the opportunity to study employment decisions between 1980 and 1990 for a nationally representative group ranging in age from 17 to 35. The expectation is that if a crisis occurred during the 1980s, some evidence in the NLSY should reflect lower quality in federal sector entrants than their private sector counterparts."[34]

Crewson argued that past discussion of the quality issue had frequently been anecdotal or based on surveys gauging supervisors' perceptions of changes in employee quality rather than on hard data. He also said that even this evidence was often contradictory, citing as examples Office of Personnel Management studies of the qualifications of scientists and engineers (1991) and computer specialists (1990), which "found no decline in the quality of federal employees when measured by education, experience, class standing, or GPA."[35] In evidence particularly germane to those concerned about the quality of future top-level executives, Crewson stressed that a study of students entering the programs of major public affairs teaching institutions "failed to find a decrease in numbers [entering] or qualifications."[36]

His finding, succinctly put, is this: "When holding sex, race, occupation and economic status constant, federal employees hired during the 1980s have AFQT percentile scores that average 5.5 points higher than private sector employees." Crewson concludes:

> Evidence supporting the premise that the federal civil service is not attracting quality personnel is very elusive. Not only do detailed studies within the federal government fail to consistently discover an alleged decline in quality, but the results from a comparative

analysis between the public and private sectors of a nationally representative sample of job entrants suggest that those entering the public service are of higher ability than anecdotal evidence or simplistic assumptions about human behavior would predict. Although there has been an influx of women and minorities during the 1980s, the federal government does not appear to have imperiled quality in its effort to increase diversity. In fact, the federal sector is becoming more diverse while still attracting more able entrants than the private sector. [37]

Some might contend that the controls in Crewson's analysis for sex, race, and family income (all statistically significant factors) undermine the strongly stated conclusion that the federal sector is attracting more able entrants than the private sector. Females, nonwhites, and people with lower family incomes tend to score lower on the AFQT. Crewson, however, argues that he should include the controls because of the differing incidence of employment in the public and private sectors of the groups represented by these variables.[38] But there is little doubt that the federal government is still doing quite well in attracting quality personnel.[39] Indeed, Crewson redid his analysis in 1997 to take account of criticisms of his approach. He and a colleague found that removing the ethnicity and gender controls from his model removed the quality difference between the public and private sectors but did not result in any advantage for the private sector.[40] In brief, there is little in the available evidence to suggest that those who reach the top of the federal civil service in the near future will be any less accomplished than those who were there in 1991–92, and the latter group is quite impressive.

Some Concluding Observations

There is a debate about the quality of the public service in the United States. The Volcker Commission endorsed the view that there is a "quiet crisis" in the public service, with a trend toward a government of the mediocre. The National Performance Review, led by Vice President Gore, sees a problem, but not in the quality of the people. Rather it stresses the notion of "good people trapped in bad systems."

We discuss system problems later in the book. This chapter centered on the people themselves. Our findings give little support to the notion that the public service is "dangerously eroded." Indeed, what we see at the top of the public service, the focus of our examination, is a group of people who have impressive educational credentials and significant experience in government. Data we present in chapter 7 on the educational levels, experience, and morale of SES executives in the reinvention era reinforce these conclusions.

Of course, there have been some important changes, particularly with regard to diversity. While the evidence indicates only modest changes in the racial and ethnic composition of the top career civil service (and a more volatile pattern for political appointees), it is clear that the administrative elite is no longer an almost exclusively male province. And, we should note parenthetically, while the women who have reached the top of the career service generally have less experience in government than the men, they have slightly higher levels of education.

Federal executives continue to come disproportionately from the upper middle class and to have extraordinary levels of educational achievement, even when compared with their professional and managerial "peers" in the rest of society. The educational accomplishments of top career civil servants in particular were more impressive in 1991–92 vis-à-vis their private sector peers than they were in 1970. There is evidence of a trend away from the prestigious private universities as a source of both political appointees and top career civil servants, but that trend is actually more pronounced for political appointees. To the extent that one believes that civil servants' attendance at such institutions is a sign that the "best and brightest" are in government, the trend for political appointees is the more worrisome one.

Most top civil servants have spent the bulk of their careers in one agency. However, there are clear signs in our data that a presidential administration can now promote greater interdepartmental mobility among career executives if it chooses. Our data confirm that political appointees tend to stay in each position they hold for relatively brief periods, a fact with mixed implications. The overall picture, however, indicates that the experience level of top administrators has not declined.

Most of our indicators, in fact, suggest that the "people" situation in the federal executive is still quite healthy. Many top federal executives may be reluctant to recommend a career in government to their children, but there is no evidence of an actual decline in the percentage of political appointees or career civil servants who come from families active in government or politics. Further, evidence available from a recent study suggests that the quality of recruits into government service is on a par with private sector recruits, and perhaps even better.

Finally, federal executives still like their jobs, though there are some signs of deterioration here. The high point in our data for job satisfaction was

1970, with a modest drop-off after that in the overall level of satisfaction and a more pronounced drop-off in the intensity of satisfaction. As we noted, these are clearly warning signs but hardly indicators of an imminent crisis.

In short, like the reports of Mark Twain's death, the Volcker Commission's worries about an "erosion in the quality of America's public service" seem greatly exaggerated. The National Performance Review's conclusion that "people are not the problem" seems closer to the mark, particularly for career executives and federal agency heads. However, this does not necessarily mean that all is well. Able people may be trapped in inappropriate habits of thought or be unresponsive to the legitimate demands of their superiors. Bad systems may discourage the full use of the considerable talents that may be available. Or inadequate resources and outside pressures may keep quality administrators from delivering the kinds of services they and the citizenry would like. These are matters to which we now turn.

CHAPTER FIVE

Reponsiveness Dilemmas

WHO ANSWERS TO WHOM is at the core of any system of delegation. And administration is inherently such a system. Authorities delegate others to act on their behalf. In any system, including absolute monarchies and dictatorships, bureaucrats respond imperfectly to the authorities' direction. In authoritarian systems, bureaucrats' lack of responsiveness or even just a suspicion about their loyalty has often resulted in suspect administrators losing not merely their jobs, but also their heads. Democracy makes the problem of bureaucratic responsiveness considerably more complex because, among other things, the sanctions for suspect loyalties are far less severe. Also, there is likely to be less continuity of authority in democratic than in authoritarian systems. Democratic politicians do not get elected or anointed for life. Adjustment is difficult. Bureaucrats in a democracy get new bosses with considerable frequency. In a democracy, the chain of command is a bit more convoluted. Louis XIV may have felt relatively little need to answer to others, but democratic politicians cannot afford such self-indulgence. They know they have to answer to others and therefore need to deliver the goods. The flip side of responsiveness is responsibility. In democracies the political leaders are held responsible, so it stands to reason that they are apt to demand responsiveness from the bureaucracy.

Bureaucracy and democracy are thus in inherent tension with one another. First of all, democratic processes are used to select politicians, but not bureaucrats. Despite contemporary pressures for increasing representativeness among civil servants on the basis of characteristics such as gender, race, and ethnicity, bureaucrats still do not have to stand for popular approval at the ballot box. Second, as we noted in chapter 1, bureaucrats may reflect the preferences of previous regimes and be reluctant to adjust to new policies and leaders. Third, as we also noted in chapter 1, bureaucrats may be especially averse to novelty. Fourth, as policy gets more complex, so does policymaking. The bureaucracy (and in the American case, also the courts) becomes an important venue for policymaking because passing laws is merely the beginning of the policymaking process.[1]

In sum, bureaucrats are involved in policy decisions (even if the fiction remains that they are not), but they are unelected decisionmakers. Moreover, career civil servants, much like federal judges, have lifetime tenure. And this, in turn, brings up yet a further source of tension between bureaucracy and democracy—the expertise of the bureaucrat in contrast to the generalist role of the politician. Most bureaucrats acquire expertise in a particular domain and get to know a great deal about the programs they administer. Politicians, by contrast, can ill afford the luxury of committing so many resources to one of many problems they have to cope with, unless that problem is getting reelected.[2]

Bureaucrats are involved in policymaking mainly because bureaucrats do the details, and, as the saying goes, the devil resides therein. Because political leaders are unlikely to know the details (at least not as well as the bureaucrats do) and because there is inherent slippage in delegation, bureaucrats usually wind up defining the exact terms for implementing what it is that leaders want. In a similar vein, bureaucrats can outline possible paths for their political superiors to follow within the bounds of technical feasibility, legal restriction, and even political reality. These powers are nowhere articulated in formal job descriptions, but to a greater or lesser degree they are real nearly everywhere. The expression "bureaucrats need to be on tap, not on top" is a prescription to counter the reality that the knowledge and experience that career bureaucrats possess make them the professionals of government and give them considerable potential to influence the course of policy.

In this chapter, we explore the issue of bureaucratic responsiveness and its relationship to democracy. We note why the issue of responsiveness is perceived to be so important, but also why responsiveness rarely can be, or ought to be, perfectly realized. Among other things, an exclusive premium on the value of responsiveness may clash with other ways in which we want the bureaucracy to perform—with equity and respect for precedent, for example.

There is another form of responsiveness that we do not directly touch upon in this chapter, but which we discuss in chapter 7. This is the idea of "bottom-up" responsiveness—thinking of citizens as customers endowed with purchasing power of a sort and expecting governmental agencies to respond to their preferences. "Bottom-up" responsiveness is a major feature of governmental reinvention both here and abroad. However, even the so-called "top-down" model of responsiveness begins with the notion that those at the top arrived there, either directly or indirectly, through the democratic electoral process and have therefore earned a legitimate right to command.

What Is Responsiveness and Why Is It Important?

Responsiveness is a simple concept in theory but a complicated one in practice. In a democracy, it has to do with the straightforward notion that bureaucrats, who are not elected, should be responsible to elected politicians (or their appointed agents). That is the simple part. In practice, it is probably impossible for any set of bureaucratic agents in a truly democratic and constitutional system simply to follow the dictates of their political superiors. In fact, a bureaucracy that consistently did this would likely be regarded as a mere appendage to whichever party happened to be in power. Such a bureaucracy might well become complicit in denying access to the regime's opponents.[3] Indeed, a system of this sort would be regarded as flagrantly violating the democratic rules of the game.

There are four problems with the idea or practice of making bureaucrats completely responsive: signals and directions from political leaders may lack clarity; conflicts sometimes occur between responsiveness to the chain of command and accountability to the law; there is potential conflict between the demand for responsiveness and the need for stability and memory in government; and institutional complications can arise that pit authorities against one another, thus sowing confusion, or fragmenting authority, and thus segmenting responsiveness.[4]

The Problem of Clarity

The problem of directional clarity arises because political leaders sometimes do not know exactly what they want or may even wish to avoid the risk of choosing. Deciphering signals or directions under these circumstances is difficult. This is one reason politicians often resort to ex post judgments rather than ex ante guidance. The marching orders that President Bush twice articulated to his cabinet are one extreme example of the problem of interpreting political will. Among them were such inspiring messages as "think big" and "challenge the system." The problem was that "the marching orders covered no policy goals for the administration, nor did they provide guidance on policy development."[5]

While political leaders may not be clear about what they do want, they usually know what they do not want. One thing they do not want is the appearance of chaos. They also do not want policies that endanger their political coalitions. Such dangers are easier to spot once a disaster has happened than they are ex ante. Everyone is wiser in hindsight.

Not surprisingly, political leaders get irritated by administrative failures to act as they might wish. Perhaps even more, they get irritated by a bureaucracy that specifically acts in a way they do not wish. But for one's wish to be one's command, it is essential to first articulate the wish. Whether the wish can be regarded legitimately as a command is a different sort of problem, one to which we now turn.

The Problem of Legality

The second problem arises because not everything political leaders want is consistent with prevailing law. Bureaucrats are supposed to be responsive to the chain of command yet also accountable to the law. Political leaders often want to stretch the boundaries of legal constraints that keep them from doing what they want. In theory, bureaucrats achieve accountability by complying with the chain of command, but this assumes that those up the chain are operating lawfully. To be fully responsive to political authority under such circumstances may well violate the rule of law. A system of divided authority further complicates both accountability and responsiveness. It gives civil servants more potential leeway or cover since they are responsible to more than one set of political authorities and can play one off against the other. It also allows civil servants to delay implementing what they regard as ill-advised directives so as to give other authorities opportunities to act and possibly countermand them. But what gives cover to civil servants fuels the suspicions of political leaders, particularly those in the executive branch.

The Problem of Stability

The third problem arises when political leaders try to budge a recalcitrant bureaucracy. For the most part, politicians tend to think bigger, or perhaps simply more grandiose, thoughts than do bureaucrats. Politicians tend to focus on symbols and desired end states; bureaucrats tend to focus more on the relationship of means to ends and the transaction costs attached to altering existing equilibria. We have noted elsewhere that, untempered by bureaucrats, politicians can be susceptible to a frenzied debate about symbolically laden and ideologically driven proposals with no roots in the past and no assessments of costs, benefits, or feasibilities. But we also observed that, undirected by politicians, bureaucrats would be weighted down by inertia derived from past commitments and thus would be susceptible to "directionless consensus."[6]

There is a sort of yin and yang in government between dynamism and ballast. Politicians tend to provide the dynamics and bureaucrats the ballast. Leadership, drive, and vision are essential to government, but continuity, connections to the past, and an appreciation of policy practicality and political feasibility are equally important. These traits are obviously in tension with one another. Harmonious balance between them is desirable, but it is not self-evident exactly how this can be achieved. To the contrary, as the visions of political leaders widen and the changes they contemplate become more expansive, the tensions are likely to become more pronounced.

Thus, the greater and more controversial the changes a new political leadership wants, the bigger the problem of responsiveness is likely to grow.[7] This is so for several reasons. One is that bureaucrats, like most people, tend to be more comfortable dealing with what they know than with the unknown. A second is that bureaucrats develop networks to support their present programs and are reluctant to upset these arrangements. A third is that, beyond the commitments inherent in program networks, bureaucrats often have ideological commitments to the programs they administer. A fourth involves the aforementioned problem of clarity—to what extent can the big ideas of a presidential administration be translated into administrative reality? A fifth is the problem of the institutional divisions along which different policy preferences align. Big and controversial change under divided government places bureaucrats in a political minefield. Whatever they do or fail to do will be regarded as unresponsive to someone. And whatever they do officially or formally, they will often be suspected by the presidential administration under which they serve of unofficially or informally seeking to undermine its plans.

The Problem of Institutions

The problems we allude to above are inherent to the responsiveness issue. That is, they are likely to occur anywhere. There is one key exception, however, and that is the institutional problem. The division of authority built into the U.S. Constitution complicates a problem that exists everywhere.

Theorists have noted that U.S. political institutions have different constituencies.[8] This is also true under unified government, when the same political party is in control of the institutions.[9] Even when these relatively favorable circumstances for presidential-congressional comity prevail, informal treaties may be reached so that congressional and executive territory are effectively agreed to, producing what Charles Gilbert referred to as "segmented responsiveness."[10] Under such arrangements, some agencies are more sensitive to key congressional constituencies and interest groups than to the leadership of the executive branch.

In their most extreme form, arrangements of this sort have been characterized as "iron triangles," in which agencies, congressional committees or subcommittees, and interest groups happily coexist.[11] In this setting, at least according to lore, agencies could escape central direction by providing goods to congressional and interest constituencies with a high demand for them. The congressional committees and interest groups would then defend agency interests politically.[12] These arrangements, of course, are merely implicit understandings and do not last forever. They occur when presidential administrations are indifferent to the situation or decide that the costs of dislodging certain agencies from the grip of Congress are too high or the probability of success in such an endeavor too low. However, as divided government has increasingly become the norm, and as policy disagreements across the parties have intensified about such issues as the size and role of government, the stakes for control of the bureaucracy have grown. From this perspective, the political costs of upsetting the prevailing equilibrium, costs that once appeared so formidable, have seemed to decrease in marginal terms precisely because control of the bureaucracy has become so fundamental to an administration's policy success.

Policy disagreements have often been constructed around the parties' strategies for building winning coalitions. In the 1970s the Democrats became a magnet for various avant-garde social causes and groups, while the Republicans sought to gain the support of whites in the formerly Democratic South and to solidify their hold on middle-class white families. During the Nixon period especially, all of these tensions bubbled to the surface, the effects of which can still be observed. And the way these conflicts played out embroiled the bureaucracy (or at least chunks of it) in open controversy. In short, the separation of powers in the U.S. government compounds the inherently complicated problem of responsiveness.

Responsive to Whom?

We have emphasized that responsiveness is a seemingly simple concept that is very complicated in practice. Even when institutions appear to make the question of who holds authority a straightforward matter, the superior knowledge and experience of career bureaucrats can often be used to manipulate outcomes. The "Yes, Minister" model of the tactful but cunning civil servant manipulating his discombobulated political master is, of course, a parody. But the success of the BBC television series was based on an underlying grain of truth—namely that if politicians want bureaucrats to respond to them, they must first know what they want and then they must ensure that their wishes can be translated into the realities necessary for implementation. In the presence of political drift and uncertainty, bureaucrats are by default often given the power to decide. That power typically lasts until the decisions generate adverse political consequences.

Under the best of institutional conditions, responsiveness is highly imperfect, though it certainly helps when politicians know their minds and pursue what they want persistently. It helps, too, when politicians have sufficient knowledge to engage those who have been delegated to act on their behalf. And it always helps when politicians and bureaucrats are in agreement on the general directions to be pursued. Unfortunately, these circumstances occur infrequently.

Bureaucracy in the Madisonian System

We noted earlier the special difficulty that shared authority across government institutions adds to the responsiveness problem. The framers of the U.S. Constitution gave little thought to bureaucracy and said equally little about it. They, and especially James Madison, the chief architect of the Constitution, did have a strong belief that different institutions organized around different constituencies would decrease the risks of tyranny. In a more contemporary vein, such a system of competitive institutions makes it extremely difficult to develop coherent majorities, such as those one finds in the British Westminster system. There is, of course, a government at the federal level in the United States, but not *the government*.

In theory, the division of power among the branches of government implies a division of labor among the institutions. There is some truth in that, of course, but the reality is that while institutions are separated, power is shared, though often uneasily.[13] One of the areas in which this sharing takes place is in control of the executive branch—that is, the bureaucracy. The Constitution helps muddle the matter of responsiveness more by what it fails to say than by what it does say. While the powers of the legislature are spelled out in the most detail of any of the three branches of government, control of the executive lies in the nether world of implied powers. One of the explicit powers of the executive is to see that the laws are faithfully executed (art. 2, sec. 3). In more contemporary terms, one might loosely infer from this provision the responsibility for managing the administrative state.[14] But article 1, section 8, clause 18 gives Congress the power to make all laws necessary to execute the powers of government. Implicit in this grant is the notion that Congress is to judge whether or not the laws it has written have been faithfully followed. As Norton Long noted, "The unanswered question of American government—'who is boss?'—constantly plagues administration"[15] and makes it likely that there will be a struggle between the executive and legislative branches for control of the executive apparatus.

Epic struggles have in fact occurred between the branches with regard to the reach of their authority, even when the same party has controlled both the legislative and executive branch.[16] But these struggles are apt to become greater when the branches are divided by party and to become titanic when party cleavages are ideologically sharp. Moreover, when divided government is persistent and the same party remains in control of an institution for a long time, an expectation develops in Washington that the controlling party has a proprietorship over it. From the standpoint of the other party, there is little to be lost and seemingly much to be gained by trying to restrict the prerogatives of the "opposing" branch. As Charles O. Jones puts it, each branch seeks to maximize its share of governmental control. In a system in which each branch is given incomplete resources to govern by itself, each has a tendency to stretch its prerogatives as far as they will go—"to round the O" in the words of Sir Ernest Barker, meaning, to complete the circle of governance by itself.[17]

The bureaucracy frequently becomes the battleground for interbranch conflict because it applies concrete meaning to policy. One of the ways each branch tries to control the bureaucracy is through micromanagement, which is simply another way of limiting administrative discretion. In the years encompassed by our interview studies, 1970–92, it is fair to say that executive and legislative political leaders have greatly increased their micromanagement of the bureaucracy. As chapter 6 makes clear, senior federal executives strongly believe that micromanagement is rampant.

The tools administrations have brought to this contest for control have been budgetary and regulatory restrictions, reorganization efforts, selective interpretations of statutes, and aggressive use of personnel policy. On the whole, presidents have been sharpening their existing tools as well as using new ones. Congress also has turned to a variety of tactics to exert control, from very exact specifications in statutes and committee reports of what it wants administrators to do, to legislative earmarks, to indefinite delays on approving appointed personnel, and, sporadically, to seeking redress through the courts. All in all, the period from 1970 to 1992 featured a growing contest of wills, through fair means and foul, between the executive and legislative branches (with the courts frequently adding yet another voice). The contest was exacerbated by the decreasing resources available for new, particularly costly policy initiatives (and decreased availability of side payments), by the growing cohesion of the parties and sharpened differences between them, by the growth of attentive political constituencies with stakes in administrative outcomes, and by a clear willingness on the part of Congress and presidents to try to prevent the bureaucracy from following someone else's will.

Conflict and Control

During the recent period of divided government, which has existed in some fashion for all but six years between 1970 and 1998, the most common situation has been one with a Republican president and a Democratic Congress (or, at a minimum, Democratic control of the House of Representatives). Certainly, the controversies over many policies were (and still are) rooted in partisan division and in the different constituencies served by the political parties. Examples are abundant. Richard Nixon's strategy to create a political base among white voters in the South, for example, meant overriding civil rights enforcement (a policy identified with the Democrats) in the former Department of Health, Education, and Welfare.[18] The Reagan administration, wishing to curry favor with the religious right, created a new unit for family affairs in the Department of Health and Human Services (HHS) and gave it the authority to deny funds to family planning agencies advising abortion as an option. The Reagan administration also consummated the Nixon administration's southern strategy, while serving the religious right, by seeking favored treatment for the evangelistic Bob Jones University, which had refused to comply with federal civil rights regulations. Even the Bush administration, which was otherwise not highly directional and often relatively indifferent toward the bureaucracy, reacted to what it perceived to be regulatory excesses (or perhaps merely to regulations that hurt its political allies) by creating the Competitiveness Council, chaired by Vice President Dan Quayle. The role of the council was to make the job of the agencies responsible for regulation more difficult, and it became notably more active in the latter stages of the Bush administration, when the White House was concerned about shoring up the support of its own constituencies.

Our examples come from Republican presidential administrations because all the years of divided government between 1970 and 1992 featured Republican presidents and Democratic Congresses. Only after the 1994 election has that been reversed. But this is not the only explanation for the conflict. The Democrats created programs to deal with social problems, public works investment, and problems of the workplace, the environment, labor markets, and civil rights. This identified them as the party associated with the big state and its bureaucracy. Simultaneously, much of the bureaucracy became identified with the Democratic party, particularly its liberal wing. When Richard Nixon wrote his memoirs, *RN*, he specifically noted his problems with the bureaucracy, claiming it was full of liberals who were unsympathetic to his more conservative policy agenda.[19] After Ronald Reagan's election to the presidency in 1980 and again upon his reelection in 1984, but before George Bush took office in 1989, a conservative think tank, the Heritage Foundation, provided blueprints for how their champions in the White House should deal with the bureaucracy in order to gain the upper hand. In chapter 6 we examine whether the suspicions of Republican presidents that the bureaucracy is riddled with career civil servants unsympathetic to their policy positions and political party is true.

Mitigating Factors

Clearly, when the conditions for conflict ripen, it is likely that the bureaucracy will be caught in the middle. Nevertheless, the degree to which the bureaucracy itself is caught up in these conflicts depends on the nature of the conflicts. If they are focused on budgets at the macro level or on broadscale program enactments, the battles will most likely, at least initially, take place in the legislative arena. But if they have to do with shifting the balance of power among the interests that influence agencies (the Reagan administration's policy of "defunding the left," for example), regulatory enforcement, and legal interpretations of executive discretion, the interbranch struggle is more likely to find its way into the administrative arena. One thing experience teaches us is that a presidential administration that is given the responsibility to run programs it does not like will usually find it easier to use the administrative than the legislative arena to alter the programs.[20]

The extent to which partisan political struggles have centered on the bureaucracy has lessened somewhat since the Clinton administration settled in Washington. This is partly due to the fact that the major political struggles have been over macro-level issues, such as budgets, taxes, and health insurance. (Some of these issues, especially welfare reform, might well result in major administrative battles down the road.) It also has to do with the lack of clear policy direction—or even a clear theory of executive prerogative—from the Clinton White House.[21] Clinton, in fact, has proved himself remarkably adept at assimilating the agendas of others when that is politically advantageous. But even he continued to use many tools of the administrative presidency when he felt the need for them.[22]

In the last few years, a shift of issues and especially a shift in the style of governance have mitigated the effects of political division on the bureaucracy to some degree. However, the Clinton administration's efforts to "reinvent government" are apt to bring about renewed conflicts with Congress and possibly with the courts because reinvention, responsibility, and accountability have been disconnected from one another. Reinvention turns out to be essentially executive-centered, downplaying the role of other branches in exercising their constitutional prerogatives in control of the bureaucracy. We say more about this initiative in chapter 7.

Conclusion

Questions of bureaucratic responsiveness themselves raise questions. To whom should bureaucrats respond? How much responsiveness should there be, and what kind? Traditionally, the civil service was responsible to the crown as the sovereign. Democracy made the people sovereign, at least in theory. But elected politicians carry the "mandate" of the people through an elected government—a theory with complications even in parliamentary systems. These complications, however, are truly massive in the American constitutional system of separated powers. Partisan division across institutions exacerbates these problems still further, especially when the policy stakes are high and the loyalties of bureaucrats are deemed suspect by one or the other political protagonist. Conditions of divided government help explain why bureaucrats in the United States are thought to be particularly unresponsive to political leadership. A high degree of political conflict under these conditions tends to place the bureaucracy in the midst of withering policy disputes. As the policies the bureaucracy implements come under fire, so too does the bureaucracy itself.

Responsiveness has limits, both realistically and normatively. It is necessary for the bureaucracy to put some space between itself and any particular set of governing authorities. In this sense, the bureaucracy represents the continuity of government above and beyond the particular needs of its present incumbents. Of course, this is the heart of the problem. How can the bureaucracy be both independent and democratically controlled? Political authorities may brand such independence, or even a questioning of its proposals, as sheer recalcitrance. Moreover, there is always reason for current authorities to believe that the bureaucracy is more committed to the legacies of the past than the policy agendas of the present.

A bureaucracy wedded to any given political perspective or any particular party inevitably presents problems for the democratic alternation of power. The career civil service may need to be responsive to the present incumbents (a task made difficult by the American system, with its diffused political authority), but it also needs to be regarded as essentially neutral and fair. A senior civil servant from our 1986–87 sample stated in a particularly folksy way the core problem faced by civil servants trying to balance adaptation and neutrality:

> We have to start with the frame of reference of the statute that's passed and to be implemented with a given administration in power. The way that law can be administered can vary within a spectrum, depending upon the lineage of the statute. . . . I think it's our job to try to follow what the administration wants to do in its approach to accomplishing that particular statute's objective, without allowing that statute to be distorted. . . . Let's say I'm a politician; you're the bureaucrat. I'm gonna stand over there and wave at you, and I'm gonna say come on over here in the burro pen and I'm going to get you as far as I can get you, but you better not get there. If you do, you're gonna be in trouble. I try to live by that because I know that the administration is gonna try to pull you to their way of thinking as far as they can, and the next administration is gonna do it the other way. And I think it's our job to keep the objective on the highway without getting into the burro pit.[23]

In chapter 6, we examine empirically the answers to a set of questions relevant to the responsiveness issue. The data we analyze help us understand how top federal civil servants have changed as the political environment has changed. They also suggest the extent to which political authorities have gained control over the bureaucracy. And they show broadly the ways that the political authorities themselves adapt to the bureaucracy. We cannot settle the large normative questions attached to the responsiveness problem—indeed, no one can—but the data give us a realistic portrait of changes occurring within the top levels of the federal executive and of efforts made by political authorities to control the bureaucracy. Ultimately, the empirical analysis reveals the extent to which there is a true crisis of responsiveness in the U.S. federal bureaucracy.

CHAPTER SIX

Political Responsiveness: Facts and Fables

WHAT WE HAVE over the period of our interviews is a wonderful natural experiment for those interested in bureaucratic responsiveness. As described in chapter 2, President Nixon was obsessed by a need to control behavior in his administration and fearful that both his appointees and the career administrators would be unresponsive to his policy directives. The political conditions and civil service rules he operated under reinforced these feelings of vulnerability and spurred often bizarre attempts to assess the political views of top administrators and to control their behavior. By the time Reagan became president, political changes (particularly Republican control of the Senate) and rule changes (the provisions of the 1978 Civil Service Reform Act in particular) made it easier for a determined administration to control who got top posts and which career civil servants would rise to the top in the agencies. Reagan and his associates had the will to use these advantages. The Bush administration, one less obsessed by the need to control, then came to office and apparently concentrated less on responsiveness.

In this chapter we analyze the changing political complexion of those at the top of the federal executive. We examine the political loyalties, policy views, and roles of federal executives over time. The answers to the questions we address are particularly relevant to the debate about the responsiveness of

An earlier version of the first part of this chapter appeared in "The Political Views of Senior Federal Executives, 1970–92," *Journal of Politics*, vol. 57 (August 1995).

the federal executive to presidential direction. Empirically, the questions are straightforward. What were the partisan and ideological views of top appointees and career executives under Nixon, Reagan, and Bush? Were Nixon's fears realistic? What impact did the changing political climate of the country and the reforms of the executive system under the Civil Service Reform Act have on the role and composition of the top civil service? Were the top career people more likely to be Republicans in later years? Were they more conservative? Did their role in policymaking appear to change? Did other actors in the political system react to the changes? How are civil servants likely to react when they disagree strongly with an administration's policy positions? What can we say about the process of adjustment between political appointees and career civil servants over the life of an administration?

In broader terms, is there a responsiveness crisis in the federal government? How well grounded are the fears of elected politicians, particularly presidents, about the responsiveness of the people who administer the federal government to political directions? Is the system one that adapts to change, or is it impervious to influence by changing political currents? Is the often contentious and deep-rooted distrust of the bureaucracy that is prevalent particularly among conservative Republicans justified? Cross-sectional survey data (comparative statics) cannot provide definitive answers to all questions about responsiveness, of course, but the data present a compelling picture of the nature and degree of political change in the American bureaucracy during each of the three decades represented in our surveys.

Partisan Complexion of the Federal Executives

One of the many distinguishing characteristics of the Nixon administration was its tendency to state its fears about the bureaucracy in an open and frank manner. From the notorious *Federal "Political" Personnel Manual* (sometimes called the "Malek Manual" after its main author, personnel chief Fred Malek) to the many comments on the White House tapes, President Nixon and his associates emphasized their belief that Democratic opponents dominated the career civil service.[1] And they were almost equally suspicious of those they themselves initially appointed to executive positions. As Nixon noted in his autobiography:

> I regretted that during the first term we had done a very poor job
> in the most basic business of every new administration of either
> party: we had failed to fill all the key posts in the departments and

agencies with people who were loyal to the President and his programs. Without this kind of leadership in the appointee positions,
there is no way for a president to have any major impact on the
bureaucracy. . . . I was determined that we would not fail in this
area again, and on the morning after my reelection I called for the
resignation of every non-career employee in the executive branch.[2]

We collected our data on the Nixon administration in 1970, before the
full implementation of the administrative presidency strategy. Relations
between the administration and the domestic policy bureaucracy were not
yet marked by unrelieved hostility. Nixon at first tried the traditional practice of appointing cabinet members "to represent the major interests in the
inner councils of government,"[3] and he allowed cabinet secretaries to
choose their own subordinates. He worked to develop legislative proposals
for presentation to the Congress but also signed legislation sponsored by
liberals. As the administrative presidency strategy evolved, Nixon tried to
bypass Congress, put loyalists in appointive positions, and dealt ruthlessly
with the career bureaucracy. Our interviews came as he was beginning to
implement this strategy but well before it reached its most aggressive phase.
    Our interviews in the Reagan years, by contrast, came well into the
administration. Reagan, like Nixon, was hostile to the domestic bureaucracy
and to many of the welfare-state policies identified with earlier administrations, but he enjoyed many advantages over Nixon. He had from the beginning appointed cabinet and subcabinet-level officials who were loyal to his
program. This was particularly important because Reagan's program was
much clearer and more coherent than Nixon's, thereby giving his appointees
(and career civil servants too) a good guide to what he wanted, one they
could easily discern. Reagan also profited from a Republican Senate for the
first six years of his administration, which meant that his appointees did not
have to run a serious gauntlet of Democratic opposition. In addition, the
political climate had changed significantly so that conservative policies now
seemed much more mainstream and legitimate. Finally, he had all the
opportunities to influence the senior civil service made possible by the Civil
Service Reform Act.
    We interviewed Bush administration appointees and senior civil ser-
vants in the third and fourth years of the administration. In contrast to the
Reagan administration, the Bush administration gave cabinet secretaries significant input into the choice of subcabinet-level officials, although the
Office of Presidential Personnel still played an important role. As James

Pfiffner notes, "Mutual accommodation was the rule."[4] In symbolic contrast to his predecessor, Bush addressed a group of senior career executives soon after taking office, and he publicly praised the career service.[5] While Bush drew closer to the right wing of his party after the 1990 budget deal wounded him politically, and he asserted presidential policy prerogatives very strongly in a manner consistent with the right-wing presidentialist style of his party,[6] his attitude toward the civil service was always more positive than that of Reagan and Nixon. He rarely stated fears that the civil service was a likely hotbed of liberal and Democratic resistance to presidential wishes.

We begin our exploration of the questions we outlined above with a look at the party affiliations of top federal executives. Party affiliation, of course, does not necessarily imply partisan behavior on the job, but it is clearly a matter of great concern to many of the politicians who direct the bureaucracy. Party is measured here by answers to survey questions about the executives' actual voting behavior. Table 6-1 demonstrates the extent to which the partisan coloration of top executives has changed. The data are broken down by year and by the status of executive personnel, with political appointees first, followed by Career I executives (the top career officials in their administrative units), and then Career II executives (SES civil servants who report not to political appointees but to other civil servants).[7]

The data in table 6-1 tell some clear stories. First, President Nixon's fears that he faced a lopsidedly Democratic civil service were hardly unfounded. Indeed, there was a three-to-one ratio of Democrats to Republicans among top civil servants in 1970. And we know from more detailed analysis of the data that the large number of independents among the civil servants (people who insisted that they regularly voted for candidates in both parties) looked more like Democrats than Republicans when we measured their attitudes on policy issues.[8]

However, things changed between 1970 and 1986–87, the next time we sampled top-level executives. In 1986–87 the modal Career I civil servant was a Republican. In fact, the percentage of Republicans among Career I civil servants went from 17 to 45 in the sixteen years between the times that we drew the two cross-sectional samples of top administrators. Republicans now outnumbered Democrats by about 7 percent. And by 1991–92 the Republican plurality was slightly more pronounced, with Republicans outnumbering Democrats by 11 percent. Looked at from the Democratic side, the proportion of Democrats fell modestly between 1970 and 1986–87 but by 1991–92 had dropped to less than one-third of Career I personnel. As we noted elsewhere, "This may not have been the top career bureaucracy of

Table 6-1. *Party Affiliation by Job Status and Year*

Percent

Sample and formal job designation[b]	Party affiliation[a] Republican	Independent	Democrat	N
1970[c]				
High political appointee (PAS designation)	81	6	13	(16)
Middle level appointee (NEA, Schedule C designation)	59	12	29	(41)
Supergrade career	17	36	47	(58)
1986–87[c]				
High political appointee (PAS designation)	94	6	0	(18)
Middle level appointee (SES-NA)	98	2	0	(44)
Career I (CSI)	45	17	38	(64)
Career II (CSII)	27	19	54	(63)
1991–92[c]				
High political appointee (PAS designation)	100	0	0	(21)
Middle level appointee (SES-NA)	100	0	0	(24)
Career I (CSI)	42	27	31	(52)
Career II (CSII)	42	19	40	(53)

Collapsed values (shown via arrows between the first two rows of each group): 1970 — Republican 65, Independent 11, Democrat 25; 1986–87 — Republican 97, Independent 3, Democrat 0; 1991–92 — Republican 100, Independent 0, Democrat 0.

a. Party affiliation was measured by asking the administrators whether they normally vote for one party or the other. Those who said that they did not normally vote for one party or the other were coded as Independents.

b. Because of the small number of PAS-designated appointees in our samples, hereafter most analyses involving the job status variable collapse political appointees into a single category (labelled "political executives" in the tables). PAS indicates a presidential appointment, by and with the advice and consent of the Senate. NEA stands for noncareer executive assignment. SES-NA indicates a noncareer appointment in the Senior Executive Service. Supergrade career civil servants held ranks GS 16 to 18. Other terms are defined in the text.

c. For 1970, Gamma = .58. For 1986–87, Gamma = .74 (excluding CSIIs, Gamma = .91). For 1991–92, Gamma = .64 (excluding CSIIs, Gamma = 1.00).

Republican dreams, particularly Reagan's, but its Republican plurality stands in sharp contrast to the marked Democratic plurality under Nixon."[9]

Turning from Career I to Career II civil servants, there is also evidence of significant change. In 1986–87 a majority of the Career II SES civil servants were Democrats. They outnumbered their Republican colleagues by two to one. The figures had changed quite dramatically by 1991–92. By then Republicans actually were more common than Democrats, although the percentage difference is small. In essence, the Career II group went from a bastion of Democrats to a group evenly split in partisan terms.

What happened? Cross-sectional data do not permit us to answer precisely, as we are not dealing with the same individuals over time, but the data suggest a combination of factors. Some people left. As one of our 1986–87 respondents noted, during the Reagan administration some career SESers who did not share the Reagan administration's philosophy "either were forced to leave or left because of their own frustration." Some people changed their party affiliations, either for opportunistic reasons or as part of the general rightward drift in elite politics. For the ambitious people who populate the top rungs of the civil service, there would be a tendency for some to become Republicans because Republicans were emerging as the majority party at the presidential level.

Raw ambition is almost certainly a factor for some, but a more subtle and complex set of factors is clearly at work for many others. Top civil servants are among the most literate people in Washington. They read scholarly and opinion journals and are well attuned to the changing currents of intellectual thought, which during the period of our study went from a concern with equity in the 1970s to a concern with efficiency in the 1980s and 1990s. Republicans, of course, were identified with efficiency concerns. They were widely seen as the party expressing the dominant set of ideas in this period. To quote one of the 1986–87 respondents: "In the 1960s the Democrats espoused ideas that moved and inspired the country. Now it's the Republicans who are doing that, while the Democrats drift about."

Besides changes in individual attitudes, however, there are systemic reasons that explain the shift in party affiliations. Top civil servants must be selected, and human biases inevitably enter into the selection process. In the case of career SES executives, selection is accomplished by means of an executive resources board, which is chosen by the agency head and is supposed to include career and noncareer appointees. There are numerous safeguards to try to ensure that the board chooses high-level executives based on merit. These include reviews by qualifications review boards chosen by the Office of

Personnel Management; a majority of the boards' members must be members of the career SES.[10] However, the method of appointing the agency executive resources boards provides an obvious avenue for partisan considerations to creep in.

In addition, the rank-in-the-person provisions of the Civil Service Reform Act allow political executives to move career executives into any position for which they are qualified. There is a 120-day waiting period after new agency heads or noncareer supervisors are appointed to prevent "peremptory reassignments,"[11] but in the end determined political appointees have much leeway in getting the people they want into given positions. The data in table 6-1 suggest that the Reagan administration used the provisions of the act to sort out career executives so that those who shared its partisan orientation were more likely to be in Career I than Career II positions.

Over time, the subtleties of the selection process apparently helped to produce a more Republican top career service. The selection process for political appointees also changed, although no formal statute was involved. As table 6-1 indicates, the political appointees of the early Nixon administration looked very different from those of Reagan and Bush. Recall that Nixon used a traditional selection process at the outset. He appointed notables, mainly but not exclusively Republican, and then allowed them to select their subordinates. The result was that about 80 percent of those who required Senate confirmation—people designated "high political appointees" in table 6-1—were Republicans, while those less-visible appointees at the "middle level" who did not require Senate confirmation were slightly less than 60 percent Republicans.

We know that some non-Republican appointees in 1970 remained in place from the previous administration and were probably slated for eventual replacement, but the data indicate less concern about the partisan affiliations of appointees in the early Nixon administration when contrasted with the Reagan and Bush presidencies. Appointments were more centralized in both the Reagan and Bush administrations, and the results are evident in table 6-1. There was not a single Democrat at any level in either sample of political appointees.

One important result of this pattern of political appointments is that the partisan gulf between political appointees and top career civil servants did not diminish over time even though there was a significant change in the partisan composition of the top career civil service. While Republicans became more and more prominent in the top career civil service, the almost total dominance of Republicans among appointees in the Reagan and Bush

administrations meant that there was still a big gap between the party affiliations of the two groups. This sets up a situation that at first might seem
paradoxical: the partisan composition of the career civil service has
changed, indicating significant responsiveness to changes in the political climate; but the partisan composition of the corps of political appointees has
also changed so that the gulf between the two remains. Thus, a suspicious
administration could be as discontented and concerned about responsiveness in the later period as in the earlier years.[12]

Changes in the Law

Democratic administrators were especially prominent in the social service
agencies during the Nixon administration. These agencies (the Department
of Health, Education, and Welfare, the Department of Housing and Urban
Affairs, and the Office of Economic Opportunity) had responsibility for
programs expending large sums on social services, and their constituencies
and supporters have traditionally been oriented toward the Democratic
Party. A Republican administration aiming to control the social service
agencies faced not only the natural tendency of their administrators to view
the world from an agency perspective, but also the barrier of few partisan
supporters among the executives who would be called upon to implement
its policies. As Richard Nathan points out, Nixon's New Federalism program, with its heavy focus on the activities of the social service agencies,
aimed to "*weaken the federal bureaucracy*"[13] (emphasis in original) and
thereby heightened the level of suspicion already existing between the president and administrators whose programs were targeted. Nixon's impaired
state after Watergate and his eventual resignation made the problem moot
for awhile, but it flared again in the Reagan administration, which also
sought to weaken the social service agencies and their constituencies.

Our purpose here is not to analyze the policy disputes, but to illustrate how
the Reagan administration apparently used the rank-in-the-person provisions
of the Civil Service Reform Act to install what it regarded as more acceptable
administrators at the top of the social service agencies. Table 6-2 presents data
that show that the Reagan administration had little trouble moving around SES
career personnel in order to staff the top positions of these targeted units with
those it considered compatible or, at least, acceptable.

The table shows the contrast in the political affiliations of Career I and
Career II civil servants in social service agencies in the Reagan administration. The Departments of Education (ED), Health and Human Services

Table 6-2. *Party Affiliation by Agency, Job Status, and Year (Career Executives Only)*[a]

Percent

Sample and job status	Party affiliation[a]			N
	Republican	Independent	Democrat	
1986–87				
Career I (CSI)				
Social service agencies[b]	67	0	33	(12)
Other agencies	40	21	39	(52)
Career II (CSII)				
Social Service agencies[b]	12	12	77	(17)
Other agencies	33	22	46	(46)
1991–92				
Career I (CSI)				
Social service agencies[b]	33	28	39	(18)
Other agencies	47	27	27	(34)
Career II (CSII)				
Social service agencies[b]	36	18	46	(11)
Other agencies	43	19	38	(42)

a. Totals may not equal 100 percent due to rounding. For 1986–87, CSI Gamma = .32; CSII Gamma = −.55. For 1991–92, CSI Gamma = −.25; CSII Gamma = −.13.

b. Education, HHS, and HUD.

(HHS), and Housing and Urban Development (HUD) were particular targets during the Reagan administration, as they had been in the Nixon administration, but Reagan's people succeeded in configuring agency career personnel more to their liking. While 77 percent of the incumbents in Career II positions in these agencies under Reagan were Democrats and only 12 percent were Republicans, the numbers look quite different at the Career I level. Here two-thirds are Republicans and only one-third are Democrats.[14] In short, the Reagan administration managed to get the type of people it wanted into the top positions of these controversial agencies.

In the Bush administration Democrats had a slight plurality in the social service departments at both the Career I and II levels. This supports what we suggested earlier: that the Bush administration was more ideologically indifferent than its predecessor. It could have put Republican SES career personnel into Career I positions, but its appointees apparently had little interest in doing so.

Political Ideology

Administrators' political beliefs may not always mirror their partisanship. Indeed, administrators' beliefs concern political leaders at least as much as their partisanship because beliefs are an even better indicator of the core values of the individual and therefore of their likely decision biases at important moments. This section focuses on a single indicator of ideology—beliefs about the appropriate role of government in the nation's economic affairs—because it captures a fundamental cleavage point in the political debate during the period covered by our study. For simplicity's sake, we will not go into more complex work done to establish the validity of the indicator. However, supplementary measures show that it is strongly correlated to other measures placing respondents along the left-right continuum on government's role in social and economic affairs.[15]

If ideology is a key test of whether there is change at the top of American administrative hierarchies, then there can be little doubt that the overall system is quite responsive to changes in the political climate. Table 6-3 shows startling changes from 1970 to 1986–87. The measure we use is reproduced in a note to the table. Administrators who strongly supported an active government role in the nation's economy were coded at one end of the scale (designated "left"). Those who strongly opposed an active government role in the nation's economy, preferring instead that decisions in this area should be in the hands of the private sector, were coded at the other end of the scale (designated "right"). Intermediate categories are indicated in the table.

In 1970, 52 percent of all administrators sampled were to the left of center on this measure. But by 1986–87 only 22 percent of administrators in the domestic agencies were left of center on the same measure. The percentage left of center increased to 35 percent in 1991–92, higher than in the Reagan administration years but still well below the total during the Nixon administration.

What can we say about the causes of this shift? First, it is partly, but by no means exclusively, caused by the increase in the percentage of Republicans among administrators. A look at the party affiliation section of table 6-3 should make this clear. While Republicans are well to the right of Democrats in every year, they were more to the right in 1986–87 than in any other year and more to the left during the Nixon administration. Democrats, similarly, were most to the left in 1970, much less so in 1986–87, and the numbers shift back (but not all the way) in 1991–92.

Table 6-3. *Beliefs about Active Government Role in National Economy, by Year, Party Affiliation, Agency, and Job Status*[a]

Percent

Sample	Strongly supports (left)	Sum of left and left-center	Supports with reservations (left-center)	Pro/con views, balance (center)	Opposes with reservations (right-center)	Sum of right and right-center	Strongly opposes (right)	N	Gamma
Marginal Distributions									
1970	28	52	24	32	15	16	1	(115)	
1986–87	4	22	18	26	39	52	13	(197)	
1991–92	9	35	26	20	36	45	9	(149)	
Party Affiliation									
1970									
Republican	7	32	25	43	25	25	0	(44)	–.50
Independent	36	50	14	41	5	10	5	(22)	
Democrat	46	77	31	13	10	10	0	(39)	
1986–87									
Republican	5	10	5	20	48	71	23	(106)	–.62
Independent	0	24	24	32	44	44	0	(25)	
Democrat	5	43	38	36	20	21	2	(56)	
1991–92									
Republican	5	19	14	20	49	62	13	(87)	–.56
Independent	17	38	21	21	29	42	13	(24)	
Democrat	16	70	54	19	11	11	0	(37)	
Agency									
1970									
Social services	39	60	21	30	9	9	0	(33)	.27
Other	23	49	26	33	17	18	1	(82)	

1986–87									
Social services	4	(24)	20	28	39	(48)	9	(46)	.10
Other	4	(21)	17	26	38	(53)	15	(151)	
1991–92									
Social services	16	(40)	24	24	26	(37)	11	(38)	.15
Other	7	(34)	27	17	40	(49)	9	(111)	
Job Status									
1970									
Political executives	17	(40)	23	42	19	(19)	0	(53)	–.35
Career supergrades	37	(63)	26	24	11	(13)	2	(62)	
1986–87									
Political executives	2	(7)	5	19	45	(74)	29	(62)	–.50
Career I (CSI)	3	(21)	18	28	42	(51)	9	(67)	
Career II (CSII)	7	(36)	29	31	29	(32)	3	(68)	
1991–92									
Political executives	2	(13)	11	18	51	(69)	18	(45)	–.42
Career I (CSI)	12	(35)	23	27	31	(39)	8	(52)	
Career II (CSII)	14	(54)	40	14	29	(33)	4	(52)	

a. The survey item read as follows: "It is argued by some people that government must play a greater role in the nation's economic affairs, while others say that decisions in this area should be left to the private sector. On the whole, which of these positions comes closest to yours? (Probe: How strongly do you feel about this?)"

Breaking the respondents down by job category shows similar results. Nixon's appointees were the most "leftist" of all appointees in the three surveys. The same is true of the top career executives he had to work with. Career I and Career II executives were least to the left under Reagan, with the results showing a moderation under Bush (although certainly not a return to the situation in the Nixon years).

By breaking the data down further and looking at beliefs about the role of the government in the nation's economy in each year by the party affiliation of the administrator while controlling for job status, we see more refined evidence of a great deal of responsiveness in the system.

Because the number of controls necessary to produce the findings in table 6-4 reduces the subsample sizes significantly, one must be cautious in claiming too much for the results. However, the overall pattern is clear. Reagan administration appointees, almost exclusively Republicans, were way to the right of their Nixon administration counterparts. Bush's appointees, all Republicans in our sample, were slightly more moderate on this measure than the Reagan administration's Republican appointees, yet clearly closer to the Reagan administration's appointees than to those of the Nixon administration.

Among the very top career administrators (labeled "supergrade career" in 1970 and "Career I" in the other years), Republicans show a similar pattern. The Republican Career I executives sampled in 1986–87 were well to the right of their counterparts in 1970, and the Republican Career I executives sampled in 1991–92 were somewhat to the left of their 1986–87 counterparts. Basically similar findings are apparent for the Democrats. They were most to the left in 1970 and least in 1986–87. We have no 1970 data, of course, for the executives we label Career II, but here also the Democrats are less to the left in 1986–87 than in 1991–92. Parenthetically, the pattern is broken for Republicans in this category, who are slightly more right of center in 1991–92 than they were in 1986–87.

These are complex data worth much detailed analysis, but for our purposes certain points are quite clear:

—There has been a clear shift to the right in top executives' views on the role of government intervention in the economy.

—Differences in executives' views on government's role in the economy have been strongly related to party in every period.

—The shift to the right during the Reagan administration was somewhat reversed during the Bush administration. The overall figures do not move as much as one might expect between the Reagan and Bush administrations

Table 6-4. *Survey Response on Active Government Role in National Economy, by Party Affiliation and Year, Controlling for Job Status*[a]
Percent

Sample and party affiliation	Left and Left-Center	Center	Right and Right-Center	N	Gamma
	Political executives				
1970					
Republican	29	47	24	(34)	
Independent	0	75	25	(4)	−.53
Democrat	83	8	8	(12)	
1986–87					
Republican	5	20	75	(60)	
Independent	50	0	50	(2)	n.c.
Democrat	0	0	0	(0)	
1990–91					
Republican	13	18	69	(45)	
Independent	0	0	0	(0)	n.c.
Democrat	0	0	0	(0)	
	Career executives				
Supergrade career					
1970					
Republican	40	30	30	(10)	
Independent	61	33	6	(18)	−.38
Democrat	74	15	11	(27)	
Career I (CSI)					
1986–87					
Republican	7	21	72	(29)	
Independent	9	46	46	(11)	−.62
Democrat	39	35	26	(23)	
1990–91					
Republican	24	29	48	(21)	
Independent	29	21	50	(14)	−.34
Democrat	50	31	19	(16)	
Career II (CSII)					
1986–87					
Republican	29	18	53	(17)	
Independent	33	25	42	(12)	−.36
Democrat	46	36	18	(33)	
1990–91					
Republican	24	14	62	(21)	
Independent	50	20	30	(10)	−.76
Democrat	86	10	5	(21)	

n.c. Not computed due to empty cells.

a. For question and response category wording see footnote in table 6-3, note a.

because Democrats in 1991–92 were an even smaller proportion of the federal executive than they had been during the Reagan years.

—Party and role are each related to ideology, although party is clearly more important than role. Focusing on party, Republican appointees are to the right of Republican career executives in every year (although not much to the right of Career I executives in 1986–87, when the Reagan administration apparently filled these posts quite carefully). And in the years for which we have the relevant data (1986–87 and 1991–92), Career II Democrats are to the left of Career I Democrats.

Overall, the findings on ideology reinforce the conclusions we drew from the data on party affiliation. There is much movement in the ideological profile of those at the top of the U.S. federal executive. That this occurs in samples of political appointees is indicative of changes in the center of gravity within the Republican Party, and perhaps the country as a whole. We should expect change among the political appointees in response to changes in the party and the policy dispositions of the presidents they serve. But it is more surprising to see such changes in the samples of top career executives. From the point of view of the system as a whole, this is evidence of considerable responsiveness in what is sometimes characterized as an insulated institution. To presidential administrations, especially those endowed with ideological gusto, the changes may not look quite so impressive because a large gap between the views of top career executives and political appointees can still exist. For these administrations, the shift that has occurred may look quite inadequate. Indeed, they may not even notice it, concentrating instead on the differences they perceive. And it is really this gap between what presidential administrations perceive and the underlying reality that may be what the "noisy crisis" is about. Presidential administrations may want total commitment from senior career officials, who are certainly supposed to give them their "best" (that is, their best judgments) but not necessarily give them their "all" (meaning, share their political views).

Place in Decisionmaking

One goal of the administrative presidency strategy was to cut off civil servants from their access to certain key decisionmakers (those outside the control of the White House) and to groups in the broader society. If one fears that civil servants are acting in their own interests or in defense of the interests of their programs, limiting civil servants' contacts with actual or potential allies is a natural thing for an administration whose goals threaten the existing power of government agencies.

We asked political appointees and civil servants to tell us how frequently they had contact with officials and others in the policy arena. Table 6-5 suggests that the Reagan White House, in particular, had significant success in influencing contact levels.

Compared with the early years of the Nixon administration, there were fewer contacts in 1986–87 between career civil servants and the Congress, interest group representatives, and the public at large. The appropriate comparison here is at the Career I level, where the samples are most comparable over time. The overall decline in contacts with Congress after 1970 is clear, even though the number of congressional staff grew substantially after that year. Great effort was expended to deter civil servants from generating policy appeals outside the executive branch, and these efforts clearly bore fruit. The level of contacts was also down between civil servants and the heads of their own departments (secretaries and similarly situated officials) as well as the heads of other departments. The one place where contacts increased was with the White House, suggesting that this is where civil servants increasingly look for information and orders.

The pattern for political executives is more complex. Like senior career civil servants, political executives report more frequent contact with the White House and decreased contacts with both their own and other department heads, but their contacts with interest groups and the public at large show no discernible pattern of decrease. The one anomaly is contacts with the Congress, where there is a slight increase for political executives in the Reagan administration and then a drop-off in the Bush administration. We believe that the data on increased contact with the White House and decreased contact with department heads is a reflection of the increased role in policy development, monitoring, and coordination played by the White House, its policy councils, and key players in White House staff agencies such as the Office of Management and Budget (OMB).

It is important to recognize that where these data indicate a drop in contacts, it is not from frequent contacts to none at all, but rather an attenuation in their frequency. Civil servants and political appointees have not suddenly become totally isolated from other actors. Rather, their contacts with them have become notably less frequent. In other words, the changes are noticeable but not revolutionary. As in the data on party and ideology we have examined, this change in magnitude can lead to very different conclusions, depending on the roles and goals of the actors involved. To civil

Table 6-5. *Frequency of Federal Executives' Contacts with Others in the Policy Arena, by Year*[a]

Percent reporting weekly or more contact

Contacts with	1970			1986–87				1991–92			
	PE	CSI	Gamma	PE	CSI	CSII	Gamma	PE	CSI	CSII	Gamma
White House	25	5	(.53)	41	20	3	(.44)	36	13	8	(.43)
Own department head	61	31	(.45)	48	23	5	(.50)	56	19	4	(.57)
Other department heads	19	18	(.29)	6	2	3	(.47)	18	4	2	(.37)
Congress	42	43	(.05)	48	20	20	(.36)	22	25	6	(.30)
Interest group representatives	69	69	(-.04)	67	45	40	(.24)	57	56	32	(.21)
Public at large	55	55	(.02)	67	40	45	(.24)	51	51	36	(.19)

a. Entries are percentages of each sample.

PE = political executives (political appointees).

CSI = career civil servants who occupy the top rungs in their administrative units and report to political appointees. Members of this group were called "supergrade" career civil servants in 1970; in 1986–87 and 1991–92 they were drawn from career civil servants in the Senior Executive Service (established in 1979).

CSII = career Senior Executive Service members who report to other civil servants, not political appointees. Data for 1986–87 include only line personnel for purposes of comparability. (CSI and CSII staff respondents report higher levels of contacts with the White House and department heads and lower levels with interest groups.)

servants in particular, it may look like a very meaningful sign of diminution in their influence in Washington policymaking. To the White House, it may look like a small gain in its ability to control the executive branch, but hardly a victory. The White House is more likely still to see a well-entrenched and savvy opponent with contacts on every corner of the policy neighborhood.

One thing we can say for sure is that there is a remarkable falloff in the perceived influence of senior civil servants, especially as seen by the senior civil servants themselves. At each point in time we asked political appointees and senior civil servants to indicate how much influence they thought each of the actors listed in table 6-6 had over policymaking. Where almost half of the senior civil servants sampled in 1970 thought that they and their peers had "a great deal of influence" over policymaking, that percentage dropped to 18 percent in 1986–87 (in the CSI category) and actually declined some more among those sampled in 1991–92.

The drop-off in influence is clearly stark. But as with the measure on contacts, only the very top category of our influence scale is shown in the table ("a great deal of influence"). In fact, the decrease is not from the top of the scale to the bottom, but mostly down to the next gradient or two. For example, in 1970, 79 percent of senior civil servants thought that they as a class had "a good bit of influence" (the second level on the scale). By 1986 the comparable figure dropped to a still significant 50 percent among the CSI group, and in 1991–92 the figure increased to 59 percent. While the civil servants sampled in 1986–87 and 1991–92 do not think they have dropped completely from the set of influentials in policymaking, it is a fair conclusion that over time civil servants believe that as a group they wield less influence.

When it comes to other actors, there is relatively little change in the influence over policymaking that agency heads are perceived to have. However, members of Congress receive lower influence scores and party leaders in Congress are rated more important in the later years than they were in 1970. Interest groups, never as influential in the eyes of the political executives and senior civil servants as they are in the eyes of many academic and journalistic observers, received lower influence scores in 1986–87 than in 1970 but showed some signs of a comeback in 1991–92. The fact that perceived interest group influence shows any decline is somewhat surprising in view of the growth in the number of interest groups active in Washington.[16] Perhaps the larger the number of groups, the more they exert a countervailing influence upon each other and the more they pluralize policy sectors that once represented only embedded interests (the "iron triangles" discussed in chapter 5).

Table 6-6. *Federal Executives' Evaluations of Influence over Policy Decisions, by Year*[a]

Percent reporting a great deal of influence

Influence attributed to	1970			1986–87				1991–92			
	PE	CSI	Gamma	PE	CSI	CSII	Gamma	PE	CSI	CSII	Gamma
Senior civil servants	35	46	(–.18)	22	18	15	(.19)	33	8	12	(.26)
Department secretaries (agency heads)	64	43	(.33)	65	43	62	(.06)	75	53	54	(.27)
Members of Congress	63	51	(.19)	35	41	43	(–.11)	47	34	38	(.12)
Party leaders (in Congress)	22	19	(.23)	27	43	49	(–.21)	27	37	34	(–.01)
Interest groups (general)	26	34	(–.06)	18	16	13	(–.09)	18	32	19	(.08)

a. Entries are percentages of each sample. Executive categories are explained in table 6-5, note a.

The key point we want to make here is that top career civil servants are less and less likely to ascribe to themselves great influence over policymaking. In fact, perceptions of which actors have great influence in the policy process and which have less have changed quite noticeably. These data do not support the idea that presidential administrations in Washington are prisoners of the bureaucracy and therefore cannot alter bureaucrats' influence on policy. As with our other data, however, the data on influence also show why administrations may be frustrated by bureaucratic sway over policy. Because the changes are ones of relative magnitude rather than either/or, presidential administrations may look at the same evidence and conclude from it that civil servants still have too much influence.

Micromanagement

The administrative presidency strategy for control of the bureaucracy has numerous facets and has generated responses from the Congress as well as the courts. To an increasing degree, political authorities specify in detail what administrators are to do in implementing policy. The term commonly used for this phenomenon is "micromanagement." Its principal effect is to shrink the room for discretion within the agencies and to make the administrator's job one of following specific orders rather than one of making judgments under broad guidelines.

Congress micromanages mainly through detailed legislation and through the language of committee reports. The White House micromanages through such devices as regulatory review and detailed specifications as to how budgeted monies may be used. As part of the struggle for control exacerbated by the Nixon administration and escalated in the administration of Ronald Reagan and in the latter part of the Bush administration, micromanagement became a more and more prominent part of the political game in Washington.

Our only data on micromanagement were collected in 1991–92, so we cannot trace changes in perceptions of the amount of micromanagement or evaluations of it. But we can examine the perceived extent of micromanagement in the early 1990s and the attitudes of the agencies' executives toward that control. And we can compare views on micromanagement by the Congress and the presidential administration.

OMB has generated considerable capacity for central control of administration where there is the political will to enforce it. OMB reviews regulations before agencies issue them, and it has an influence, often quite strong,

Table 6-7. *Federal Executives' Experience and Evaluation of Micromanagement by OMB, 1991–92*[a]

Percent

	Experience of OMB micromanagement				
Sample	Experienced a great deal	Experienced it	Experienced a little bit	No experience of it	N
Political executives	32	36	14	18	(44)
Career I (CSI)	29	31	14	27	(52)
Career II (CSII)	19	28	23	30	(53)

	Evaluation of OMB micromanagement				
	Strongly Approve	Approve	Neutral	Disapprove	Strongly Disapprove	N
Political executives	3	14	22	31	31	(36)
Career I (CSI)	5	8	13	31	44	(39)
Career II (CSII)	0	6	18	36	39	(33)

a. For experience of micromanagement by OMB, Gamma = .20; and for evaluation, Gamma = .15.

over how the agencies spend their budgeted monies. These powers can be exercised with a light hand, of course, and in close conformity with a good-faith interpretation of the law's intent, but they can also be used to exercise close White House control and to enforce the will of the White House over the intent of Congress.[17] If exercised lightly, they are not likely to be perceived as pervasive or intrusive. If exercised heavily, the opposite is likely to be the case.

Table 6-7 indicates that, as expected, most federal executives, especially those closest to the top, have experienced at least some micromanagement by OMB. Political appointees report the most and Career II executives the least. OMB micromanagement tends to be unpopular with all groups of executives, but particularly with career civil servants. In theory, political executives are on the same team as OMB, so their tendency to approve of OMB micromanagement more than career executives do is less surprising than the fact that a majority of them are willing to state a clear dislike for OMB's role in this regard.

Table 6-8. *Federal Executives' Experience and Evaluation of Micromanagement by Congress, 1991–92*[a]

Percent

	Experience of congressional micromanagement				
	Experienced a great deal	Experienced it	Experienced a little bit	No experience of it	N
Political executives	48	36	5	11	(44)
Career I (CSI)	47	29	6	18	(51)
Career II (CSII)	30	26	8	36	(53)

	Evaluation of congressional micromanagement				
	Strongly Approve	Approve	Neutral	Disapprove	Strongly Disapprove	N
Political executives	0	3	0	38	60	(37)
Career I (CSI)	0	0	22	32	46	(41)
Career II (CSII)	3	3	21	32	41	(34)

a. For experience of micromanagement by Congress, Gamma = .29; and for evaluation, Gamma = .29.

While OMB has hardly been passive in the war for control of administration, micromanagement is one of Congress's most frequently used tools in its efforts to maintain its position vis-à-vis the executive. Indeed, as table 6-8 demonstrates, more administrators at all levels report experiencing more micromanagement by Congress than by OMB (table 6-7). And there is more marked disagreement between executives at different levels about congressional micromanagement. Even though most executives tend to disapprove of it, disapproval is just about unanimous (and most intense) among political executives, while a little over a fifth of the civil servants express neutrality about it, and a small percentage of Career II civil servants even express approval.

In sum, the data clearly indicate that micromanagement of all types is unpopular among executives, a finding that is not too surprising since micromanagement impinges on their freedom to act. However, the reaction differs depending on who is doing the micromanaging and who is on the receiving end of it. Thus political appointees disapprove of congressional micromanagement more then career people do, and to a lesser extent career executives are more likely than political appointees to disapprove of OMB micromanagement. Attitudes toward an intrusive management procedure, in other words, are conditioned by position, with Congress a more "legitimate" participant in the eyes of those in the permanent government than it is in the eyes of political appointees. The reason is clear: in the years when these data were collected, Congress often defended agency programs against a presidential administration bent on limiting program scope and budgets. Administrators, particularly career administrators with an ongoing interest in the health of these programs, are more likely to accept interference with their management prerogatives under such circumstances.

Perceptions of the "Other"

One of the most interesting things about the relationship between civil servants and political appointees is the way in which their relationship solidifies over time. Political appointees, in particular, often grow to appreciate the qualities civil servants bring to the job.[18] And experienced civil servants recognize this occurs, even though they may be frustrated by the nature of the relationship before this trust develops. One senior civil servant in a social service agency, for example, made this comment about the way relationships developed in the often-hostile atmosphere of the Reagan administration:

> I think there were a host of [political appointees] who came into the Reagan administration prepared to dislike the bureaucracy. And then, when they left, at their going away party, extolled the bureaucracy as being the most wonderful thing they had ever seen—how hard we worked, how dedicated we were. So, they turned around completely. And I always thought, well, you know, he will never be back. We are going to have to start with a new one. But they do that. They soon identify with the organization and come to like the career people.[19]

Not all relationships develop in this manner, of course, but the data in table 6-9 indicate how positively most political executives come to evaluate civil servants. Each top senior civil servant and political appointee interviewed in 1991–92 during the Bush administration (the only time we used this set of measures) was asked to rate career civil servants and political executives on the traits and qualities listed in the table. As a result we can see

Table 6-9. *How Political Executives and Civil Servants See Themselves and Each Other, 1991–92*[a]

Percent[b]

Characteristic	Political executives on political executives	Civil servants on political executives	Political executives on civil servants	Civil servants on civil servants
Bring valuable experience to the job	82	60	98	98
Have good leadership qualities	64	52	59	82
Have good management skills	55	28	61	71
See job as an opportunity to make positive long-term improvements to government service	90	59	75	92
Work hard to carry out administration initiatives and priorities	100	91	71	90
Are comparable to the best executive talent in the private sector	55	43	29	79

a. Data for Civil Servants I and II are combined.

b. Percent of respondents who agree or strongly agree that senior agency political executives or career civil servants have a given characteristic.

how the incumbents of each role view both themselves and their counter-parts. While the ratings are certainly positive overall, the exceptions and the differences in the ratings that civil servants and political executives give also suggest a certain amount of skepticism about each other, but with more expressed by the civil servants.

To reiterate the initial point, these data indicate that political executives tend to give high marks to senior career civil servants. They are most impressed with the value of the experience senior civil servants bring to the job (98 percent of political executives strongly agree or agree that this is so), but they also see civil servants as dedicated people who work hard to carry out administration initiatives and policies. Close to 60 percent of the political executives questioned even think that senior civil servants have good leadership qualities.

However, political executives tend to think that senior civil servants are not comparable to the best executive talent in the private sector. This view is disputed by top civil servants, four-fifths of whom (79 percent) see their colleagues as comparable to the best in the private sector. Senior civil servants, in fact, see themselves in positive terms on every quality and trait in the list, with the lowest positive ranking given on management skills. Even there, 71 percent of civil servants rate themselves and their colleagues quite positively.

One might suspect that comparable data for the Reagan years—certainly a more difficult period in the civil servant–administration relationship—would not show political appointees giving such positive ratings of civil servants. However, data gathered in 1988 by the Merit Systems Protection Board (MSPB) suggest that political appointees either start with or come to appreciate the qualities of civil servants. (Cross-sectional survey data do not allow us to say which is the case, since we do not know how the political executives felt when they were appointed, although it is a good guess that they did not start with very positive impressions of civil servants.)

These data come from an August 1988 mail survey of former SES political appointees who had left government between January 1, 1983, and June 30, 1988.[20] They show that Reagan-era political executives were almost as positive about the traits and qualities of civil servants as their successors in the Bush administration. Eighty-three percent agreed that civil servants bring valuable experience to the job (as opposed to 98 percent for Bush appointees), and 54 percent agreed that civil servants have good leadership qualities (as compared with 59 percent of Bush appointees). The item about the private sector was not asked in the MSPB survey, so we cannot compare on that dimension.[21]

Turning back to the 1991–92 data in table 6-9, the contrast between the way civil servants rate themselves (the last column) and the way political executives think of themselves (the first column) is quite striking. On management skills, for example, only 55 percent of political executives think that political executives as a class have good management skills. And the same percentage—barely more than half—see political executives as comparable to the best executive talent in the private sector. Political executives, in addition, are less likely than career executives to see themselves as having good leadership qualities. Not surprisingly, they are also less likely to see themselves as bringing valuable experience to the job.

Perhaps the most notable thing about the table is the relatively low regard senior civil servants have for political executives. Only about a quarter of the senior civil servants believe that political executives have good management skills, and less than half believe that political executives are comparable to the best talent in the private sector. Indeed, after giving political executives high marks for working hard to carry out administration initiatives and priorities (91 percent of career civil servants believe that political executives do this), the percentages drop off noticeably for the rest of the traits. Only between 50 and 60 percent of senior civil servants believe that political executives have good leadership qualities, see the political executives' jobs as an opportunity to bring long-term improvements to government service, or even that political executives bring valuable experience to the job.

In sum, the 1991–92 data suggest that if there is a problem with the traits and qualities of federal executives, the group to focus on is political appointees. Not surprisingly, the MSPB data from former career executives who served under Reagan are even more pronounced in supporting this interpretation. Of the career federal executives who retired during the Reagan administration, only 15 percent thought that the political executives they served under had good management skills, only 18 percent thought that political executives had good leadership qualities, and only 25 percent thought that political executives brought valuable experience to the job.[22]

We return to the problem of the appropriate role and quality of political appointees later, but for now we want to emphasize how relatively little dissatisfaction experienced political executives express about civil servants. The relationship may well be rocky to begin with, but whatever suspicions political executives start with apparently fade. It may be possible that Bush administration political appointees fell victim to the charms of career civil servants and the seductive attractions of the agencies and their clientele groups—that, in the rather infamous phraseology of John Ehrlichman, they went off and "marr[ied] the natives."[23] However, it is highly unlikely that the carefully selected and even more carefully prepared Reagan appointees— people who were told that civil servants would be one of their major problems—were so easily won over.[24] The more likely conclusion is that the survey data reflect the simple fact that Reagan's political appointees found top career civil servants to be competent professionals. This does not imply that Reagan's political appointees necessarily liked civil servants or felt comfortable with them—just that, on average, once political appointees got to see civil servants perform, they were reasonably satisfied with them.

Exit, Voice, or Loyalty?

The fear of bureaucratic sabotage is never far from the minds of political appointees, especially when the administration they serve wants to make significant political changes. In one of the more insightful discussions of the subject, Hugh Heclo argues that active sabotage is actually quite rare. Instead, bureaucrats simply fail to share information with appointees or passively accept what they are told to do rather than provide the kind of information (including opposing arguments) appointees may need to achieve their objectives.[25]

We know from our comparative studies that top American civil servants are quite feisty. For example, in the mid-1980s we asked executives in Germany and the United States what courses of action they felt would be appropriate if an administration came to power with relatively clear policy proposals (in their areas) that the executives felt were "very undesirable or ill-considered."[26] Eighty-two percent of the German career civil servants felt obliged to support their government's policies even if they personally disagreed, while only 42 percent of the American civil servants felt this obligation.[27]

However, the modal response among U.S. civil servants was not sabotage. Far from it. Only about 10 percent of the total sample of career SESers (concentrated heavily in the Career II category) favored opposing the administration outright by seeking allies outside the administration or leaking information if necessary.[28] Instead, the most typical action advocated— by about 47 percent of the top career federal executives—was to oppose the administration's policy inside the councils of the government, resigning if persuasion fails and the disagreements are too great to bear. The latter is hardly a stance likely to please people with the strong convictions found among many Reagan-era political appointees, but it falls well within the bounds of conventionally acceptable behavior by civil servants. Indeed, "speaking truth to power" (as the civil servant sees truth) is one of the roles of a top civil servant, so long as the conversation does not become too loud.

As in many considerations of bureaucratic responsiveness to authority, the picture here is complicated once one does further analysis. It is the Democratic career civil servants who are most likely to endorse outright opposition to the administration by a margin of almost three to one (a little more than 19 percent of the Democrats versus a little less than 7 percent of the Republicans). Yet the other side of the coin is that more than 80 percent of the Democratic civil servants say that ultimately they should either go along or resign. The overall picture, then, is one of bureaucratic compliance with political authority, although not without debates and attempts to influence policy.

Overview

As we noted in chapter 5, the problem of bureaucratic responsiveness to political authorities is particularly large in the United States. Our system of separated institutions sharing powers magnifies the complex issues already inherent in putting into practice the deceptively simple notion that the bureaucracy ought to be responsive to officials chosen by the people. There is constant jockeying between the president and the Congress (and often the courts) over control of policy and administration, even in the most tranquil of times. When there is split partisan control of the main institutions, the struggle is likely to become much more contentious, particularly when significant changes in the status quo are proposed.

Numerous problems can come into play. The bureaucracy represents continuity in government, so those who want change are often suspicious of it. The bureaucracy also is the leading enforcer of rules, and those who want to change the rules (especially if they cannot change statutory language to their satisfaction) are likely to be dissatisfied with the bureaucracy's behavior. The bureaucracy is supposed to be both neutral and responsive—a delicate task under the best of circumstances and an almost impossible one when those who oversee administration have different views about what policy should be. Add to this mix the fact that high-level civil servants are part of the political process—as policy analysts, advice givers, policy implementers, and sources of information to and negotiators with interested parties—and one has the makings of great controversy.

The issue of bureaucratic responsiveness has been a major concern of political leaders and concerned citizens over the years covered by our study. Our data allow us to examine many aspects of responsiveness. The results suggest that the American bureaucracy is in many ways a remarkably flexible and adaptive instrument. That is not to suggest that it is perfect, or even that it is likely to satisfy its many critics, but simply that the data indicate that the system is quite responsive to a changing political environment and that instruments are in place to promote responsiveness.

Changes over the years of our study in the party affiliation profiles of top career executives have been little short of remarkable. Our data indicate that Richard Nixon inherited a set of supergrade career civil servants who were Democratic by a three to one ratio. The picture was fundamentally different by the time of the Bush presidency. The comparable group of top career civil servants (now part of a corps called the Senior Executive Service) was clearly more Republican than Democratic, and even the group of career SES executives we label Career II was now slightly more Republican than Democratic. We have put forth a variety of explanations of these changes, including the sensitivity of civil servants to changes in the political climate. But the fact of change is clear and unmistakable.

One important element in producing change was the Civil Service Reform Act of 1978. The Senior Executive Service created as part of the act put rank in the person rather than in the position the person held, as was previously the case. This made it possible for administrations to move civil servants around in a way previously not allowed (at least not if the rules were followed). The Nixon administration produced a notorious guide for political appointees (the "Malek Manual") to assist them in getting rid of suspect civil servants or moving them to out-of-the-way positions. The 1978 legislation provided legal means for an administration to put career people of its choosing into key positions, and our data indicate the Reagan administration took great advantage of the opportunity provided.

Our analysis of a major indicator of political ideology—views on the role the state should play in the nation's economy—buttresses the points developed in our examination of the party allegiances of federal executives. In fact, one could argue that these beliefs are more important than party because they are closer to the core of an individual's values and therefore even more likely than party affiliation to affect behavior. Certainly those who believe it is important for an administration to have kindred spirits in its top posts are likely to take such beliefs quite seriously. Our data show dramatic evidence that there has been much movement in the ideological profile of those at the top of the federal executive. The overall shift, certainly before the Clinton presidency, was to the right.

When it comes to the role of the bureaucracy in decisionmaking, the White House has been able to influence the frequency of contacts of career civil servants with Congress, interest groups, and the public at large. And there has been a very marked falloff in the perceived influence of senior civil servants, particularly as seen by the civil servants themselves. These are clear signs of the influence the White House can exert on the bureaucracy when it wants to do so.

There have been reactions to the increased activism and influence of the White House, of course. Micromanagement by OMB has been a part of that activism, and Congress has countered with its own virulent micromanagement. Whoever is to blame, it is clear that administrators, both career and noncareer, dislike micromanagement, with each tending to show the greatest dislike for the micromanagement that hurts it the most.

Relations between political appointees and career civil servants are surprisingly good, especially after the passage of enough time so that the two adjust to one another. Political appointees are particularly positive about the traits and qualities of top career civil servants. Career executives, on the other hand, tend to be more skeptical of political appointees. Less than half of them think that political executives have good management skills or are comparable to the best talent in the private sector.

Regardless of the tensions these negative evaluations by civil servants may cause, they overwhelmingly reject sabotage as a tool for dealing with administration policies they believe to be very undesirable or ill-considered. Top career civil servants may well debate the issues with political executives or exit the service if they feel strongly enough, but there is clearly a strong norm against carrying their opposition too far.

So what is the problem? Why should people even speak about a "responsiveness crisis"? Obviously, political leaders are concerned about bureaucrats' responsiveness to the extent that their goals might be stymied or responded to without commitment or enthusiasm. The more a political leader wants a shift from the status quo, the more concern he or she is apt to have about responsiveness, especially in a system where there are multiple and often conflicting overseers of the bureaucracy. The more the bureaucracy is filled with people who are in tune from the outset with a president's preferences, the more comfortable a president is likely to feel about it. Conversely, the greater the distance in their predispositions, the more uncomfortable a president is likely to feel about the bureaucracy. A good bit of the "responsiveness crisis" is inevitably a matter of perception— of the ideological distance between the presidential administration and the senior civil servants in a political system where the latter are widely perceived as having many opportunities to foil presidential ambitions. How much these perceptions are founded in reality is a different and more complicated matter.

Our data help provide answers both to the question of why there is talk about a responsiveness crisis and how legitimate the concerns are. There is no doubt that the civil service has changed to reflect better the political balance in the country. But it is still not the instrument that a Richard Nixon during his administrative presidency stage or a Ronald Reagan wished for. This is mainly because each wanted the bureaucracy to be fully compliant and subservient. While the changes in the personnel system implemented through the Civil Service Reform Act give administrations a tool to alter the composition of top career personnel in agencies they regard as strategically important, even the CSRA would not allow presidents, within the time frame of their administrations, to create a senior career executive in full accord with their own political goals. Because presidents, especially when their party controls the Senate, can make a more immediate impact on the partisan and ideological makeup of the corps of political appointees than on the top civil service, the partisan and ideological gap between political appointees and top career civil servants hardly changed over the twenty-odd years covered by our empirical work. Political appointees and civil servants, in other words, have shifted in tandem but from different points of origin. In an earlier article we referred to the "shifting, yet still clashing, beliefs of the federal executive."[29] That continues to sum things up quite well.

The data on contact patterns and influence tell a story similar to those on party and ideology—at least in terms of why presidential administrations might not be satisfied. On the one hand, civil servants' contact levels and perceived influence are not what they once were. They have definitely declined. On the other hand, the drop-off is not from the top to the bottom of our scale, but rather down a gradient or two at the most. In other words, top career executives may be less central to decisionmaking than they were before, but they have not fallen out of the loop. Looked at from the perspective of a president who wants them to have little or no role in decisionmaking, that may seem insufficient.

The same sorts of arguments can be made about the other evidence we discussed. Federal executives may be heavily micromanaged by OMB, but they resent it (particularly the career executives), and, more important, they are even more heavily micromanaged by Congress. The fact that political appointees, even in the Reagan administration, apparently came to appreciate the qualities of top career civil servants may be a positive sign of adaptation to some, but it was almost certainly a source of distress to many in the Reagan White House. That civil servants tend not to approve of sabotage as a means of dealing with administration policies with which they strongly disagree, but rather advocate voicing their objections inside the councils of government and then resigning if the disagreements are too great to bear, is almost surely small comfort to those who demand reflexive loyalty of the "when we say jump, their only question should be 'how high?'" variety.

Most disinterested observers familiar with the evidence would judge the current system to be quite adequate.[30] By almost any reasonable standard, the U.S. bureaucracy appears to be an unusually flexible and responsive institution politically. In addition, presidential administrations now have the tools, *if they choose to use them*, to limit bureaucratic influence or to shape parts of the bureaucracy more to their liking. There might have been legitimate complaints (as distinguished from legitimate actions) about a lack of presidential influence over the bureaucracy during the Nixon administration, but the situation is now very different.

However, the degree of responsiveness one thinks adequate is clearly a function of what one wants from the bureaucracy. Political leaders, after all, are rarely disinterested observers. Indeed, they may be passionate seekers of control (Nixon) or of policy changes (Reagan). In such cases, presidents want to control who will serve in top civil service and appointee positions. That means people who are loyal to them personally or who resemble them ideologically and who will carry out their policies with a minimum of questioning or dissent. However adaptable it may be, the U.S. system does not change rapidly enough for such presidents. They are likely to be particularly frustrated when they must deal with bureaucrats playing their traditional roles as bearers of institutional legacies and cautionary agents when it comes to proposals for change. The most acceptable solution from such a perspective is one in which political appointees (chosen solely on the basis of compatibility with the president) fill all key positions and career civil servants are totally isolated from policy decisions. In brief, the role of the civil servant would simply be an "intelligent tool." Politics and administration would finally be as separate as the Progressives hoped they would be.[31]

Whatever other changes may take place, such a situation is not likely to come to pass. Aside from the fact it would be unacceptable to most of the citizenry, who already react negatively to the degree of "politics" in Washington, Congress is unlikely to yield such power to any president. In addition, separating politics from administration is doable in theory but not in practice.[32] A system such as the one used in Germany might make presidents more comfortable. There, top career civil servants can be placed on sabbatical by an incoming administration, which can then fill important positions with administrators with whom it feels comfortable.[33] However, Congress, especially in a period of divided partisan control, would probably not look with favor on such a solution.

An inescapable conclusion, we believe, is that what remains of the responsiveness crisis (now better termed a problem) in the United States is not likely to be resolved soon, nor would most people want it resolved once they considered the consequences. Some of the problem is grounded in the inability of presidential administrations to build enough support to pass legislation mandating the kinds of changes they advocate (for example, Nixon and Reagan) or even to gain support for nominees (Clinton). Presidents facing such situations are tempted to adopt the administrative presidency strategy in order to bypass Congress. This is not likely to be a viable long-term solution to their problems in a system based on separation of powers, but it has great appeal to incumbents who are otherwise stymied. Some of the problem is basically epiphenomenal; political leaders scapegoat the bureaucracy for enforcing provisions of the law many citizens do not like (for example, civil rights and environmental and safety regulations). And some of the problem is due to politicians' frustration with the role of bureaucrats as bearers of institutional memory and cautionary agents. Many political leaders simply want to march forward without dissent or analysis of any sort, but this is often self-defeating.

In brief, our evidence indicates that the U.S. bureaucracy is now a quite flexible and responsive institution, one that is demonstrably responsive to changes in the political climate of the country. Whatever is wrong with the higher civil service (and administrative system), it is not that it is unresponsive or insulated from influence by presidential administrations or changing ideas about the role of government. The Civil Service Reform Act of 1978, in particular, has given presidential administrations the ability to manipulate which top career executives will serve where in the departments and agencies. The evidence indicates, too, that the civil service is much influenced by general factors that are pushing ideas in a given direction. In other words, the system is not rigid. It is responsive to the environment and quite adaptable.

This does not mean that presidents will instantly get what they want—a fact that frustrates them but is not necessarily a flaw. The civil service is supposed to provide a brake on radical change and to supply historical and institutional memory to policymakers. It is also supposed to be responsive to executive authority, although in the American system that is supposed to be tempered not only by the law but by the will of the Congress as well. Just where the right balance lies is impossible to say, but there is little doubt that the current system is far from the crisis zone in this respect. Political authorities clearly have the upper hand. We asked in chapter 5 whether there is a "true crisis of responsiveness in the U.S. federal bureaucracy." Our considered answer is an emphatic no, especially if one accepts, as we do, the notion that changes do not have to instantly and totally mirror changes in presidential administrations.

CHAPTER SEVEN

Reinventing Government

OUR ANALYSIS INDICATES that both the "quiet crisis" story of a diminution of quality along with a drop in morale among senior civil servants and the "noisy crisis" story of a lack of responsiveness in the bureaucracy to changing political currents are, at a minimum, exaggerated. But what about the hot topic of today—the need to reinvent the government?

Reinvention is actually a worldwide phenomenon. Its most prominent manifestation in the United States is Vice President Al Gore's National Performance Review (NPR), now officially retitled the National Partnership for Reinventing Government but still usually referred to as NPR or simply as reinvention. Gore's goal is a government that "works better and costs less."[1] There is little argument about such an admirable goal but many questions about the means to achieve it.

NPR focuses much more on management systems than on personnel (either quality or political responsiveness) per se. In fact, a major conclusion is that good people can manage badly. As NPR's report states: "The federal government is filled with good people trapped in bad systems: budget systems, personnel systems, procurement systems, financial management systems, information systems. When we blame the people and impose controls, we make the systems worse."[2]

The NPR report clearly rejects most of the "quiet crisis" story. And it sidesteps most of the political responsiveness story. Indeed, it seems little concerned, at least on the surface, about the political affiliations and loyalties of civil servants, and it overtly encourages contact between career bureaucrats and interest groups, which would clearly be part of the "customer" base of agencies that NPR sees as a major focus for agency attention. NPR is a public management and a systems design/incentives–based explanation for government administrative problems. It blames the current management system for failing to produce results and for failing to motivate civil servants properly.

This chapter lays out the core of the reinvention argument in the United States, relates it to similar movements under way in many nations, and examines reinvention's problems and prospects. It also reviews experience so far with a major piece of legislation related to reinvention: the Government Performance and Results Act of 1993. Finally, it considers some broader issues about what reinvention can and cannot be expected to accomplish.

Origins and Elements of Reinvention

President Clinton asked Vice President Gore to lead a major review of the federal government early in his administration. The review was conducted by a team of approximately 250 government employees and yielded a mound of documents and a summary report that has become an object of interest and controversy among government insiders and academics. The first phase of NPR focused on how the government works; the second phase focused more on what government does. The review is now in its third phase. It is increasingly focused on outcomes and on "high impact" agencies such as the Internal Revenue Service, where failure "could prove managerially and politically damaging" to the administration and, not coincidentally, to the vice president's political prospects. The third phase of reinvention emphasizes its linkage to the goals of the Government Performance and Results Act, which requires that agencies specify clear objectives and then measure whether the objectives have been achieved.[3]

NPR is part of a worldwide movement known as the New Public Management (NPM). There are several variants of the New Public Management, but a key notion is plainly stated early in the NPR report in a section entitled "The Root Problem: Industrial-Era Bureaucracies in an Information Age":

> Is government inherently incompetent? Absolutely not. Are federal agencies filled with incompetent people? No. The problem is much

deeper: Washington is filled with organizations designed for an environment that no longer exists. . . .

From the 1930s through the 1960s, we built large, top-down, centralized bureaucracies to do the public's business. They were patterned after the corporate structures of the age. . . . With their rigid preoccupation with standard operating procedure, their vertical chains of command, and their standardized services, these bureaucracies were steady—but slow and cumbersome. And in today's world of rapid change, lightning-quick information technologies, tough global competition, and demanding customers, large, top-down bureaucracies—public or private—don't work very well. Saturn isn't run the way General Motors was. Intel isn't run the way IBM was.[4]

President Clinton put it more bluntly in his remarks announcing the establishment of NPR: "In short, it's time our government adjusted to the real world, tightened its belt, managed its affairs in the context of an economy that is information-based, rapidly changing, and puts a premium on speed and function and service, not rules and regulations."[5]

New Public Management, in brief, rests on the assumption that government bureaucracies (and many government policies, too) need to adapt to a changed world. The rule-driven bureaucratic structures and cultures of the past are to be replaced by smaller, flexible, customer-oriented organizations. New management systems are key. Providing managers with the proper incentives and giving them latitude to manage free from constraints in a highly competitive and performance-driven environment, NPM advocates say, should produce results that will restore confidence in government and get the most for each tax dollar. The goal is a lean state performing only needed functions efficiently and effectively.

It is one thing to talk about reinventing such venerable institutions as "industrial age" bureaucracies and another thing to do it. To the surprise of many, nations such as Great Britain, New Zealand, Sweden, and Australia, which have had "big states," set about doing precisely that—and the NPR staff was well aware of their activities.[6] The Organization for Economic Cooperation and Development (OECD) has a web page devoted to the subject.[7] The World Bank preaches this gospel. It is a full-blown movement.

One obvious question is why. Another is, why now? These are not easy questions to answer. The NPR's answer, given above, is that the movement developed because "the needs of information-age societies were colliding with the limits of industrial-era governments." In essence, regardless of the ideologies of those in control, nations have been pushed to reinvent by necessity.

But what precisely makes NPM a necessity? Christopher Hood, a noted British analyst, explored a set of competing explanations and settled, somewhat skeptically, on an answer not very different from the Gore report. He sees NPM as "an administrative reflection of that broader set of social changes triggered by 'postindustrialism.'"[8] Changes in technology, particularly the introduction of powerful, networked computers, presumably allow governments to contract out more than before and to run flatter, more flexible organizations. And changes in occupational structures associated with technology-driven changes in the economy, by shifting employees away from unionized industries, have undermined the traditional electoral coalitions supporting government growth. The median voter, according to this argument, now has a new (higher) position on the income distribution scale and is no longer willing to pay the price of supporting many of the programs and structures of the welfare state, which they believe do not benefit them.

Others, such as World Bank analyst Malcolm Holmes and the OECD's David Shand (who now works for the International Monetary Fund), say that the "reform of public sector management has been a reaction to the perceived excesses of the welfare state, both in a macro sense, as reflected in the growing size of government and associated fiscal deficits, and in the micro sense, in the perceived recognition of limits to government's ability to solve all of our problems."[9] One does not have to agree with the charged term "excesses" to accept the basic thrust of this explanation. Many benefits in the modern welfare state, particularly retirement benefits, have become harder to pay for simply because increased longevity has changed the ratio of working to retired people. This problem will become even more severe when the baby boom generation retires. And there is little doubt that people are more skeptical today of government's ability to solve problems, although that is partly because government has taken on more and more difficult problems.

As a recent analysis succinctly puts it: "By the beginning of the 1980s, stagnation, inflation, unemployment, and weakening productivity and investment had severely affected budgets, resulting in large and persistent deficits."[10] The cost-cutting, leaner-state elements of NPM were particularly attractive in this environment because they promised to limit the growth of public expenditures, help address deficit problems without necessitating unpopular tax increases, and help revitalize the private sector.[11]

Yet another explanation, again addressing NPM's emphasis on cost cutting and a leaner state, is that governments are losing policy autonomy due to globalization.[12] Global competition and the amazingly quick movement of capital that is now possible make governments compete more intensely than before for capital and investment. To be competitive, they need to bring budgets under control and restrain the taxation that is the lifeblood of the welfare state.

States downsize, according to Richard Rosecrance, to make themselves efficient competitors in a global economy featuring the increasingly free flow of technology, capital, and labor. He argues that the flow of international factors of production is swamping domestic economic power and making the state reliant on outside forces to solve domestic economic problems:

> Countries must induce foreign capital to enter their domain. To keep such investment, national authorities will need to maintain low inflation, rising productivity, a strong currency, and a flexible and trained labor force. These demands will sometimes conflict with domestic interests that want more government spending, larger budget deficits, and more benefits. That conflict will result in continued domestic insecurity over jobs, welfare, and medical care. Unlike the remedies applied in the insulated and partly closed economies of the past, purely domestic policies can no longer solve these problems.[13]

In addition to these factors, it seems clear that the public, especially in the United States, has grown increasingly dissatisfied with the way many regulatory programs are enforced. This is not a simple matter. The situation is roughly analogous to welfare state issues, where many want high benefits and low taxes. People simultaneously want the benefits produced by many regulatory regimes—clean air and water, and safe food and drugs—without inconvenient requirements. And they often do not like the goals represented by regulations in areas such as affirmative action. The antiregulatory tone of the National Performance Review may not derive from the same concerns as the public reaction to regulation, but political leaders appreciate its popular appeal.

Finally, technological change, changes in the economic environment, and the many problems faced by the state have apparently contributed to a widespread feeling that the methods used in the private sector are superior to those used in the public sector. When New Public Management advocates call for privatization, more contracting out, deregulation, and the like, they are in tune with a current of political opinion that has shown great vitality of late across much of the political spectrum.

In brief, there are a variety of explanations for the emergence of the New Public Management (including the American version, the National Performance Review) as a potent force in contemporary government. There is probably some power in each of the explanatory factors put forward, although, like Hood, we remain skeptical that the argument or evidence for any of them is yet dominant or compelling enough to settle comfortably on a major cause. This is one of those areas that cry out for more research. What is abundantly clear is that U.S. government executives and those in most industrialized nations face a changing environment brought on by efforts to implement many of the proposals espoused by NPM advocates.

According to Donald Kettl, a leading student of NPM, the global revolution in public management has had two basic variants. In one that he terms "*let* managers manage," employed in countries such as Australia and Sweden, "Reformers . . . believed that managers knew the right things to do, but that existing rules, procedures, and structures created barriers to doing it."[14] The managers, reformers argued, were restrained by standard operating procedures and limited in their vision of what could be done by existing policies and practices. Reforms should be designed to free managers so that they could focus on the problems to be solved and react to them in flexible and creative ways. "At the core of let the managers manage is the customer service movement," Kettl says, "which focuses managers on serving citizens instead of the needs of the bureaucracy, on the 'works better' side of the 'works better/costs less' dilemma."[15]

The second variant Kettl labels "*making* the managers manage." This approach is particularly identified with the reforms in New Zealand and Great Britain. Reformers emphasized that "because most government agencies and programs are monopolies, managers had little incentive to manage better. The only way to improve government performance, they believed, was to change the incentives of government managers by subjecting them to market forces."[16] A variety of techniques have been used. In Britain's Next Steps initiative, agencies (separate from policy framing departments) were established to carry out policies under contracts specifying goals and performance standards. In New Zealand, managers are now hired on performance contracts and can be fired if their units do not achieve performance standards set for them. Both nations have privatized programs and contracted out, much as rational choice economists advise.

Kettl argues that the "let managers manage" and "make managers manage" philosophies "drive in opposite directions."[17] The "let managers manage" approach increases managers' responsiveness to consumers. It empowers them to act flexibly to improve service, all the while driven by consumer demand and preference. The "make managers manage" approach has goals set from the top, with managers then given freedom (within some limits, of course) to do what is necessary to achieve the goals. Kettl notes that the Americans who shaped the reinvention initiative borrowed widely, drawing on both approaches without paying much attention to how they fit together. The result is a set of proposals with many facets but not much coherence.[18]

Exactly what are the main elements of the reinvention initiative in the United States? At first blush, the initiative looks rather simple. The original NPR report lists four key "principles" and then organizes its proposals within those principles. These are supposed to focus mainly on how government should work. As we noted earlier, a later set of proposals, often called NPR II, gives greater emphasis to what government does—and what it should be doing.[19] And the very latest phase, NPR III (or Phase III using Kettl's label) focuses on improving thirty-two "high impact agencies" and on using "outcomes measures to transform federal management."[20]

The four key principles of NPR I are cutting red tape, putting customers first, empowering employees to get results, and cutting back to basics. Despite the emphasis on the "how," the last clearly has strong implications for the "what" of government.

Cutting red tape involves a long series of steps to deregulate and streamline government. In what has gained the most attention from analysts, the NPR report suggests cutting regulations at the federal level and cutting federal regulations for states and localities. This includes a proposed process to allow agencies to obtain waivers from regulations and a suggestion that Congress impose fewer mandates on the agencies—that is, limit what critics like to call congressional micromanagement. The report also includes proposals to allow states and localities to consolidate separate grant programs and to allow cabinet secretaries to grant states and localities waivers from federal regulations. The NPR report also suggests minimizing many restrictions on agency spending imposed by the Office of Management and Budget (OMB) and the Congress, allowing budget rollovers between fiscal years, and streamlining the budget process by introducing biennial budgeting. It advocates decentralization of the personnel process to give managers greater authority to hire, promote, reward, and fire workers. It calls for reforming the procurement process, especially eliminating rigid procurement rules and relying more on the marketplace. And finally, it suggests that departmental inspectors in general change their orientations from rules enforcement (punishing violators) to improving agency performance.

The NPR report contains numerous suggestions for putting customers first. Agencies are to get customers' views on services (using surveys and similar techniques). Where feasible, they should be made to compete for their customers' business: internal service agencies would compete with each other and with external service providers, and externally oriented service agencies would compete with private companies that can perform similar tasks. When a government monopoly is deemed absolutely necessary, as in the case of the air traffic control system, the organizations should be run more like business enterprises, emulate the best practices of the private sector, and be given incentives to respond to customers. Finally, the report urges that some federal functions be shifted to markets, including job training and workplace inspection.

NPR makes numerous proposals that it says will empower employees to get results and "create a culture of public entrepreneurship."[21] Decision-making power should be decentralized, giving lower-level employees more authority to make decisions while simultaneously cutting the number of supervisory personnel. Employees must be held accountable for results. Here the NPR enthusiastically embraces the Government Performance and Results Act of 1993 and calls for its full implementation, which includes strategic plans, annual performance plans with measurable goals, and opportunities for exemption from administrative regulations ("management flexibility waivers"). NPR also calls for the president to develop written performance agreements with department and agency heads. The report uses Britain's performance contracts as an example and implies that agency heads (and agencies) failing to achieve the agreed-upon objectives will suffer dire consequences. Finally, the NPR report asks that federal employees in the reinvented government receive the tools and training they will need to do their jobs and insists that they "make sure they use them."[22]

The final principle of NPR I is cutting back to basics. This is the section of the report that overlaps the "what" of government supposedly reserved for NPR II. The first element of cutting back to basics specifies that the federal government should "eliminate what we don't need."[23] Obviously, "what we don't need" is at least partially a function of one's political values and interests. The report focuses on what it terms the obsolete, on duplication (including overlapping programs), and on the elimination of "special interest privileges."[24] The examples the NPR report gives of the latter would be regarded by most as noncontroversial, but some might put a large number of federal programs under this rubric. Other suggestions for "getting back to basics" include raising user fees (and giving agencies greater freedom in this regard), working harder to eliminate fraud, investing in greater productivity, and reengineering programs to cut costs.

NPR I called for savings of $108 billion over five years, almost 40 percent of it through "streamlining" the bureaucracy by eliminating about 252,000 jobs (later raised to 272,900 by Congress). NPR II called for additional savings of nearly $70 billion over five years through program changes, terminations, and privatization.

An analysis we did of the NPR II savings indicates that of the specifically allocated changes (some agencies, such as NASA, did not break proposed savings out by program), 84 percent required legislative changes.[25] Savings, in other words, cannot simply be achieved by administrative changes. Many of the "inefficiencies" in administration are legislatively mandated, suggesting a political source for the problem rather than an administrative source—a point to which we return later.[26]

NPR I was widely criticized for its emphasis on savings over performance improvement and for its lack of a strategy for dealing with Congress, whose support would be needed in a variety of ways, including legislation. The president and vice president trumpeted the reductions in the size of the bureaucracy and the projected cost savings. The "costs less" part of NPR, in short, dominated the "works better" part—no surprise to any political observer. But it did constitute a problem because, as Donald Kettl put it so well, "seeking big savings in short order can undermine the broader effort for management improvement and increase costs in the long run." [27]

In brief, the NPR aims to cut programs, save money, contract out government functions, privatize, rely on competition and markets, and adopt private sector techniques in a redesigned administrative system that emphasizes results. It also endorses bottom-up management and a focus on customer satisfaction. It says little about what should happen if the elements clash.

One could write volumes about the various management tools NPR advocates. In fact, people have. And many of the NPR proposals contain exciting ideas for freeing federal managers to manage effectively. When we criticize some of the notions of the performance review, as we do in the next section, the spirit is constructive. Indeed, we do not want to pour cold water on many of the management reforms NPR suggests (or at least on the need for management reforms), but we do want to comment on difficulties with the reforms and then emphasize that the problem is deeper than NPR or NPM suggests.

Critique of Reinvention: Problems and Prospects

As noted, many parts of the National Performance Review proposals are attractive. It is always useful to review the mass of regulations, which can frustrate federal workers and executives even more than they frustrate citizens whose direct contact with federal programs is relatively infrequent. Few would deny the advantages of careful thought about what might be done better or more flexibly in the private sector, although this is likely to yield greater payoffs in nations where the public sector has historically run transportation systems and provided other quasi-commercial services. More contracting out might prove successful, although much of the government's previous experience in this area demonstrates how difficult it can be to manage the contracting process.[28] Certainly, most objective observers can only applaud efforts to use modern information technology to make organizations run better and to flatten them out so that fewer workers provide a better product. And all who care about how government works should want to see those it serves receive courteous, polite, and satisfying treatment in government offices.

We do not aim in this section to critique each of the many changes NPR suggested. Rather, we want to look for areas that need rethinking and probe beneath what looks appealing on the surface to see if its underside contains a hidden problem. We start with a critique of the four basic principles of NPR and then follow with a discussion of other issues raised by the NPR exercise, including broader issues that affect the political system.

Cutting Red Tape

The first major goal of reinvention is "cutting red tape." This goal is as close to motherhood as one can find in the world of administrative reform. Red tape is a pejorative term that few people are likely to endorse.

However, a thoughtful and dispassionate analysis of red tape by Herbert Kaufman should make one think twice about red tape's uses as well as its abuses. Kaufman argues that these binding, official constraints on behavior were created to protect people from abuses, to ensure due process (fairness), to make sure that interests can be represented in the policy process (and in an orderly, rational way), to promote effectiveness in administration, and to make sure that administrative actions are open to public scrutiny.[29] These are values most people in a democratic society favor. Unfortunately, procedures to promote them sometimes make things inconvenient or irritating. That is the dilemma of red tape—balancing the costs and benefits. By simplifying the issue, the NPR is open to the criticism of ignoring the need to consider proposed procedural changes very carefully—including those proposed in the laudable effort to deregulate and streamline government—to make sure that the costs as well as the expected benefits are taken into account.

James Q. Wilson, drawing on Kaufman, argues that guarantees of fairness and predictability in the public sector—such as rules governing how agencies hire, purchase, and contract—provide fundamental protections for individuals and organized interests in the society. Rules guarantee that there are established procedures for developing and promulgating regulations (the Administrative Procedures Act) so that people with an interest can learn what the government plans to do and have their say. Sometimes the rules are established to make sure that a particular group has access to public resources (minority-owned businesses or local governments are two of the examples Wilson uses). Here rules are used to protect an interest or to record the victor in a policy dispute.[30]

The obvious conclusion is that administrative flexibility is likely to be regarded as a virtue until some basic interest is damaged by it. Then there will be a demand to have procedures put back into place to ensure fairness, transparency, predictability, and related values. As Peter Aucoin notes in an essay that focuses on countries other than the United States: "The crucial tests are whether politicians, especially executive authorities, will restrain themselves from demanding new regulations or reregulation when the inevitable administrative mistakes and thus political embarrassments occur or when deviations from newly accepted norms, such as employment equity, are discovered."[31] Because of its focus on Westminster parliamentary systems, Aucoin's essay does not consider the even greater likelihood that elected politicians in an institution such as the U.S. Congress would quickly demand new rules and procedures in response to scandals or abuses. Indeed, Congress instigated many of the most restrictive rules now in place.

Putting Customers First

"Putting customers first" is the next principle of NPR. This is another idea that looks simple and desirable at first glance. Clearly, the public wants government agencies to satisfy those they serve and to provide them with the best possible treatment. However, not all customers are alike.

When a government agency such as the U.S. Postal Service has the general citizenry as its customers (and the customers are paying a fee for services received), there is not likely to be much debate about providing services according to customer preferences and demands. But often the customers are regulated interests or recipients of targeted benefits (such as welfare). Many others in society have a stake in these policy areas. They may be providers of the funds through redistribution of general tax revenues or they may be affected by the regulated interests (such as broadcasters or food processors). Who are the appropriate customers to consider in these cases? Whose interests should be given primacy? These are basically questions about legitimacy and equity, and they are political problems of the first order. In short, it's not always clear who the customers are and who should be "put first."

A related criticism of the putting customers first principle is the way it conceives (or, more accurately, fails to conceive) of citizens. Some analysts even go so far as to characterize reinvention as a denial of citizenship: "As citizens we expect government to act in a way that not only promotes the consumption of services . . . but also promotes a set of principles and ideals that are inherent in the public sphere."[32] There is a difference, in other words, between private sector providers of products and those things a nation's citizens strive to do collectively through government.

A major figure in the design of the reinvention initiative, John Kamensky, indirectly addresses this criticism by drawing a distinction between giving customers a say over service delivery and giving them a say in policymaking. He argues that the NPR advocates "increasing the role and voice of customers in the service delivery (but not the policymaking process)."[33] Government leaders are to set the basic policy framework within which customer satisfaction can be pursued. This distinction should help in many instances but sidesteps the basic contradiction discussed earlier in this chapter—the tension between what customers may want and what government policy requires, particularly if managers are evaluated on performance criteria beyond customer satisfaction.

Finally, there is some doubt that the NPR's market analogies about customer service are entirely on the mark. The assumption in NPR is that businesses have customer satisfaction as their primary goal. The fact is that their primary goal is profit. Satisfying customers is a means to that end, but not the end in itself. When they can, businesses eliminate competition and squeeze what they can out of customers. And even when there is competition, businesses must gauge the trade-off between what customers would like (excellent service) and what they prefer to pay (low prices). Anyone who flies the domestic airlines is well aware of this trade-off.

There are, in short, many unresolved problems with the appealing idea of putting customers first.

Empowering Employees to Get Results

"Empowering employees to get results" is the third NPR principle. Decentralizing authority so government workers may be free to contribute creatively to organizational performance is another goal few would dispute. Like the other NPR goals, however, significant difficulties will arise in achieving employee empowerment. The first and most obvious is the danger of scandal. Wilson quotes the following line approvingly from the NPR report: "In Washington's highly politicized world, the greatest risk is not that a program will perform poorly, but that a scandal will erupt."[34] He assumes, reasonably in our view, that this dynamic will continue. It is not fertile ground for successful, sustained employee empowerment.

Another difficulty with employee empowerment is the problem of agreed-upon expectations. Again we return to the tension between goals defined by employees (and customers) and those defined by elected officials or decisionmakers at the top. Just how much flexibility should democratic systems give to administrative employees, especially as it is the administration of policy that often defines what policy is? If the political system gives administrators vague goals, as is often the case, how free should government employees then be from interference (supervision) by the central authorities? And what happens when Congress and the executive disagree about goals and then give conflicting signals about what agency goals or behavior should be?

Many of these questions will arise again when we discuss early implementation of the Government Performance and Results Act (GPRA). The NPR report holds up GPRA as an excellent example of empowering employees to achieve results and then making them accountable.[35] Of course, there are huge advantages in developing measurable objectives for agency employees to achieve. The problems in implementing a statute such as GPRA come when, as is commonly the case, the political process leaves goals unsettled or the level of resources for programs may be in dispute. (And often both goals and resources are in dispute.)

Cutting Back to Basics

The fourth and final goal of NPR is "cutting back to basics," with eliminating "what we don't need" as a first step. Few would disagree in principle with the idea that government should eliminate what isn't needed. However, there is likely to be quite a dispute about what should be considered basic. Indeed, the core of the problem, far more important than questions of administrative systems or mechanisms, is in reaching consensus on what government should be doing.

As James Q. Wilson notes, the original NPR made relatively noncontroversial suggestions, such as closing down some agency field offices and targeting wool, honeybee, and mohair subsidies.[36] As we noted above, NPR II makes more substantial program suggestions, but most of its proposals require congressional action because the programs or modes of service delivery targeted for deletion or change have been established by legislation. The key to making the changes is political, not administrative. There are supportive constituencies behind most government programs. Supporters regularly claim that the nation needs their favorite programs (and often have suggestions for improving the programs by extending them in some way). It usually takes conflict and the expenditure of political capital to make authoritative decisions about what is basic and what is not needed.

Other analysts make similar points. Ron Moe, for example, in a scathing analysis of NPR, concludes that after all is said and done "what we really need today . . . is to rethink what it is that we really expect from our government."[37] George Frederickson argues that reinventing government is plagued by the "wrong-problems problem." He says that "in the wrong-problems problem a government seeks to avoid making tough policy choices that deal with real public problems and instead turns to better management as the universal solution."[38] Of course, NPR does suggest some policy choices, but very few really tough ones. And it is these tough choices that Frederickson means when he talks about "real public problems."

Other Problems and Inconsistencies

For a reform package that is concerned with efficiency and the way government organizations operate, NPR gives relatively little attention to the role of high-level managers. NPR calls for cutbacks among middle-level supervisory personnel as a means of reducing the size of the civil service and simultaneously increasing spans of control, but it is curiously silent about the increasing size of the corps of political appointees. Their numbers have risen dramatically since 1960, part of a phenomenon Paul Light refers to as "thickening government." A review of Light's book puts the problem well:

> As [Light] so effectively points out, early justifications for limited spans of control rested on the innate limitations of leaders; current motivations for thickening rest on a desire by presidents for tighter control of bureaucrats they do not trust. By not systematically addressing political appointees in its recommendations the Gore report fails to remove a major obstacle toward achieving a thinner and better performing federal bureaucracy. [39]

One problem is that with so many appointees at the top, it is difficult to hold any particular person accountable for outcomes—one of the goals of NPR. Another, raised by the Volcker Commission, is that the talents and expertise of top career officials are not used effectively when so many key positions are held by political appointees.[40] The NPR says a great deal about personnel hiring, training, and use of modern technology, but it shies away from the politically sensitive problem that there are probably too many presidential appointees, many of whom lack the skills of the careerists serving beneath them.

Kettl stresses another missing piece in NPR: the need to tie the rein-vented management system to budgeting. One huge potential advantage of a performance-based management system is that it can help clarify thinking about policy goals and provide data on whether those goals are being achieved. That, in turn, should "help elected officials weigh competing claims for scarce resources and put the money where it will do the most good."[41] The Government Performance and Results Act is certainly meant to have a profound effect on the performance clarification and measurement side of the equation—although how it will finally work out in practice is still unclear, and the budgeting side of the equation is still quite problematic. Indeed, the General Accounting Office (GAO), in an understated manner, reports that "due to the great variability among agencies' program activity structures, Congress and the executive branch will likely be challenged as they attempt to link performance goals with the budget's program activity structures."[42]

We could go on in this vein, but it should be clear that there are numerous problems with the NPR blueprint (and with NPM) that require careful thinking and difficult choices. The more consistent the elements of the reform, the better the chance that it will succeed. Some proposals can be put into effect easily, and many have. More contracting out, streamlining the hiring process, use of various devices to gauge agency customer opinion and to respond to it, greater and more effective use of information technology, streamlining some aspects of procurement, and attention to a variety of internal agency management reforms all seem to have been implemented with some success.[43] The long-term question is whether the inconsistencies and problems with NPR such as those identified above will be resolved.

Of particular note are the following issues:

—How will the "let managers manage" and "make managers manage" elements of NPR be reconciled?

—How will the error-sensitive U.S. political system respond to the inevitable major mistakes and scandals that will occur in a reinvented government, just as they occur in the private sector?

—Can a bureaucracy as flexible and adaptive as that envisioned in the NPR report also be held accountable, and to whom? Kettl, certainly no opponent of the reforms, goes so far as to say that the performance measurement and customer-based emphasis of reinvention and NPM "subtly transforms the relationship between elected officials and administrators. At the least, it introduces new standards by which administrators can assert autonomy from policymakers; at the most, it uncouples the existing leverage that elected officials typically use in asserting their control over public managers."[44]

—How would the reinvented government deal with the inconsistencies inherent in the American separation of powers system, especially when there is divided control of Congress and the presidency? To which institution would agencies be accountable for results? What would happen if Congress failed to appropriate the funds the president and the agency have agreed are necessary to achieve results specified in agency plans? How would managers *then* be evaluated?

—What would the relationship between managers and elected officials look like under an implemented NPR? Would elected officials, especially the Congress, be willing to refrain from interference in administration, even assuming there is agreement on goals? More broadly, why would Congress accept the limited role implied by the reinvention initiative?[45]

—What, if any, will the political and social consequences be if, as appears to be the case, "the near-term emphasis on efficiency in reinventing government has taken a toll on social equity"?[46] Will the emphasis on "basics," the lean-state philosophy, and the devices of reinvented government hold up to the increased demands for equity likely to accompany the next major economic recession?

GPRA: Dilemmas of Reinventing

The Government Performance and Results Act was passed by the Congress and signed by President Clinton in 1993, the year of the initial NPR report. The report embraces this legislation. It sees it as an essential tool in getting agencies to set measurable goals for their programs and in holding top managers accountable for results.[47] And, as Kettl points out, GPRA is a cornerstone of NPR III, with its emphasis on achieving results in "high-impact agencies."[48] It is much too early to pronounce judgment on the act, but early results are informative about problems in implementing a key element of NPR/NPM in the U.S. context.

The GPRA is meant to "encourage greater efficiency, effectiveness, and accountability in federal spending by establishing a new framework for management, and subsequently budgeting in federal agencies. The framework requires agencies to set goals, measure performance, and report on the results."[49] The act requires agencies to produce strategic plans (covering a five-year period, updated at least every three years), annual performance plans, and annual reports on program performance. Performance plans must include performance goals expressed in "an objective, quantifiable, and measurable form," and "establish performance indicators to be used in measuring or assessing the relevant outputs, service levels, and outcomes of each program activity."[50] Agencies are to consult with Congress and OMB and solicit the views of others in developing their strategic plans. The statute also allows the director of OMB to exempt programs from certain nonstatutory rules and regulations if the exemptions will help to improve program results.[51] Five agencies were to be designated as pilots for testing performance budgeting for fiscal years 1998 and 1999, thereby providing a direct link to the budgeting process.[52]

It is easy to understand the NPR report's enthusiasm for this statute. And because the statute called for GAO evaluations, significant evidence is already available on its implementation, though full implementation was to take seven years (to 2000) from its passage in 1993.

GAO produced two reports in 1998 that are particularly enlightening.[53] The reports examine the statutory framework for performance-based management and accountability and review the twenty-four major agencies' strategic plans, which were formally submitted to Congress and OMB in September 1997 in the first full cycle of strategic planning. While the agencies' September plans were judged better than earlier trial submissions, the

GAO had numerous criticisms. Indeed, the strategic plans were delicately described as "very much a work in progress."[54]

The problems with the plans are quite revealing. Some difficulties are merely disappointing, but not too surprising for the early stages of such an endeavor. Many agencies, for example, listed "goals that did not focus on results to the extent feasible," and goals were not "always expressed in a manner conducive to assessing progress in terms of actual performance." Agencies also often did not discuss how they would accomplish goals.[55] Time and experience could conceivably solve these problems, at least to the extent they are not related to more fundamental difficulties.

However, there are indications that some shortcomings go beyond mere adjustment to a changing environment. For example, GAO identified agency difficulties in addressing overlapping and fragmented program efforts and competing policy priorities in their plans. These are not a function of agency administrative problems but are related to legislative mandates produced in the complex U.S. political environment. A GAO report, for example, commented on the Forest Service's inability to reconcile conflicts about the use of its lands and cited the example of promoting timber sales versus protecting wildlife. It goes on to say that "striking the right balance is a continuing and difficult challenge because forging the political consensus needed to create and sustain a program often results in that program having competing and/or broadly stated goals."[56]

Indeed, striking the right balance is a difficult political challenge for many federal agencies. The GPRA leaves it to the agencies to propose goals.[57] That can put them in jeopardy with congressional committees and constituencies, not a place savvy agency executives like to be. It is hardly surprising that agencies have often shied away from stepping on this potential land mine.

It is also not surprising that some members of Congress have been quite critical of the agencies' strategic plans. For example, House Majority Leader Dick Armey castigated agencies for failure to address the overlap in federal programs.[58] A less-than-friendly critic of Armey's position, writing in the journal *Government Executive*, reacted by asking: "But who created all those redundant programs, anyway?" She suggested that Congress take the lead in cutting the redundant programs "no matter whose district or which lobbying group they were created to please."[59] This is not likely to happen, but it points to a fundamental difficulty. Most overlapping programs and responsibilities derive from the authorizing legislation agreed to in the political process. GPRA tells the agencies to state their goals clearly, even though that may often be close to impossible legally or politically or both.

A related problem is that the GPRA calls for the agencies to consult with Congress in developing their strategic plans, but it was left unclear exactly what consultation means.[60] Agencies clearly must communicate with relevant congressional bodies and try to reach an accommodation with them, but no one knows precisely what will happen if Congress and OMB disagree, or in the quite possible situation in which the two chambers disagree. The statute also allows Congress to add, amend, or abolish a performance goal. This would be the ultimate form of "making the managers manage." Frederick Kaiser and Virginia McMurtry of the Congressional Research Service, however, point out that "it is uncertain . . . just how any such goal replacement might be achieved."[61] Holding managers responsible in the manner envisioned by NPR and the GPRA may be difficult indeed.

There are other significant problems that are likely to arise, even if goals are agreed upon or Congress raises no immediate objection to the goals specified in agency reports. Kaiser and McMurtry ask: "How should the failure to reach certain goals be assessed if, subsequent to approval of a plan, an agency's budget were reduced; if funding were earmarked for other purposes and thus indirectly limited for certain goals; or if reprogramming and rescissions affected the agency's ability to achieve the unmet goals?"[62] These are good questions, in a similar vein to those we raised earlier about likely problems of New Public Management approaches when applied in the United States, with its separated powers system of government.

Other problems GAO mentioned include the fact that the federal government often has a quite limited or indirect influence in determining whether a desired goal is achieved: "GAO work has shown that measuring the federal contribution is particularly challenging for regulatory programs; scientific research programs; and programs to deliver services to taxpayers through third parties, such as state and local governments."[63] These are major elements in the program array of the U.S. government. GAO also is concerned that agencies' quality performance data are often of low quality, due in part to factors that are difficult to control, such as "the need to rely on third parties to provide data."[64] Managers in the GPRA/NPR environment are clearly going to have to be more skilled than ever in securing and evaluating data from states and localities and from the many additional contractors envisioned by the NPR report.

Finally, as we noted earlier in the chapter, GAO is concerned about the difficulties likely in linking agencies' performance plans to the budget process. These difficulties arise because "the extent to which the budget's program activity structure can be linked to a results-oriented performance framework varies widely among activities." The problem is not that adjustments are difficult to conceive or implement, but that Congress and the executive branch disagree and that reaching agreement will "be a time-consuming and difficult process that will take more than one budget cycle to resolve."[65]

Despite the existence of all of these problems (and perhaps unforeseen others), it is likely that GPRA will have many positive effects. By going through the exercise of producing strategic plans, annual performance plans, and annual performance reports, agencies will be forced to consider their goals in a clearer and more measurable way. They will improve their use of information technology and will almost surely be better supervisors of states, localities, and contractors. GPRA will also highlight differences between Congress and the executive branch over policy and perhaps stimulate greater clarity in legislation and efforts to decrease program overlap and fragmentation. But in the end, the most sensitive problems of goal definition, program fragmentation, and uncertain and changing levels of program budgetary support are at base political problems. Management reforms can highlight such problems, but they cannot solve them.

Reinvention and the Public Service

The ultimate effects of reinvention are unknown, and even the full implications of what has been achieved so far remain unclear. We can, however, look at the impacts, if any, of the reinvention effort on some aspects of federal service we considered earlier. The available data limit what we can examine quantitatively, but many important issues can be addressed, especially in reference to the Senior Executive Service (SES), based on data available from government and other studies.

First, we look at the impact of efforts to downsize the federal service—one of the areas where the reinvention effort is touted for its impact. Second, we turn to questions of quality. Have educational levels changed? If so, how? Are those at the top of the federal executive less experienced than their predecessors? If so, by how much? Third, are top executives less satisfied with their jobs amidst all the hubbub of reinvention? Has morale collapsed?

Cuts in the size of the federal work force are often proudly cited as an accomplishment of the reinvention effort. And it is clearly the case that the federal civilian work force (as well as the armed forces) has experienced a meaningful decline. Not counting the U.S. Postal Service, the number of civilian employees of the federal government declined from just over 2,250,000 in 1990 during the Bush administration to a little under 1,872,000 in 1997.[66] Donald Kettl, in his fifth-year report card on reinvention, cites a reduction of just over 330,000 positions during the Clinton administrations.[67] Most of the cuts, however, were in Department of Defense civilian employment, where downsizing was already under way; but as Kettl and others point out, they also affected some non-Defense agencies.[68]

An interesting aspect of the employment cuts is that they were concentrated in the lower ranks of the General Schedule (GS). Statistics collected by the U.S. Office of Personnel Management (OPM), for example, show that federal civilian employment in the GS ranks dropped by 9.4 percent between 1986 and 1997. The cuts were immense in the GS 1–4 category, where the number of employees declined by 59.1 percent in this period; less severe in the GS 5–8 category, where employment fell by 12.0 percent; barely noticeable in the GS 9–12 category, where there were 1.5 percent fewer workers; and nonexistent in the GS 13–15 category. In fact, GS 13–15 employment actually increased by 39.4 percent.[69]

These changes are a function of many factors, especially the spread of technology in the federal workplace, making lower-level jobs superfluous (as in the private sector), and the increased use of contracts and grants by many agencies.[70] GS 13–15s are needed to administer these contracts and grants, which, as Light points out, should also be considered in determining the true size of government because of the many government-supported employees they create. While Americans now have a government that is shaped differently from the pyramid of the past, the public sector is still quite large and meaningful.

The Senior Executive Service has not been untouched by changes in direct federal employment levels, but the impact is complex. There were close to 6,900 charter members of SES in 1979[71] and 6,742 in 1986 during the heyday of the Reagan administration.[72] There were 6,804 in SES in 1998, the last year for which we have data. Looked at from this perspective, there has been relatively little change in SES—reinvention notwithstanding. However, there was a big run-up in SES totals during the Bush administration, reaching a high of 8,200 in 1992. From that perspective, there has been a decline under President Clinton of approximately 16 percent in SES membership. Membership, however, was relatively stable from 1996 to 1998, averaging 6,891 and indicating that SES has simply returned to approximately its historic norm. Because of the increase in personnel during the

Bush period, it was evidently relatively easy for the Clinton administration to find slack in the system and thus to appear more efficient.

Has this movement in the size of the SES from the high of the Bush administration back to the norm affected either the educational level or experience of SES executives? OPM data indicate that the impact has been quite modest but positive. The overall percentage of SES members with advanced degrees increased from an average of 66 percent in 1990 and 1992, around the time we interviewed SESers in the Bush administration, to an average of 69 percent in 1994, 1996, and 1997.[73] The changes are hardly dramatic, but they clearly show no decline. In addition, the average age of SES executives remained in the low fifties, and the average length of service remained in the twenty-two- to twenty-three-year range. SES people in the reinvention era, in other words, continued to be extraordinarily well educated and quite vigorous, assuming that people in their early fifties are at the height of their professional careers.

Despite these data, we cannot discount the possibility that the tensions and changes brought about by reinvention may have hurt morale in the SES. We know that federal employees tend to be skeptical in their overall evaluations of NPR. The Merit Systems Protection Board (MSPB) conducted a survey of a representative sample of the nation's full-time, permanent civilian employees in 1996. It found that only 35 percent of government workers who said that their organizations had made NPR a priority agreed with the statement: "The efforts of the National Performance Review, which has been working on reinventing Government, have had a positive impact in bringing change to Government." The figure for those whose organizations had not made NPR a priority was a paltry 10 percent.[74] While figures were quite a bit higher on individual items—such as whether unit productivity had increased over the preceding two years or whether workers had been given more flexibility in how they accomplished their work goals (with organizations making NPR a priority scoring highest)— the overall view of reinvention was not overwhelmingly encouraging. Workers were very negative about the impact of downsizing, and many spontaneously wrote comments on the survey instruments indicating "that as far as they were concerned, the NPR was simply a way to reduce the size of the Government work force and thereby save money."[75]

Nevertheless, in this same survey 70 percent of federal workers indicated that they were generally satisfied with their jobs, and 87 percent described their work as meaningful to them. These figures were comparable to the results from similar surveys conducted in 1989 and 1992, before the reinvention effort began. And the data indicate that satisfaction was actually highest among those who worked for organizations that had made the goals of NPR a priority.[76] Clearly, whatever else it has done, NPR has not damaged morale among the broad cross-section of federal workers.

The same is true for SES executives examined separately. Results from the Merit Systems Protection Board's 1992 survey of all federal workers broke results down by job type. It indicated that 86 percent of SES executives were satisfied with their jobs.[77] That is an extraordinarily high number—higher than our own figures reported in chapter 4, using a different measure. However, a 1997–98 survey of SES executives by the Pew Research Center for the People and the Press indicated an even higher level of job satisfaction than that reported in the MSPB survey. When asked, "All things considered, how satisfied are you with your job overall?" 56 percent of SES respondents indicated "very satisfied" and 38 percent indicated "mostly satisfied" for a total of 94 percent satisfied. Only 1 percent were "very dissatisfied," and 4 percent "mostly dissatisfied."[78] Members of the SES also reported that they are proud to tell people they meet for the first time where they work and that they believe that government does a better job than it is generally given credit for.[79]

There are many possible reasons SES executives are satisfied with their jobs despite their general skepticism about reinvention, including Hawthorne effects (the positive effects of being the object of study) and the possible departure from government of dissatisfied executives. We are not in a position to add anything other than speculation as to why morale remains high. But the evidence is incontestably clear that reinvention has had no negative effects on the Senior Executive Service in terms of the educational levels of those in the service, their level of experience, or their morale.

The Larger Issues

Lurking behind much of our discussion of NPR is a difficult question: how important are management concerns in the total scheme of things? The reinvention initiative, and the New Public Management of which it is a part, assume that reforming management is a major answer to the problems faced by contemporary governments. Reinvented government will not only work more efficiently, they say, providing a government that works better and costs less, it will cut the services of the state back to basics, eliminate what is not needed, and restore the people's trust in government. The reinvented government will also be more in tune with the advantages modern information technology can bring and will put the country in a better position to compete in the globalized economy.

Many of the NPR proposals are relatively noncontroversial. There is little debate about the desirability of courteous and efficient service in government offices, or about using communications and information processing technology to make organizations run more smoothly and efficiently, or even about considering the costs and benefits of contracting out and privatization in many areas. And most observers would agree that rules and regulations should be carefully reviewed and culled, although there might be great disagreement about which rules are necessary.

Indeed, the difficulties arise from the political side of reinvention. Though stated as a set of management reforms, the core of reinvention is political. It raises the whole set of fundamental issues we mentioned in the opening pages of chapter 1 that usually underlie proposed changes in management technique or personnel policy. NPR proposes changes in the distribution of power, although it does not resolve who will gain. There is a tension in NPR between increasing the influence of those at the center and increasing the influence of people the reinvention report terms "customers." And NPR is understandably vague about who at the center will gain power, although the NPR report deemphasizes Congress and thereby implies an answer. On the question of discretion and judgment, the NPR endorses an increase in the discretionary power of lower-level officials, but at the same time the goals of those at the top (or customer preferences, depending on the section of the report) are supposed to dominate. It makes assumptions about cutting red tape that, as we have seen, are highly questionable. Concerning accountability (who is legally responsible for what?), NPR is unclear. Certainly when it comes to the vexing question of responsiveness in U.S. government (to which principals in a system of separated and often divided powers are bureaucratic agents to respond?), the issue remains as unresolved and contentious under NPR as it was before.

Perhaps the biggest problem comes in "cutting back to basics" and "eliminating what we do not need." While NPR treats these as management issues—indeed, emphasizes them in a management context—they are only to a small extent issues of management. In short, these are political questions: they cut to the core of what a society expects of its government and what it is willing to pay, questions that remain central even if one makes optimistic assumptions about the benefits to be achieved from increased government efficiency.

The United States, like most Western-style democracies, has confronted a package of political problems since the early 1970s. These include relative resource scarcity (growing entitlements), challenges to the power of the nation-state (globalization), regulatory programs that many accept in principle but do not like in practice (in areas such as environmental protection and civil rights), and the rise of political movements hostile to government and government expenditures (unwillingness to pay). If Americans could agree on how to deal with entitlements, regulatory processes, and global competitiveness—then much of the rest would fall into place. The "good people" the NPR report talks about could manage the system in a way most would accept—with or without the NPR reforms.

Better government for less would be welcome, and management reforms can help. But there is little evidence as yet that the NPR management reforms in and of themselves are the answer, even where they are adopted. It is cutbacks in programs and benefits that produce major savings. Or, alternatively, vigorous economic growth that makes cutbacks unnecessary or cushions their impact. American citizens say that they want smaller government, but they also want most of government's major domestic expenditure programs, particularly Social Security and Medicare, considered to be among the best administered. The key is for the American public to agree on what it wants and what it is willing to pay. Management reforms, judiciously applied, are also important and can help with some problems such as excessive rule-boundedness, but decisions about what government should or should not do are ultimately a job for the people's representatives (elected officials) in a democracy.

As James Q. Wilson asserts, you can't successfully reinvent government "in any serious way without rethinking what it is government ought to do."[80] Much of the reinvention initiative emphasizes management techniques, many of them important and useful, but the first question is what Americans want the public sector to do. Only when that question is answered can government consider the best way to accomplish these goals.

Another important broad issue is related to the strategic planning notions that are fundamental to the family of New Public Management reforms. Some question the appropriateness of strategic planning in the contemporary environment. For example, Jonathan Boston and June Pallot, two keen students of the New Zealand reforms, contrast strategic planning and strategic thinking:

In the face of accelerating changes (such as the information revolution, globalization, and democratization in communities and workplaces), strategic planning has come under attack because the forecasting of discontinuities is virtually impossible, predictions are almost invariably wrong, and its calculating analytical style misses "soft" information and important nuances. Unlike strategic planning, strategic thinking is based on creativity, intuition, and organizational learning; strategies often cannot be developed on schedule and immaculately conceived but must be free to appear at any time and at any place in an organization.[81]

We cannot evaluate here the differences between these two approaches to management, but it would be ironic if governments adopted yesterday's cutting-edge private-sector thinking in their rush to manage more like the private sector.

In evaluating the reinvention initiative one must also consider difficult questions about the function of government. As Kettl notes:

As much as reformers incorporate private sector models into government operations, government is not and never will be a business. In a democracy, its fundamental job is pursuing the public interest. It promotes critical values of fairness, justice, equity, and due process. Government exists . . . precisely because the private market, and market-style management, does a terrible job in pursuing goals such as these that go beyond efficiency."[82]

Kettl believes that "performance management" is quite compatible with, and indeed assists, government in pursuing the public interest.[83] By shedding light on what government programs are accomplishing, performance measures should improve management and also aid citizens in evaluating government performance. Critics tend to stress what they see as an incompatibility between the customer focus of NPR and the goals of government in the United States. James Carroll articulates this point eloquently:

In place of the purposes and values proclaimed in the Preamble to the Constitution as the objectives of constitutional government—a more perfect union, the common defense, domestic tranquility, justice, the general welfare, the blessings of liberty—it [NPR] substitutes the values of a consumer society—customer satisfaction. It converts government into an instrument of service consumption, ignoring the roles of government in resolving conflicts, settling national goals, controlling the use of force in society, investing in the nation's future, and pursuing constitutional values and policy objectives which have little if anything to do with service or with satisfying customers.[84]

At the bottom of the debate about the New Public Management is unease about its emphasis on efficiency and customer (as opposed to citizen) satisfaction. Part of the problem is the potential incompatibility between the two. As the Kettl and Carroll quotes make clear, there is also tension between accomplishing certain political ends—what might be thought of as political efficiency—and managerial efficiency. The more one accepts the notion that government exists to promote fairness, justice, equity, and due process, the more important it is to specify where NPR/NPM techniques should be emphasized and where they should retreat to the background.

CHAPTER EIGHT

The Federal Executive in the Web of Politics

AS THE U.S. FEDERAL government grew and came to be more important in people's lives, its executive apparatus, what is commonly called "the bureaucracy," became increasingly controversial. One simple reason is that a government that once did little was now doing a lot more. And some of these activities were mired in controversy.

Controversies about the bureaucracy typically have less to do with the bureaucracy per se than with the role of government and its policies. Many of these controversies about the role and purpose of government owe their origins to the New Deal reformation of the federal government in the 1930s. The reaction to the New Deal and its successor regimes, such as the Johnson administration's Great Society programs and even the early Nixon administration's refurbishing of the regulatory state, helped trigger antigovernment sentiment. The bureaucracy soon became the synonym for big government and a manifestation to some of a government gone awry. For many politicians seeking national office, running against government and the bureaucracy was their ticket to ride. Jimmy Carter and Ronald Reagan both stressed the anti-Washington, anti-bureaucrat theme, although for different reasons. The bureaucracy was a vulnerable target and could readily be scapegoated. To many politicians in Washington, or those trying to get there, the bureaucracy became a prime target because it was at the delivery point of policies perceived as failures.

The controversies enmeshing the federal bureaucracy became more intense in the 1970s, in part because divided government was almost continuous after the 1968 election and in part because the ferment of anti–big government became more powerful over time. Presidential administrations and congressional majorities frequently fought over executive turf. This was not a new phenomenon, but policy differences, magnified by divided government, made the struggles more intense. Each of the branches of government, including the courts, became more assertive in the struggle for control over policy.[1] We noted in chapters 2 and 7 that fiscal and global constraints on government were growing, and the responses to these challenges seemed to many to dictate a smaller, less burdened state with a smaller permanent bureaucracy. In short, over time the political environment delegitimized big government and its agent, the bureaucracy.

The federal bureaucracy became the symbol of big government's problems—rarely of its successes. The bureaucracy also became embroiled in the policy struggles and disputes waged between its various overseers (president, Congress, and the courts) and their very different, often conflicting, policy agendas. Consequently, the bureaucracy became the object of both reform and derision. As we noted in chapters 2 and 6, the Nixon White House, through means fair and foul, sought to make the bureaucracy responsive to its agenda alone. When the bureaucracy, including some of the Nixon administration's own appointees, did not fully comply with the White House's policy and political objectives, it became an object of presidential wrath. The Nixon White House developed an assertive strategy toward the bureaucracy known as "the administrative presidency."[2]

The two elected presidents following Nixon's downfall came to office after waging unmistakably anti-Washington campaigns, and they carried similar attitudes into the White House. Jimmy Carter made reform of the civil service one of his primary objectives. The image of the bureaucracy he emphasized was that of an indolent, inflexible federal work force too frequently unaccountable, unresponsive, and insulated.[3] Carter emphasized the seemingly intractable difficulties of actually firing a tenured career employee.[4] The Carter reform, the Civil Service Reform Act of 1978, was multifaceted, containing both carrots and sticks. The accompanying rhetoric, however, largely emphasized the sticks, and the punitive part of the package seemed more real to civil servants than the carrots. The Reagan administration had even harsher rhetoric about the federal bureaucracy (and government in general). Drawing on Nixon's administrative presidency strategy, it had a plan to gain control over the bureaucracy and put its clearly designed agenda into effect. Indeed, antibureaucratic rhetoric was a main Reagan administration battering ram.

By the mid-1980s a reaction to this assault on the bureaucratic establishment and the civil service began to take shape. It culminated in the Volcker Commission report of 1989, which expressed grave concern about the state of the federal career service.[5] The Volcker Commission argued that government and the career service had been so deeply denigrated that civil servants were demoralized, a condition that would precipitate, indeed was already causing, a decline in the quality of the career service. The antigovernment rhetoric was not simply symbolic. It was accompanied by intense efforts, especially during the Nixon and Reagan administrations, to try to make the bureaucracy more responsive to presidential wishes and more fully committed to them. Putting the two together, the logic of the Volcker Commission's argument is what we have called the "noisy crisis" (the alleged lack of bureaucratic responsiveness to the designs and needs of political leaders), and the responses of presidential administrations to this problem led to the "quiet crisis" (an alleged demoralization within the career service and a decline in the quality of its personnel).

What are the real problems of the federal executive? Political leaders, especially those who want rapid change, often emphasize what they perceive as a lack of responsiveness from the career bureaucracy. The public administration community, civic leaders, and organizations allied to civil service interests, however, emphasize something different. For them, the problem is typically perceived in terms of demoralization and concerns about the deterioration of both the quality and the stature of the public service. In this book, using data from our surveys and other sources, we have addressed the quiet crisis and its related hypotheses and the noisy crisis and its related hypotheses. We conclude there is little evidence to sustain either contention.

People Are Not the Problem

There is little doubt that for some time the federal bureaucracy and its career service have been buffeted about by unsympathetic political leaders and subjected to derision in the popular culture. The private sector is increasingly held up as a model, while the public sector, never overwhelmingly blessed with status, is much criticized. It is understandable that many sympathetic commentators would conclude that a high-quality civil service could not be sustained in such a situation. It was in this context that the Volcker Commission expressed its concern for the future and the quality of the U.S. federal service.

As we noted in chapters 3 and 4, there is no easily agreed-upon criterion by which to assess the quality of the individuals who compose the public service. In chapter 7 we note that similar difficulties exist at the organizational level. Certainly no one assessment of quality is definitive. Quality has a great deal to do with matches between qualifications and specific role demands. A good bit also has to do with the kind of civil service system Americans want or traditionally have had: whether that be, for example, a system that emphasizes management skills, or one that stresses technical specialization, or one that seeks the well-rounded qualities that presumably allow individuals to move comfortably from one position to another. The fact of the matter is that there is much controversy about just what the proper qualifications for a given job should be and to what extent these can be matched with a set of credentials.

The "quiet crisis" that the Volcker Commission refers to speaks of a thinning out of quality among those in the public service and an inability to retain and attract the best quality personnel. The commission acknowledges difficulties with operationalizing quality, but typically does so in terms of educational achievement. A first and essential step, therefore, is to evaluate this argument at its broadest level, namely educational credentials.

Using educational credentials, we examined two propositions essential to the Volcker Commission's principal hypothesis. First, has the civil service declined in quality? Second, is the civil service of lesser quality than peer groups in the private sector? Our data are complex yet consistent on this subject. We could find little evidence to support the Volcker Commission's main argument. Indeed, the preponderance of evidence indicates that the qualifications of civil servants, judged at least by the level of their educational attainments, have risen over time rather than declined. Ironically, according to these criteria, where there has been decline, it is most marked among the politically appointed executives rather than the senior career service.

Thus the evidence on behalf of a "quiet crisis" is itself very quiet. There is no doubt, however, that the public sector and the public service have been widely denigrated, especially at the federal level. It is therefore reasonable to infer that exit would be the likely response of civil servants, especially since their financial compensation is substantially lower than it is for their peers in the private sector. The reasonableness of that inference may have led the

Volcker Commission report to speculate on a qualitative decline, largely on the basis of anecdotal or incomplete evidence. Yet there is relatively little in our data to substantiate that quality has declined. Chairman Volcker set forth his view that the American civil service once attracted most of its top personnel from a small set of elite universities—what he called "our best institutions." However, it is doubtful that at any time in the modern era, with its explosion in the number of university graduates, these "best institutions" supplied the preponderance of the public sector elite (other than perhaps the foreign service) or even the corporate elite.[6] Moreover, the U.S. bureaucracy tends to place a relatively high premium on technical proficiency, frequently in fields that are not taught at many of the nation's elite universities. Thus it is somewhat surprising that top federal executives resemble private sector leaders as much as they do in their attendance at elite schools, especially in the prestige of the graduate schools they attended.[7] There are some signs of change that bear watching, but these hardly indicate a current crisis.

It is worth repeating, of course, that there are no definitive criteria by which to assess quality. That elusive term is often conceived as a compound of knowledge, skills, and ability—a nuanced combination of traits hard to measure. High-quality executives should be able to engage others effectively, to persuade them, lead them, and help them see things as they presumably should. Diplomacy and smoothness in interpersonal skills are often a big part of the implicit package that we call quality. An effective civil servant certainly requires a high degree of intelligence, but an intelligence and style very different from, let us say, a Nobel Prize–winning scientist.

This said, we have sought to deal with the argument put forth by the Volcker Commission report in a way that fairly operationalizes what the commission meant. Everyone would agree, we think, that extensive formal education is undoubtedly important for a group whose work requires intellectual agility. On those terms, there is not much of a crisis regarding the composition of the senior civil service, especially if the Volcker Commission is somehow right that the very best and brightest have already exited. If they have, then there was evidently a good deal of bench strength.

Furthermore, we found no evidence to support a drastic decline in how satisfied senior civil servants are with their jobs, despite the obviously greater frustrations attached to working in the public service by the mid-1980s and early 1990s relative to 1970. While there was some drop-off in the degree of satisfaction, the overall levels remain high, and data from the late 1990s suggest that satisfaction is even higher now than in the early part of the decade. Politically appointed executives more or less tracked the senior civil servants in this regard, with each experiencing moderate decreases in job satisfaction over time while still having high levels of job satisfaction overall.

There may be some reason for concern here, as the Volcker Commission report suggests, but certainly nothing that indicates a crisis. Our data are quite consistent with government studies showing that senior civil servants' job satisfaction remains high, if not quite as high as in the halcyon days, at least in retrospect, of 1970. Since then, the conditions for civil servants, as well as for politically appointed executives, have become more onerous. There have been more internal regulations and micromanagement from within the executive and from the Congress, as well as more antigovernment rhetoric and more bureaucrat bashing. Salaries were compressed for some of the period, and for a number of years there were no adjustments in salary for public servants. There were the usual, if legitimate, complaints about too many positions being set aside for political appointees. There certainly are complaints from civil servants, and significant political distrust hovers over the activities of the federal executive. These certainly are problems. The dissatisfaction civil servants do express appears in large part to stem from the political turmoil and controversy surrounding the federal government and affecting its operations since the mid-1960s. Nevertheless, there is no fundamental demoralization and no crisis.

A reasonable skeptic of our findings might ask, how can this be? In view of the less desirable conditions facing civil servants after the early 1970s, how could civil servants not be demoralized? As a class, how could their quality not significantly diminish? There is certainly a compelling logic for drawing these conclusions, and we believe this may have stimulated the Volcker Commission to overstate its case. We readily concede, of course, that there could be a slow seepage of quality that will cumulate and have impact later. But at some point—and we have now covered three decades—data reflecting these Cassandra-like predictions ought to be more apparent. So far, dire warnings have yet to be substantiated.

Neither in our data nor in any other source can we find systematic evidence of a massive demoralization, although we noted a clear decline in the numbers of those showing the highest level of enthusiasm in our post-1970 surveys. There are many conditions that are more frustrating to civil servants than was the case thirty years ago. Such a statement could probably be made of other professions too. Medical doctors and professors, like civil servants, do much more detailed reporting to authorities of matters previously done on the basis of trust. Symptoms of civil service demoralization and deterioration bear watching, and we have stressed that. But so far there has not been a dramatic decline in satisfaction nor in quality, as many serious observers of the federal executive have feared. Why not?

Trying to prove precisely why the dog did not bark is never easy. We have a mystery—at least a minor mystery—on our hands. We cannot be sure of the answers, but we can speculate. First, while some of the demoralized (of which there seem to be few at any given time) have exited the senior civil service, a ready reservoir of well-qualified civil servants apparently exists to take their place. This observation does not reflect a lack of concern about the conditions leading to disgruntlement among senior civil servants,[8] it only underscores the fact that at any given point there is a high level of job satisfaction among those in active service. Second, civil servants may be willing, to a significant degree, to put up with many irritants in order to do jobs they believe contribute to the public good. They may be less enamored of their environment than their predecessors of the early 1970s, but they still believe their jobs to be attractive and worthwhile. We think there is much to this explanation (although we have no hard data on it), and we also worry, as do other observers, about conditions that might eventually make these jobs less attractive. Clearly, we need to be watchful regarding signs of deterioration and demoralization, but we also need to be cautious about drawing conclusions that cannot be empirically substantiated, even when they seem logically plausible.

Whatever the problems of the federal government, there is scant evidence that they are fundamentally related to the quality or morale of the senior career civil servants who serve it. In sum, there is not convincing evidence of a people crisis.

Neither Is Responsiveness the Problem

Presidential administrations tend to be suspicious of what they inherit. The bureaucracy in particular has been the object of major White House suspicions and has been subject to sustained efforts to control it. These efforts began with special vigor during Nixon's presidency and peaked in the Reagan White House. We noted in chapter 2 the strategies various presidential administrations used to secure control of the administrative apparatus and the relative intensity of those strategies. Of course, there is a natural tendency on the part of any administration, whether it is parliamentary or presidential, to want to mold the bureaucracy, particularly when the leadership's course is clear and reflects intense conviction. Responsiveness to political leadership is an issue, and a complicated one, in all systems. It is embodied in the clash of political mandates and career mandarins, and thus of change and stability in government. The U.S. separation of powers system makes responsiveness yet more complicated, and the prevalence of divided government and intense partisan conflict since the Nixon presidency has contributed further to the complication.

A big part of the political responsiveness problem, especially as perceived by Republican presidential administrations, was that the career bureaucracy was predisposed against their agendas. This perception was based, first, on the assumption that the senior civil service was politically skewed toward the Democrats, and therefore not friendly to Republican policies. Data from the Nixon administration indicate that there was then a good bit of evidence to support this perception. Democrats vastly outnumbered Republicans in the ranks of the senior civil service, and they held more interventionist policy views. Second, since the bureaucracy administered many programs that were essentially Democratic policy legacies, Republican presidential administrations suspected that it was favorable to a status quo that benefited Democratic rather than Republican constituencies and interests. Third, because the Congress was in Democratic hands (at least in the House) from 1969 until 1995, Republican presidents could easily perceive senior civil servants and key congressional personnel as being in an unholy alliance against their policy preferences.

As with the issue of quality, responsiveness is more complicated than it seems at first. We cannot always know from people's expressed policy preferences or their political leanings how they will behave or to what extent they will carry their disagreements outside proper channels—a possibility that is readily available in our very open and leaky system. We saw in chapter 6, for example, that relative to their German counterparts most U.S. senior civil servants would not shy away from making their views known if they seriously disagreed with an administration's course of action. Yet very few of the U.S. senior civil servants (though more than their German peers) indicated that they would go beyond channels to sabotage the policymakers.

A lack of responsiveness may be more perception than reality. It may be perceived when the bureaucracy does not immediately do exactly what a political principal wishes, for reasons we discussed in chapter 5. A responsiveness problem may be perceived when the bureaucracy responds but does so with less than fully committed ardor. It may be perceived, too, when information is leaked, whatever the source, or if information is not provided when it has not been explicitly requested. Or it may be perceived if the information provided suggests a conclusion the political principal does not like. And obviously, when there are strongly conflicting political overseers (the problem of multiple principals), each will want the bureaucracy to be responsive exclusively to them. Consequently, there will be a responsiveness problem in the view of one or another or even both sets of political actors.

We examined several facets of responsiveness, focusing on areas likely to be especially important to elected politicians and politically appointed administrators. We looked at changes in the party affiliations and ideology of federal executives. We also looked at changes in their patterns of contact and in their levels of influence. And we examined officials' perceptions of processes and relationships within the federal executive, particularly in regard to such concerns as the incidence and effects of micromanagement on administrative operations and the perceived strengths and weaknesses of political appointees and senior civil servants in the federal executive.

Looking across three Republican presidential administrations, the evidence clearly shows that civil servants became more Republican and more conservative in regard to the role of government, just as the country had. There are multiple explanations for this shift. First, there are Zeitgeist influences. In times more favorable to Republicans, civil servants are likely to move in the same political direction. Second, there is the changed agenda of government, which made the civil service less attractive to Democrats and liberals than it had been when government was still looking for new policy worlds to conquer. Third, there are new tools for selective recruitment of personnel into senior civil service positions that didn't exist during Nixon's presidency. Consequently, we emphasized key provisions of the Civil Service Reform Act of 1978. The CSRA gave presidential administrations greater leverage to manipulate civil service personnel, enabling a determined administration to influence the staffing of departments critical to its policy objectives more effectively than it could have before. Under CSRA an administration could put civil servants sympathetic (or at least not hostile) to its policy objectives in top positions, where they have direct interface with presidential appointees. The Reagan administration brought a strong will to newly available ways of manipulating the personnel system.

Nevertheless, despite the presence and use of these tools during the Reagan administration, and despite the rightward movement of the senior civil service, top career officials were still sufficiently distant in political composition from the presidential appointees that they did not simply mirror the administrations they were serving. This was because the political profile of appointees of presidential administrations also moved rightward, most spectacularly from the Nixon period of 1970 to the Reagan era of 1986–87. While a plurality of SES career executives at all levels were clearly favorable to the Republicans by the time of the Bush administration, the political distance between career executives and political appointees remained basically constant.

There is also evidence that the efforts—especially of the Reagan administration—to constrict the networks that top civil servants cultivate outside the executive branch were relatively successful. The contacts that civil servants had with members of Congress and with interest groups fell, while involvement with the White House rose. Contact with the White House increased among the political executives also. The curtailing of these networks dovetails well with evidence that senior civil servants interviewed during the Reagan and Bush administrations saw their group as less influential than their counterparts had been during the Nixon administration. In short, presidential administrations bent on diminishing the entrepreneurial tendencies of senior civil servants and cutting their connections outside the executive branch have been relatively successful. In regard to these changes and the political changes noted above, the big contrasts are between the Nixon period and the Reagan presidency. The administrative presidency strategy adopted by the Nixon White House was perfected by the Reagan White House.

As clashes between the branches of the federal government became more constant and took on a sharper edge, the political leaders of each branch sought to control the latitude of the other. Micromanaging the bureaucracy was one mechanism for doing that. The Office of Management and Budget (OMB) was the main instrument used to impose control over executive branch agencies for the president, while congressional micromanagement was used to constrain presidential interpretations of statutory intent. The impact of this tug-of-war was to squeeze administrative discretion, judgment, and efficiency. The bureaucracy became the pawn in a deeper political struggle. Both political executives and senior career officials interviewed in the 1991–92 period saw a lot of micromanagement from each direction and had little good to say about it, although they differed in the degree to which they faulted Congress or OMB. While we cannot know precisely how much these conditions influenced the reinvention initiative of the Clinton administration, the National Performance Review (NPR) has removal of excessive constraints on public managers as part of its agenda.

It is ironic that, despite these efforts to secure control over policy, political appointees and senior career officials in the federal executive gradually accommodate one another, and the political executives who deal with senior civil servants usually think better of them at the end of their tenure than they did at first. Our data indicate that civil servants are somewhat more skeptical of political executives than the political executives are of them. The problem, of course, is that the turnover of political executives is so rapid that these relations must be cultivated time and again all over the government. Experience seems to build trust. How to increase that trust, maintain some measure of continuity and memory, and yet also ensure that the bureaucracy will not be insulated from the effects of significant political change is a big part of the governing problem in the United States.

On the overall question of how responsive the U.S. federal executive is to alterations in the political climate around it, the bottom line is that the federal executive changes too—though certainly not as rapidly as any given presidential administration might wish. Allowing for lags in the adjustment to political and policy change that are inherent in any career system, there is no substantial evidence that the federal bureaucracy has been unresponsive to changes in the political climate. There certainly has been much clamor over this issue, which is the reason we refer to it as the "noisy crisis." The clamor precipitated methods of control that make the lives of civil servants much more complex than was the case when we began our interviews in 1970. A system of government that separates power and in which there has been a consistent propensity since the 1968 election to divide control of governing institutions along party lines makes responsiveness especially problematic. However, new tools that emerged since 1970 have strengthened presidential administrations' abilities to get the bureaucracy to respond to their wishes.

If a measure of the bureaucracy's responsiveness is an adjustment over time to changes in the political and policy climate, then one must conclude that the U.S. bureaucracy has been responsive. We have emphasized the importance of the Carter administration's Civil Service Reform Act in promoting responsiveness. Responsiveness appears to be a function of both evolutionary adjustments to the political environment and direct efforts by presidential administrations to use the instruments available to them to "politicize" the administrative apparatus so it will more closely accord with their preferences.[9] Particularly from an evolutionary perspective, it is quite clear that there is no crisis of responsiveness in the U.S. federal executive. Over time, the bureaucracy moves in the direction of the nation's politics.

Political leaders, however, tend to look at responsiveness differently than political scientists might. Politicians' perspectives are understandably short term. They have agendas to fulfill, constituencies to satisfy, and elections always on the horizon. Mostly, they would like bureaucrats to be totally and fully committed to their agendas and responsive to their political needs. While that would certainly be a sign of a totally responsive system, it would come at the cost of any measure of continuity. Politicians seeking total power or revolutionary policy change are apt to be most obsessed with total responsiveness. More often, though, political leaders have considerable uncertainty as to what they wish to do and, above all, precisely how they wish to proceed. Under normal circumstances (the Reagan and later Nixon administrations are the exceptions), the larger issue is how to create a comfort zone between the political appointees of the president and the senior career officials in the agencies. There is little doubt that congruence in the goals of top career and noncareer executives helps ease relations between them.[10] Yet we know that continuity also helps to create that comfort zone while radical upheaval operates to destroy it, at least until the results of the upheaval create new points of departure and thus a new political or policy equilibrium. The balance between continuity and responsiveness is inevitably delicate. Both are necessary, but they do not easily coexist. No civil service system anywhere will provide a perfect accompaniment to the political tune of the day. Nor should it. In that sense, the civil service anywhere is apt to be a few beats behind, letting us know, whatever the tastes of a present political leadership, that government is a continuous business and has a past. Still, our data suggest that a presidential administration that knows what it wants and has focus can find and strategically place the personnel needed to help it reach its goals. In the fuller course of time, the senior career civil service reflects the political changes occurring in the country.

Is the System the Problem?

Although our interview data take us only to 1992, in the following year the Clinton administration unveiled a new package of reforms under the rubric of "reinventing government." The report of the National Performance Review, chaired by Vice President Al Gore, defined the fundamental problem of managing the government as a systems problem rather than a people problem. NPR argued that the federal government was encumbered by industrial-age, hierarchical, overregulated organizations that focused too much on process rather than on outcomes. According to this thesis, good people were trapped in bad systems. Reinventing government meant, among other things, making its organizations more compatible with the information era and thus more adaptable and flexible, focusing more on performance and outcomes than on process, and becoming sensitized to market forces. Bad systems were defined as industrial-age bureaucracies. The NPR report did not, however, focus on the preindustrial-age political system and its structural features (such as the system of separated authorities sharing power) in which these industrial-age relics were imbedded. Reinventing government was restricted to the machinery of its administration. The prescriptions in the reinvention package, however, often implicitly assume that the larger governmental context also has been reinvented and that governmental authority has somehow been miraculously unified.

As we have contended in chapter 1 and especially in chapter 7, the fundamental defects in the federal government's administration derive from its political structures and practices and from cleavages over policy. If consensual practices were more prominent than conflictual ones, if disagreements were essentially marginal or incremental rather than fundamental, if regulatory practices (such as cleaner air and safer workplaces, for example), were organized around cooperative rather than adversarial or litigable postures, and if political authority were unified, problems of administration would likely be dramatically reduced and less controversial. What we normally characterize as problems of administration are in reality often problems that flow from the political environment and that are political in nature, such as defining appropriate levels of public expenditure.

The "reinvention" solution to administrative problems is part of a larger paradigm of reforms known as New Public Management (NPM), which has been deployed in a number of countries and discussed in an even larger number. While these reforms have some distinctive features in different countries, one of their compelling attractions is that they claim to produce major gains in efficiency and lessen the responsibilities of government. The latter is a distinctly political and not purely administrative matter, and it is hardly surprising that governments faced with global competitive pressures and rising entitlements are looking for a fix. The "new age" flexibility and innovative ways to relieve fiscal stress of this particular reform paradigm help account for its present popularity. The U.S. federal government has been a relative latecomer to NPM. The attractions of reinvention are especially appealing for a government ensnarled in micromanagement since it claims to offer flexibility and adaptiveness, the elimination and simplification of many rules, performance orientation and information tracking, and an accessible, user-friendly government.

The problem is that these objectives, which most people would agree are admirable, are not without blemishes. As we have noted, each of them has a downside, and together they may well redefine the contours of public and private activity. We emphasized, for example, the risks of inadequate guide-lines, the risks to accountability and equity, and the absence of a public-good ethic when market criteria replace a public service orientation. Performance management, even if performance criteria were more clearly defined and measurement less problematic, might well do more harm than good. The fragile unity of government rests on the assumption that public servants are engaged in a common enterprise and that common goals can be achieved through interagency bargaining. Narrow forms of performance management produce perverse incentives that work against cooperation and that could well increase tensions within the executive branch and between the executive and Congress. Organizations fixated on narrow definitions of performance will likely wind up being as inflexible as those that have to respond to numer-ous rules and regulations. An Australian observer, reflecting upon reinven-tion there, contends that where there is deliberate subordination of the val-ues of policy coordination to purely operational demands, "organizations will lose their capacity to think on their feet."[11] Paul Light, an astute observer of administrative reform in the United States, suggests also that building capacity in organizations "by providing government and its employees with the skills, tools, and political support to be effective" may be as effective, if not more so, than a purely performance-based system.[12]

Narrowly conceived tracking systems risk reducing government to "bean counting," thereby threatening innovation and judgment just as rules-based systems do.[13] To focus government narrowly on achieving efficient manage-ment may be a way of removing it from the prospect of doing difficult things and of trying to cope with ill-defined problems that cannot be neatly moni-tored (because the criteria for doing so are either unclear or are politically controversial). A former senior British civil servant, William Plowden, asserted that while there was much that was provocative and thoughtful in the New Public Management in the United Kingdom, there were also several things missing from its conception of the world of public service. One thing missing, Plowden claimed, was an awareness of people and what is required to motivate them. Conceived of as a total management strategy, cost-effi-cient public management becomes an accountant's view of government. A second thing missing from the New Public Management is an appreciation of most things associated with the public service.[14] The preservation of insti-tutional memory is discounted, while the notion that the private sector provides an exclusive model for public sector innovation, streamlining, and customer-friendliness is promoted.

The American National Performance Review is replete with suggestions that the old bureaucratic system is broken and that, consequently, citizens have lost their confidence in government. It claims, for example, that there is a performance deficit, and that as a result "people simply feel that government doesn't work."[15] While it is certainly true that U.S. citizens trust their government much less than they did thirty years ago, evidence is scarce that this is attributable to the operations of the federal machinery.[16] Two direct answers as to why there has been a massive decline in trust since 1964 are Lyndon Johnson and Richard Nixon. Big declines in public trust in government occurred during their tarnished presidencies, primarily because of their behaviors, not those of federal bureaucrats. Vietnam, Watergate, and the deceptions and worse practiced by these presidents precipitated the decline in confidence, not the operations of the federal machinery, except to the extent that it had been corrupted by these presidents. That said, however, the continuing low level of trust seems to be the product of a number of factors: the loss of deference to authority, the growth in political partisanship, controversies about what government ought to be doing, and the growing vulnerability to global economic forces felt by many citizens in the United States and abroad.[17]

The contention that administrative operations are a fundamental cause of the loss of confidence in government in the United States is simply false. The public has much more confidence in its civil servants than in its politicians. By a margin of over four to one, "the public has more faith in federal workers than in elected officials to do the right thing."[18] Further, it is not clear whether micro-level improvements in the performance of government link up to macro-level issues of performance. As Paul Light comments in regard to administrative reform:

> It is not clear . . . why making government work would affect public confidence. The two are poorly linked at best. . . . Confidence in government rises and falls more with economic performance, the president's personal approval, and individual social trust than with real progress made on procurement reform, administrative procedures, even paperwork reduction. Thus, even the most successful management reforms might not affect confidence."[19]

If all the above is true, why then is there so much focus on the bureaucracy and its performance when the bigger problems of the political system are often ignored? One analyst, Kenneth Meier, concludes that "in contrast to what is adequate (some might even say excellent) performance by the bureaucracy, the performance by our electoral [political] institutions has been dismal."[20] How dismal or adequately our political institutions have performed is itself subject to different interpretations.[21] Whatever the reasons for the problems of government, they are not fundamentally attributable to the bureaucracy, and therefore reform of the bureaucracy will not magically resolve problems that essentially originate from the outside. In fact, such reforms may make the problems worse.[22] Meier even goes so far as to argue that while "we have readily and enthusiastically helped to reorganize, reform, and reinvent bureaucracy" and "have worked suboptimizing wonders on the bureaucracy, [we] have long since passed the point of diminishing marginal returns."[23] It is also worth noting here the late Marver Bernstein's classic statement on administrative reform: "The history of management improvement in the federal government is a story of inflated rhetoric [and] shifting emphasis from one fashionable managerial skill to another. . . ."[24] Reformers have, in other words, focused the preponderance of their energies on that aspect of the system likely to have at best marginal effects, while paying little attention to what really counts: the nature of the constraints and contradictions visited upon the bureaucracy by a political system purposefully designed to prevent efficient governance. This is the system we have. These are the politics and political incentives we have. This is where the problem lies. It is, on the whole, quite remarkable that the bureaucracy works as well as it does.

Could Reinvention Work?

Big changes in our governing system and in the incentives for politicians are part of the price of running a government consistent with both the premises and promises of the reinvention reforms. On the political side, politicians and judges would have to be immensely sensitive to the effects of their interventions and decisions on the operations of government. This also means that they (and the public they serve) would have to share the premise, long ago rejected by the framers of the U.S. Constitution, that efficient and effective government should overshadow the prevention of arbitrary government and the protection of rights. There would have to be significant constraints on intervention in administration by political executives, Congress, and the judiciary. It is, in fact, the intensely political style of governance, sig-

nificantly a function of the U.S. system of separate institutions sharing powers, and the elaborate system of constitutionally and judicially granted
rights that are responsible for many of the most egregious cases of ineffective or inefficient government.

To optimize the prospects of reinvention probably would require a truly
reinvented government, one more unified and more consistent with managerialist assumptions than the present system. Since the prospects of this
occurring are dim at best, it would be practical to ask what might be necessary for some of the reinvention proposals to succeed within the present
system of government. We think there are a combination of changes consistent with the NPR recommendations that could help make the system
work better, if not necessarily cost less. These changes, among other things,
would require substantial investment in career personnel in order to avoid
some of the pitfalls accompanying a more flexible and less rule-bound management system. But there are some things that politicians could do—and
might even find it in their interests to do—that also would help improve the
management of the federal government.

Strike a Better Outsider-Careerist Balance

The National Performance Review tells us that a fundamental problem of the
federal government is that good people (career civil servants) are trapped in
bad systems. Yet the NPR fails to address why these people are not in positions
of greater authority so they may help run the system better. Indeed, the NPR
(unlike the Volcker Commission) ignores one of the most obvious impediments to a better-managed government: the vast number of political appointments at the disposal of presidents. The United States has by far the biggest
army of political patronage appointments of any modern democracy, indeed
more than its citizens are accustomed to seeing in their state and local governments. Furthermore, as Paul Light points out, the trend is toward significantly greater "thickening" of political appointments—that is, larger numbers and more layers of them.[25] In this regard, it should be recalled from
chapter 6 that although political appointees tended to think better of civil servants over time, the civil servants themselves perceived greater deficiencies in
the political appointees (particularly their management skills and leadership
qualities) than the political appointees did in them. An implication of this is
that thickening government with more political appointments is contrary to
making it work better, unless by "working better" one means helping achieve
the president's immediate aims at the expense of other considerations.[26]

A system in which there are greater opportunities for civil servants to rise to the top has both pluses and minuses. There would be several advantages. First, there would be more continuity across administrations. In the absence of continuity, there is little incentive to think long term about the relationship of means to ends. Where transient executives are numerous, it is someone else who wrestles with the consequences of action (or inaction). Second, promotion opportunities are good morale boosters, but, above all, they allow the perspectives and experience that civil servants bring to the table to interact with the enthusiasms and freshness brought by political executives. Third, there have been a number of ethics issues associated with presidential nominees in several recent administrations. We doubt that this is because the nominees themselves are more ethically dubious than in the past, but rather that there are more ethics laws, immensely greater scrutiny, and more use of ethics considerations by political opponents to embarrass presidential administrations. We can only speculate on how much the laws and scrutiny influence who is willing to be considered for public office. However, because career civil servants spend their professional lives inside government, already tightly constrained by rules controlling their conduct, they are apt to provide less raw material for interest groups and Senate staff members to exploit. A fourth advantage, therefore, is that opening up more of the current political jobs to civil servants should help speed up the process of appointment and allow vacancies to be filled more expeditiously. The Clinton and Bush administrations in particular have had difficulties filling positions in a timely way. Putting more career officials into appointive positions (or reducing the number of appointive positions) will also reduce the costs of the search. Fifth, a key advantage would be to give civil servants more influence and more stake in management reforms, as this could increase the chance of successful reform. They would be well positioned to connect reform to the realities of administration, and they are the actors who have the most substantial long-term interest in good administration. Such a system would also probably make it easier to form an administration in the first place.

Of course, we would expect any presidential administration to select civil servants with whom it is likely to be comfortable. In that sense, the appointment process inevitably would be political. But this is no different from European systems whose cabinet ministers bring into their confidence a small set of top civil servants (in the form of a ministerial cabinet) who are compatible with their views and, above all, with whom they have some personal chemistry.

There are, to be sure, downside features to an executive branch more heavily staffed at its upper reaches by career civil servants. One difficulty is that a larger role for career civil servants would be politically controversial because it would be seen as threatening the influence of some political constituencies as well as that of Congress and the president.

The American system has been uniquely staffed by people from the outside, at least until New Public Management came into vogue in other countries (where managers are now often brought in on contract to serve in government for limited terms). Many of the U.S. political executives, of course, are "in and outers." No simple generalization adequately describes all the individuals who come to serve a presidential administration from the outside. A few are incompetent. Some are on a mission. Some are inexperienced but capable of learning a great deal if they stay long enough. Some provide political experience and savvy. Some provide intellectual energy. Some are, by any judgment, quite extraordinary. We need what the best of them can bring, but the burdens of creating an administration seem to have become greater as more positions become political, as ethical scrutiny becomes more intense, and as the intensity of political opposition swells. And those eventually selected simply do not stay the course. The system badly needs to be brought into balance—with more permanence and continuity within our government, leavened when necessary by external appointments. Only career officials are likely to have an enduring stake in managerial reforms that require some measure of persistence, yet they are not well positioned to initiate reform.

A serious concern about having an executive branch more heavily staffed at the upper levels with career officials is that it probably would be less immediately representative in certain respects. While there has been steady growth in the number of female and minority civil servants, as we saw in chapter 4, even greater representativeness can be achieved rapidly only through political appointment—a technique that goes back to the heyday of party machines and balanced tickets. This is the most effective way to infuse new personnel quickly into top positions.

Under a system in which civil servants hold higher positions, presidential administrations would also have fewer appointments to hand out to favored constituencies. While this clearly would be regarded as a disadvantage by partisan enthusiasts, it actually might work to the advantage of presidents in office, as they would need to expend less effort catering to controversial political enthusiasts. (The origins of the U.S. civil service are rooted in the excesses of a patronage system that became burdensome,

even life threatening to presidents.) Such enthusiasts often get their administrations into trouble. But it is these constituencies that provide much of
the political support and energy for candidates bidding for the presidency,
and they expect to be rewarded with posts they deem important to their
interests. For better or worse, therefore, limiting political appointments
probably would diminish incentives for political mobilization by key interests. That again, for better or worse, has implications for the U.S. political
system and also the processes of governance. There is a chance that it could
make the politics of governance smoother (and thereby create a more hospitable environment for reinvention-style reforms). At the same time it
might make the already-turbulent politics of the United States even more
turbulent if political and policy activists believe they have little chance to
enter the chambers of power.

In sum, a true reinvention of U.S. government along the lines of the
NPR would necessitate curtailing powerful political influences at work
within the federal government's administrative apparatus. Is that possible?
And if it were, would that be desirable? Substantial organizational reform of
the sort recommended by NPR is, after all, more likely to work if specialists
in organizations are given freer rein, a sentiment reflected in the oft-heard
cry to "let the managers manage." But curtailing these political influences
has consequences for both politics and democracy. At a minimum, these
include the prospect of blunting representation and the accessibility of government to intensely mobilized interests. These consequences also would
include at least a partial eclipse of both congressional and presidential
authority and the enhancement of bureaucratic power. To rationalize government and make it more productive typically means reducing the role of
politics (and of politicians) in it. We may or may not in the end like what we
get from any reform, but we should be clear about what is necessary to
achieve it.

Invest in Personnel

Reinvention requires a civil service with a high level of autonomy.
Discretionary judgment is necessary in a system that is to be less rule bound
and that emphasizes rapid adjustment. But to prepare managers to work
effectively in an environment of greater freedom and responsibility, significant investment will be required, with an emphasis in six areas: widespread
training in writing and monitoring contracts with other levels of government and the private sector, increased political experience in negotiating
between branches of government, increased mobility across levels of gov-

ernment and within and across government organizations, experience in interpreting and using methods for measuring user needs and satisfaction, increased knowledge about developments in other administrative systems where New Public Management has been adopted, and more subtle and sophisticated training in ethics.

WRITING AND MONITORING CONTRACTS.   One of the features of reinvention is its emphasis on using private contractors to perform functions once directly supplied by the government itself. While there has always been a significant amount of outsourcing in government, reinvention emphasizes it even more, especially as outsourcing can create a competitive force to drive down costs while also presumably reducing permanent overhead costs (especially personnel) inside government. Among other skills that federal executives will need in such an environment is the ability to write and monitor contracts. The opportunities for scandal or nonperformance of contracts increase with the number of services and goods under contract, particularly if there is inadequate guidance in writing the contracts and if downsizing (one of the purported benefits of outsourcing) leaves insufficient personnel to monitor contract performance. To ensure that contracts meet performance criteria, the conditions of the contract must be carefully stipulated. If outsourcing is meant to loosen or even eliminate the shackles imposed by general rules, then agreement regarding the performance outcome and the specific conditions relating to it are essential. Equally essential, once a contract is written, the government must itself meet its end of the bargain by ensuring that it has the money predictably appropriated to pay for the agreed-upon goods and services. Under our present system of fragmented authority, a contract made by a freewheeling executive could be second-guessed in the Congress and inadequate funds appropriated for its completion. That would be fatal, at least for this aspect of reinvention.

POLITICAL EXPERIENCE.   A more autonomous civil service will need to be more self-consciously political. Obviously, we do not mean political here in a partisan sense, but in terms of mediating between outside interests and the government (and mediating interests within government) and between different levels of government. Senior career officials would increasingly be negotiating operational goals with political authorities and interest groups. The trade-off for civil servants making more decisions on the ground and being free from myriad rules is that they will need to read political cues more carefully, both inside and outside the executive. Administrators operating under pressure to please customers will also have to be sufficiently astute to retain independence in their operations, lest they be dominated by their organization's clientele groups (the most likely set of customers). This is a problem in the current system, but the emphasis on customer satisfaction under reinvention will exacerbate it. The myth in the reinvention scenario of separate spheres between politics and administration would have to be dispelled. While political sensitivity is not something that can be easily taught, guidance for navigating the political environment should become an ostensible part of the continuing education of civil servants. Even more than in our current system, civil servants will need to be political without being politically partisan. That is a fine line not often understood in the hyperpoliticized environment that characterizes contemporary Washington.

DIVERSE ORGANIZATIONAL EXPERIENCES.   To foster a more integrative outlook and manage coordination effectively, it may be helpful to have career civil servants whose professional lives are organizationally diverse. This may be costly in terms of orienting executives to new agencies, but knowing how things look from different perspectives would be useful background for newly empowered and less rule-restricted administrators. Especially if the measure of accountability is to be in results achieved rather than in procedures followed, the new public manager will have to look at problems from a broader perspective. Much depends upon how performance is tracked. If it is tracked narrowly, there will be few if any incentives for a wider range of experiences and little need for career breadth. However, if performance criteria are results-oriented (as NPR and GPRA expect), then a problem focus rather than an agency focus should be prized because a great deal of interagency and interprogram coordination will be needed and expected. One of the potential problems that reinvention will have to work out is how to appraise organizations and even individuals when problems are themselves interorganizational in scope. If one is to look at results or outcomes rather than processes or structures or possibly even organizational outputs, civil servants will need a diverse portfolio of experiences.

EXPERIENCE IN SOCIAL ANALYSIS.   The reinvention emphasis on customer satisfaction implies that civil servants will have to know how to gauge customers' needs and determine whether they are being satisfied. Social scientists and market analysts apply a variety of methods to these problems. In a market system, customers may express their dissatisfaction by changing suppliers. That is not usually possible with respect to the supply of public goods, although more privatization and competition are parts of reinvention.

Another way of gauging customer preferences and needs, their satisfaction or dissatisfaction, is to discover their expressed preferences in sophisticated ways. Through surveys and focus groups, for example, civil servants can increase knowledge about customers' needs and concerns and discover how the public reacts to their efforts to make public organizations more user friendly. Their familiarity with the use of instruments developed by social scientists and used in marketing may be linked to writing and monitoring contracts effectively, in that actual data gathering will most likely be done by private sector organizations. The civil servants charged with assessing customer satisfaction will need to know a lot about what they want to find out and be capable of discussing design and interpretive options with the contractors carrying out these activities.

DEVELOPING INTERNATIONAL PERSPECTIVE.   As the NPR report notes, changes similar to those it proposes for the United States have been sweeping much of the highly developed world, and in many cases were implemented elsewhere well before the initial NPR report was issued in 1993. If these New Public Management reforms stay intact, an effective inventory of knowledge about new administrative developments, such as that generated by the Organization for Economic Cooperation and Development, should be put to widespread use, and there should be continuing encouragement for American civil servants to swap information with their counterparts in Australia, New Zealand, the United Kingdom, and elsewhere. Civil servants (and political executives) will need to keep up with the latest developments abroad (as well as in U.S. states and municipalities) to find out what works and what doesn't, what kind of learning has occurred, and what can be usefully applied here from there and vice versa. Keeping up such international contacts and learning experiences will be important for working through the reinvention process.

ETHICS TRAINING.   Faced with more choice and with greater demands to be simultaneously customer friendly and fair, career administrators will confront compelling ethical dilemmas. They will be caught between competing demands—some stemming from the requirements of lawful procedures and equitable treatment, the others from demands to be customer friendly and also results oriented. These are not exactly new problems in public administration.[27] But reinvention shifts the balance toward being customer friendly and results oriented (though these two goals often conflict, as discussed in chapter 7). Administrators are apt to find themselves in the cross hairs of conflicting demands that are ethically challenging: first, because they will inevitably have more latitude in resolving substantive conflicts between

competing social goods; and second, because it is impossible from a procedural standpoint to forgo judicial review of administrative process or ignore
a past layer of statutory and constitutional law regarding due process without reinventing government in the more fundamental sense. In other words,
administrators will have more choices to make (producing results) and be
faced with more serious second-guessing as to how they made the choices
(the extent to which they used fair procedures).

Operating under a liberated management system, civil servants will
confront hard decisions for which (if the cynics about reinvention are correct) they will be held liable politically and perhaps even legally. Navigating
between these hard rocks in a less bounded setting will require ethical sensitivity mixed with political shrewdness. As with political sensitivity, ethical
sensitivity may be the product of experience and instinct at least as much as
of formal training. To the extent that these features can be inculcated
through training, it will be essential to make appropriate investments in the
public personnel system.

Management Reform and Political Theory

Administrative reforms have a long tradition in the United States. Whatever
their actual accomplishments or consequences, they are almost always over-
sold as the cure to whatever ails government. Everyone says they want
administrative reform, but they usually want something more. The bottom
line is that the country usually looks to reform administration as a means of
reallocating power and thereby changing policy. Administrative reform proposals become a cover for deeper political change or for avoiding responsibility for hard and distasteful policy decisions. Political or policy reform
comes disguised as administrative reform nearly everywhere. Because of the
highly pluralized politics prevalent in the United States, the diverse preferences of an equally pluralized society are reinforced and stymie forceful
political leadership at nearly every turn. A great deal of administrative reform, consequently, is aimed at overcoming the complex allocation of
power so that someone or some set of actors can sit atop the system and
thus be better positioned to command it.

For example, efforts to link administrative reform to budget rationality—
Program, Planning, Budgeting, Systems (PPBS) and Zero-Based Budgeting
(ZBB), prominent in the Johnson and Carter eras, respectively—were promoted as good management expedients. Yet, had they been truly successful,
they would have shifted power wholesale from Congress to the president,

threatening the political foundations and identity of long-standing programs. In promoting these reforms, neither President Johnson nor President Carter asked Congress to make major changes in programs. Instead, they proposed to accomplish this reform through changes in the budget process linked to their newfangled management techniques. The management techniques were to serve the purposes of politics.

A different set of administrative tactics employed by Presidents Nixon and Reagan to enhance responsiveness to their agendas were also essentially efforts to overcome opposition forces among interest groups, in Congress, and in the courts. As Nixon, Reagan, and their associates saw it, the problem was that the federal bureaucracy was not completely and unequivocally responsive to them. Their gripe was really with a political system that neither cedes exclusive power to any single authority nor commands instantaneous responsiveness to it. In fact, as our study shows, a claim that the civil service lacks responsiveness to political authority has plausibility only if one expects total and instantaneous change in the partisan and ideological makeup of top career civil servants, a form of responsiveness more likely to be associated with revolutionary regimes than democratic governments. The demand for exclusive responsiveness fails to accord with the U.S. constitutional system, and the claim for instantaneous responsiveness lacks resonance with virtually any modern form of democratic government.

The Volcker Commission responded to the "bureaucracy bashing" climate perpetrated by several recent presidential administrations—Carter's, and especially Reagan's. It believed that the denigration of the bureaucracy would lead to deterioration in the quality of public servants. The Volcker Commission's emphasis was ostensibly apolitical. It assumed that good people would produce good government. Perhaps implicit in the Volcker report is the notion of an American mandarinate that would govern without political interference from self-interested politicians. Assuming this to be a proper reading of the Volcker report, such a notion, naturally, would produce a reallocation of political authority. There is a more pertinent point, though: the assumption that better people would produce better government and presumably a more satisfied citizenry avoids the fundamental problem, which is really about whether the electorate finds the policies being administered satisfactory or not. Were even the smartest graduates of Harvard or equivalent institutions recruited into the federal bureaucracy, it is an illusion to think that they alone could solve the problem of governance. When George Wallace threatened during his presidential campaigns to throw the briefcases of "pointy headed bureaucrats" into the Potomac, it was not because of their intellectual deficiencies but because he and his political constituents opposed the policies the bureaucrats were implementing. When the best and the brightest (or any others) administer controversial policies, they too will become controversial. In other words, the administrators are usually not the fundamental problem; politics and policy more often are at the core of the controversy, and administrative reform is not likely to cure that, despite claims that make the U.S. administrative system appear to be at the forefront of the nation's ills.

There are premises of political reform embedded in the latest specimen of administrative reform, "reinventing government," and it holds these in common with New Public Management movements elsewhere. Faced with global pressures to keep government lean and budgets disciplined, the NPM and reinvention reforms are consistent (or at least claim to be) with these demands. The reinvention report even talks explicitly about eliminating "unnecessary programs" in its "back to basics" section, and NPR II called for program changes, terminations, and privatization. This is not the language of administrative reform; it is the language of policy reform. Policy change in a democratic system is supposed to be a primary responsibility of democratically selected politicians. In fact, the NPM movement worldwide is not merely about administrative reform. It is really part of a wider debate about the proper role and scope of government. These are political decisions. Decisions about privatization, for example, are also decisions about the proper role of government and who should be held accountable.[28] If the public wants smaller government—and there is no clear indication that it does as a general matter—those decisions should be made openly through the political process.[29] What political leaders often want to do, however, is use the language of reinvention—with its emphasis on cost savings, job cuts, and elimination of red tape—to argue that they are cutting costs without cutting anything "basic." Blending together "works better, costs less" is at one level largely political theater—a way to look creative and justify cost constraints in a highly politicized environment.

Demands for streamlining government make it seem as though politicians played no role in making government convoluted to begin with. Different organizations are involved in what seems to be the same action precisely because politicians want them involved. No administrator on his or her own recognizance can wave a magic wand and proclaim streamlining to be purely an administrative activity and expect to continue as an administrator for long. Once key constituents and interests are adversely affected, politicians will spring into action with a demand for the administrator's head. Thus, while it may appear expedient, it is hardly appropriate to have administrators sort out what politics and politicians have created.

For the most part, what we call bad management in the public sector is a function of the constraints and rule-boundedness imposed on the agencies by politicians and courts. In the U.S. system of fragmented political authority, these constraints often lead to a high degree of administrative convolution. In the words of James Q. Wilson, "If we wish to complain about how rule-ridden our government agencies seem to be, we should direct those complaints not to the agencies but to the Congress, the courts, and the organized interests that make effective use of the Congress and the courts."[30] Despite the management problems created by complex statutes and mandated procedures, it is not at all clear that the U.S. government works poorly from a strictly management point of view, regardless of the hyperbole claiming it does. In fact, on the whole, it seems most of the time to work pretty well, inasmuch as its performance is basically predictable and often even lauded by its "customers," most of whom think they were treated fairly even by the dreaded Internal Revenue Service.[31] It might well be a good idea for politicians to loosen the constraints they have imposed on the bureaucracy. And it would be an excellent idea for them to specify realistic, noncontradictory goals for the agencies and to fund them appropriately and predictably. But it also is necessary to understand that in most cases the public, especially affected stakeholders (that is, customers), have asked the politicians to impose these constraints in the first place.

Aspects of reinvention clearly work best and in relatively straightforward ways in what James Q. Wilson calls "production organizations." In such organizations, "both outputs (or work) and outcomes are observable" and "managers have an opportunity to design (within the limits established by external constraints) a compliance system to produce an efficient outcome."[32] These organizations constitute the bulk of local governmental activities, a lesser percentage of state governmental activities, and an even smaller share of federal governmental activities. Most of these activities are susceptible to purely managerial fixes because most are relatively noncontroversial politically and because improvements in efficiency and consumer satisfaction are more readily calibrated. This is why local governments frequently have been at the forefront of such managerial remedies, and some of these are readily applicable to certain functions of the federal government. Government can certainly be improved. Truly reinventing it, however, will require fundamental political choices that go far beyond management issues.

The tasks of public managers are actually likely to become more challenging and government itself more difficult to manage in the smaller public sector envisioned by reinvention enthusiasts. When government, to use Paul Light's words, operates in a "shadow" of contractors and grantees (a nominally smaller public sector, at least), it will have less direct control over its output.[33] Where there is extensive privatization and outsourcing, there will also be intense political struggles over distributive issues and the near certain defense by elected officials of inefficient, even negligent, contractors who are politically influential. Going private will not inherently reduce politics in the administrative process; it could even exacerbate it. Substantial investments in personnel training and an emphasis on political savvy would certainly be crucial for administrators to make a less hierarchically organized system work effectively.

In sum, the problems that reinvention proclaims it will solve through administrative means are mainly problems created by the political decisionmaking process. If the U.S. system produces complexity, contradiction, bloated or inefficient programs, and unusually high degrees of restriction on managerial latitude, that is primarily the product of politicians, not bureaucrats. The most basic improvement in the management of American government would result from applying the simple aphorism: "politician, heal thyself." But we suspect that is unlikely to happen.

Sampling and Interviewing
Federal Executives

INTERVIEWS REPORTED IN the book come from samples of federal executives drawn in three periods: 1970, 1986–87, and 1991–92. Executives sampled worked for agencies of the federal government primarily concerned with domestic policy. Officials selected had to be employed full-time and work in the Washington, D.C. area.

We drew from three strata in 1970. The first consisted of officials formally appointed by the president and passed with the advice of the Senate (PAS). Some of these people were assistant secretaries, and others were at approximately that rank in their agencies.

A second set was classified as noncareer executive assignment employees (NEA). These officials had job designations at the GS-16, GS-17, or GS-18 grades. Like the PAS appointees, they held positions whose incumbents were expected to advocate administration policies and help ensure control of the executive machinery of government by the presidential administration. Hierarchically, but depending on the particular agency, they ranged from the approximate level of deputy assistant secretary through bureau or division chief to program chief. A few Schedule C appointees serving on an acting basis in NEA positions were also interviewed.

The third set of officials consisted of career civil servants under civil service jurisdiction with supergrade status—that is, GS-16 through GS-18. They held career executive assignment (CEA) status. In order to be considered within the sampling universe, such officials had to hold the top career position in their administrative units and report to a political appointee. In some cases, supergrade career officials held top positions of parallel rank within their administrative units. When this occurred, all of these officials were included as members of the sampling universe.

Staff officials and those serving in the offices of the secretary or agency director or administrator were eliminated, as were officials serving in the offices of the agency's general counsel. Executives serving in internal agency budget, finance, management, public information, or personnel offices were also excluded. In addition, we excluded members of collegial fact-finding, quasi-judicial, or quasi-legislative groups such as commissioners of regulatory agencies.

Executives were drawn randomly from cabinet departments, regulatory agencies, executive agencies, and independent administrative agencies in proportion to the number of executives in each sampling classification (PAS, NEA, and CEA) within each agency. Individuals were randomly selected within each classification using a random-number procedure. When necessary, replacements for refusals or vacant positions were drawn from the same sampling classification and agency type. The cabinet departments included were Agriculture, Commerce, Health, Education and Welfare, Housing and Urban Development, Justice, Labor, Transportation, and Treasury. The Federal Communications Commission, the Federal Trade Commission, the Federal Power Commission, the Interstate Commerce Commission, and the Securities and Exchange Commission were the regulatory agencies sampled. The Office of Economic Activity was the executive agency selected. And the independent administrative agencies consisted of the General Services Administration, the Small Business Administration, and the Veterans Administration.

We were quite successful in obtaining interviews from the respondents selected. Table A-1 gives information on the number of executives we contacted and interviewed in each year. For ease of presentation, PAS and NEA executives are lumped together under the political executive (PE) category in the table. Our success rate was always higher for NEA than for PAS respondents, with a rate of 85 and 71 percent, respectively, in 1970. Overall response rates are quite consistent across the years, with career civil servants responding at the highest rates.

The Civil Service Reform Act (CSRA) of 1978 created the Senior Executive Service (SES). This significant reform created a mild complication when we sampled senior civil servants in 1986–87. In 1970 we had sampled

Table A-1. *Sample and Interview Data for Studies of Federal Executives*[a]
Number unless otherwise indicated

Sample and action	PE	CSI	CSII	Total
1970				
Contacted	76	68	...	144
Interviewed	61	65	...	126
Interviewed (percent)	80.3	95.6	...	87.5
1986–89				
Contacted	76	78	74	228
Interviewed	62	68	69	199
Interviewed (percent)	81.6	87.2	93.2	87.3
1991–92				
Contacted	55	55	57	167
Interviewed	45	53	53	151
Interviewed (percent)	81.8	96.4	93.0	90.4

a. PE = political executives (political appointees).

CSI = career civil servants who occupy the top rungs in their administrative units and report to political appointees. Members of the group were called "supergrade" career civil servants in 1970; in 1986–87 and 1991–92 they were drawn from career civil servants in the Senior Executive Service (established in 1979).

CSII = career Senior Executive Service members who report to other civil servants, not to political appointees.

the highest civil servants in seventeen domestic agencies. The rank-in-the-person SES system created by the CSRA meant that an administration could now move career SES-level executives from position to position without fear of charges of "adverse action," since executives retained their rank no matter what SES position they might occupy.

This feature of SES opened many additional opportunities for presidential administrations to control which career people occupied key positions at the top of administrative hierarchies, and it led us to select two samples of SES career executives for interviews. The first, which we label Career I, is parallel to the senior civil servants interviewed in 1970. All those in the SES Career I sample are the highest civil servants in their administrative units and report to political appointees.[1] The second sample, labeled Career II, consists of SES career civil servants who report not to political appointees but to other civil servants. Comparison of the two groups helps us to analyze the ways administrations have used the opportunities the CSRA gave them.

In addition to adding a sample level, we also added samples of staff officials in 1986–87. These officials served at levels comparable to the program officials in our other samples. They are analysts and evaluators rather than program administrators. They do not have managerial responsibilities for a particular program and often have words such as planning and analysis in their formal titles. In most instances, and after test comparing the two groups, officials in these samples were combined with officials at the same level in the program administrators' samples for purposes of the analyses reported in this book. Where those in the two groups differed significantly, the staff officials were not included in the data reported. Such instances are indicated in the text or tables.

Finally, the CSRA allowed each agency to make noncareer SES appointments. Noncareer SES appointees may be placed in any SES general list position.[2] The law limits these appointments to 10 percent of total SES positions governmentwide and to 25 percent in any one agency. These political appointees were, of course, included in our 1986–87 sampling frame and are included in the figures for political executives in table A-1.

The cabinet departments included in 1986–87 were Agriculture, Commerce, Education, Energy, Health and Human Services, Housing and Urban Development, Interior, Justice, Labor, Transportation, and Treasury. The Federal Communications Commission, the Federal Trade Commission, the Interstate Commerce Commission, the Nuclear Regulatory Commission, and the Securities and Exchange Commission were the regulatory agencies sampled. Independent administrative agencies sampled were the Federal Emergency Management Agency, the General Services Administration, the Small Business Administration, and the Veterans Administration. The Office of Management and Budget was included as part of the effort to sample staff officials.

The 1991–92 samples were done in the same way as the 1986–87 samples, except that staff people were not included. Cabinet departments included were Agriculture, Commerce, Education, Energy, Health and Human Services, Housing and Urban Development, Interior, Justice, Labor, Transportation, Treasury, and Veterans Affairs. The Federal Communications Commission, the Federal Trade Commission, the Interstate Commerce Commission, the Nuclear Regulatory Commission, and the Securities and Exchange Commission were the regulatory agencies sampled. Respondents were also drawn from the Environmental Protection Agency and the Federal Emergency Management Agency.

All respondents were interviewed using an interview instrument containing both open-ended and close-ended questions. The interviews were conducted using a conversational format (though questions were structured) appropriate to interviewing elites. Most interviews were tape-recorded.[3] This meant that we usually had an excellent record of each respondent's exact words—a huge advantage for coding interviews, where one aim is to capture the subtleties of response from highly sophisticated and involved individuals.

We took great care in coding the interviews. In 1970, the first round of the study, we had all interviews coded twice and then reconciled any discrepancies. In 1986–87 we check-coded (that is, had a second coding done) for 19 percent of the interviews, and in 1991 we check-coded 20 percent of the interviews.

Notes

Chapter One

1. For example, the Ash Council (the President's Advisory Council on Executive Organization), the Grace Commission (the President's Private Sector Survey on Cost Control), the Volcker Commission (the National Commission of the Public Service), and the National Performance Review (NPR). The motif of each of these reports was to strengthen the executive by weakening congressional authority. The Ash Council focused on reorganization, the creation of a supercabinet, and the Office of Management and Budget, among other things. The Grace Commission focused on costs. The NPR focus is on deregulation of management and cost reductions.

2. See Allen Schick, "Systems Politics and Systems Budgeting," *Public Administration Review* 29 (1969): 137–51.

3. See David Osborne and Ted Gaebler, *Reinventing Government: How the Entrepreneurial Spirit Is Transforming the Public Sector* (Addison-Wesley, 1992); Donald F. Kettl and John J. DiIulio Jr., eds., *Inside the Reinvention Machine* (Brookings, 1995). In addition, the Organization for Economic Cooperation and Development sponsors the Public Management Committee and Public Management Service (PUMA), whose mission is to provide information, analysis, assessment, and recommendation on public management, exchange good practices, and report on issues and developments in public management.

4. The traditional conception of bureaucrats as performing administration while politicians did policy is referred to as Image 1 in Joel D. Aberbach, Robert D. Putnam, and Bert A. Rockman, *Bureaucrats and Politicians in Western Democracies* (Harvard University Press, 1981), especially pp. 4–6. This view is articulated with crystal clarity by a notable political scientist of his era, Woodrow Wilson: "Administration lies outside the proper sphere of politics. Administrative questions are not political questions. . . . The field of administration is a field of business. It is removed from the hurry and strife of politics." Woodrow Wilson, "The Study of Administration," *Political Science Quarterly 2* (June 1887): 9–10, as quoted in B. Guy Peters, *The Politics of Bureaucracy*, 4th ed. (Longman, USA, 1995), pp. 3–4. Note here also Peters's important statement (p. 4): "As

long as it was assumed that administration was a simple non-discretionary action, it was useless to think of it in the more general context of the political system."

5. The image of politicians imparting energy to government and policymaking while bureaucrats provide equilibrium has considerable empirical evidence behind it. This conception accepts bureaucrats as playing a role in policymaking but one that is different in style from that which politicians tend to play. This has been referred to in our previous work as Image 3 (Aberbach, Putnam, and Rockman, *Bureaucrats and Politicians*, pp. 9–16).

6. Norton Long, "Power and Administration," *Public Administration Review* 9 (1949): 257–64.

7. See Matthew Holden Jr., "Political Power and the Centrality of Administration," paper presented at the annual meeting of the American Political Science Association, Chicago, August 31–September 1995. Also see Hugh Heclo, *A Government of Strangers* (Brookings, 1977).

8. On this point, see Paul C. Light, *The Tides of Reform: Making Government Work, 1945–1995* (Yale University Press, 1997).

9. Note the following passage in the report of the NPR (p. 6): "We discovered that several other countries were also reinventing themselves from Australia to Great Britain, Singapore to Sweden, the Netherlands to New Zealand. Throughout the developed world, the needs of information-age societies were colliding with the limits of industrial-era government. Regardless of party, regardless of ideology, these governments were responding. . . . In the United States, we found the same phenomenon at the state and local levels." (National Performance Review, *From Red Tape to Results: Creating a Government That Works Better and Costs Less* [Government Printing Office, 1993]).

10. For a general discussion of these reforms in New Zealand, Britain, and Australia, see the following set of articles, all found in *Governance* 3 (April 1990): Graham Scott, Peter Bushnell, and Nikitin Sallee, "Reform of the Core Public Sector: New Zealand Experience," pp. 138–67; Michael Keating and Malcolm Holmes, "Australia's Budgetary and Financial Management Reforms," pp. 168–85; Peter Kemp, "Next Steps for the British Civil Service," pp. 186–96. More recently, see Colin Campbell and Graham K. Wilson, *The End of Whitehall: Death of a Paradigm?* (Blackwell, 1995); B. Guy Peters and Donald J. Savoie, eds., *Governance in a Changing Environment* (McGill-Queen's University Press, 1995). In Sweden as well, more emphasis has been given to decentralized administration. A Swedish economic historian notes that public service agencies have decentralized authority and accountability in decisionmaking and financing. As a consequence, market-like relations have been introduced both within the public sector and between the public and the private sector. Also, the roles of principal and agent as between political and administrative bodies, respectively, have been more clearly delineated. As a consequence, transaction costs have increased in comparison with the previous more centralized system. Bo Gustafsson, "Foundations of the Swedish Model," *Nordic Journal of Political Economy* 22 (1995): 11.

11. Barry Karl, *Executive Reorganization and Reform in the New Deal: The Genesis of Administrative Management, 1900–1939* (University of Chicago Press, 1979).

12. See, for example, R. Shep Melnick, *Between the Lines: Interpreting Welfare Rights* (Brookings, 1994).

13. Edward J. Lynch, "Politics, Nonpartisanship, and the Public Service," *The Public Interest* 98 (Winter 1990): 118–32.

14. There has been a precipitous drop in public confidence in government. In 1958 about three-quarters (73 percent) of the American public indicated that they trusted the government to do the right thing. This figure fell to 61 percent in 1968, 36 percent in 1974, and to 25 percent during the recession of the early 1990s. There have been fluctuations in this trend, but even during a peak recovery period in the Reagan administration, it failed to move even to 50 percent. See Gary Orren, "Fall from Grace: The Public's Loss of Faith in Government," in Joseph S. Nye and others, eds., *Why People Don't Trust Government* (Harvard University Press, 1997), especially p. 81.

15. William T. Gormley Jr., *Taming the Bureaucracy* (Princeton University Press, 1989).

16. See Jack L. Walker, "The Origins and Maintenance of Interest Groups in America," *American Political Science Review* 77 (1983): 390–406.

17. A survey in 1997, for example, conducted by the *Washington Post*, Harvard University, and the Kaiser Family Foundation found that "more than three-quarters of Americans believe that the federal budget can be balanced without touching Social Security (retirement) and Medicare benefits. . . ." Moreover, while "the poll shows that most Americans believe dire forecasts that Social Security and Medicare . . . will go broke in the next century unless Congress takes action soon . . . the action most favored by respondents is for Congress to eliminate perceived fraud, waste and abuse in the programs" (cited in the *International Herald Tribune*, April 1, 1997, p. 3).

18. John W. Kingdon, *Agendas, Alternatives and Public Policy*, 2d ed. (Harper Collins College Publishers, 1995).

19. For a highly developed, if also stylized, argument propounding this thesis, see Terry M. Moe, "The Politicized Presidency," in John E. Chubb and Paul E. Peterson, eds., *The New Direction in American Politics* (Brookings, 1985), pp. 235–69.

20. Jack L. Walker, "The Diffusion of Innovations among the American States," *American Political Science Review* 63 (1969): 880–99.

21. See, for example, the Occasional Papers Series on Public Management, issued by OECD's PUMA. See also Patricia W. Ingraham, "The Reform Agenda for National Civil Service Systems," in Hans A. G. Bekke, James Perry, and Theo A. J. Toonen, eds., *Civil Service Systems in Comparative Perspective* (Indiana University Press, 1996), pp. 247–67. More generally, see Johan P. Olsen and B. Guy Peters, eds., *Lessons from Experience* (Scandinavian University Press, 1996).

22. Tom Christensen, "Structure and Culture Reinforced—The Development and Current Features of the Norwegian Civil Service System." A paper presented at the

conference on Civil Service Systems in Comparative Perspective, Indiana University, Bloomington, Indiana, April 1997, p. 31.

23. Joel D. Aberbach and Bert A. Rockman, "Civil Servants and Policymakers: Neutral or Responsive Competence?" *Governance* 7 (July 1994): 461–69.

24. Dean E. Mann, "The Selection of Federal Political Executives," *American Political Science Review* 58 (March 1964): 81–99.

25. Because of the public availability of documents concerning what went on in the Nixon presidency in this regard, there is an ample harvest of Nixonian commands to supercede the law. See, for example, U.S. Senate Select Committee, Hearings, *Watergate and Related Activities, Responsiveness Program*, 93 Cong., 2 sess., 1974, books 18 and 19. Also see Stanley Kutler, ed., *Abuse of Power: The New Nixon Tapes* (Free Press, 1997).

26. Roundtable discussion with Bush administration political appointees, Brookings, May 27, 1992, transcript, p. 50.

27. Richard Rose, "The Variability of Party Government: A Theoretical and Empirical Critique," *Political Studies* 17 (December 1969): 413–45.

28. Richard Rose, *The Problem of Party Government* (Macmillan, 1974), p. 418. Rose's contention is that civil servants are apt to be suspicious of change until it actually occurs and thus becomes the new status quo. His contention is that this skepticism is a temperamental, not a partisan, phenomenon.

29. Robert D. Putnam, "Bureaucrats and Politicians: Contending Elites in the Policy Process," in William B. Gwynn and George C. Edwards III, eds., *Perspectives on Public Policy-Making*, Tulane Studies in Political Science, vol. 15 (Tulane University Press, 1975), pp. 179–202.

30. NPR, *From Red Tape to Results*, p. 2.

31. Hood attributes one of the explanations for the rise of the New Public Management syndrome to "a new-look form of Treasury control, a set of convenient doctrines fastened upon by central financial controlling agencies to destroy the administrative bases of the 'public service welfare lobby' and to increase their own power vis-à-vis the professionalized line departments." Christopher Hood, "De-Sir Humphreyfying the Westminster Model of Bureaucracy: A New Style of Governance?" *Governance* 3 (April 1990): 206.

32. Herbert Kaufman, *Red Tape: Its Origins, Uses, and Abuses* (Brookings, 1977).

33. Charles Goodsell illustrates this process in a welfare agency where administrators are constrained by law from taking certain steps that they would otherwise like to take. Charles T. Goodsell, "Looking Once Again at Human Service Bureaucracy," *Journal of Politics* 43 (1981): 763–78.

34. Theodore J. Lowi, "The Public Philosophy: Interest Group Liberalism," *American Political Science Review* 61 (1967): 5–24, and by the same author, *The End of Liberalism: Ideology, Policy, and the Crisis of Public Authority* (W. W. Norton, 1969). Also see the 1979 version of this book.

35. See, for example, Mathew McCubbins, "The Legislative Design of Regulatory Structure," *American Journal of Political Science* 29 (1985): 721–48.

36. See here James Q. Wilson, "The Bureaucracy Problem," *The Public Interest*, no. 6 (1967): 3–9.

37. The distinction is sharpest between "production" organizations and "coping" organizations, as defined by James Q. Wilson. Production organizations produce observable outputs and outcomes, whereas in coping organizations, neither is observable. James Q. Wilson, *Bureaucracy: What Government Agencies Do and Why They Do It* (Basic Books, 1989), pp. 154–75.

38. Roundtable with federal executives interviewed during the Reagan presidency, Brookings, December 13, 1990, transcript, p. 46.

39. For a discussion of this issue, see Aberbach and Rockman, "Civil Servants and Policymakers," pp. 461–69.

40. For evidence of greater partisanship, see David W. Rohde, *Parties and Leaders in the Postreform House* (University of Chicago Press, 1991). See also, for some other arguments suggesting greater strife in the system, Eric M. Uslaner, *The Decline of Comity in Congress* (University of Michigan Press, 1993), and Benjamin Ginsburg and Martin Shefter, *Politics by Other Means: The Declining Importance of Elections in America* (Basic Books, 1990).

41. Volcker Commission, *Leadership for America: Rebuilding the Public Service* (D. C. Heath and Company, 1990), p. xiii.

42. One analysis focusing on the New Public Management in the United Kingdom notes the growth of "public entrepreneurialism," there defined as "the range of perks, discounts, and performance-related pay awards that is an integral part of the private sector management environment." The analysts worry that "if new public entrepreneurialism is an integral feature of new public management" the challenge facing British governments will be "to ensure that new public entrepreneurialism is harnessed to deliver public services more effectively rather than new public management being harnessed to benefit new public entrepreneurialism." See Alan Doig and John Wilson, "What Price New Public Management?" *The Political Quarterly* 69 (July/September 1998): 271, 274.

43. See, for example, Daniel Bell, "'American Exceptionalism' Revisited: The Role of Civil Society," *The Public Interest* 95 (1989): 38–56. For an interesting, if unsubstantiated, commentary dating back to the 1940s, note Harold Laski's statement "that the American Civil Service, both in the federal and the state governments, has been the Cinderella of the American democracy to which no prince appears at midnight with a glass slipper." Harold J. Laski, *The American Democracy: A Commentary and an Interpretation* (Augustus M. Kelley Publishers, 1977), pp. 20–21. Laski goes on to say: "It is pretty true to say that the posts available [because of political appointments in the top rungs] were not likely to attract men of first-rate talent whose qualities had a marketable value elsewhere. And when . . . there is added the continuous, often profound hostility of Congress to the idea of positive administration, it was pretty inevitable that . . . not many men of outstanding capacity would suffer the humiliation it was the special delight of Congress . . . to inflict upon them."

44. Alexis de Tocqueville, *Democracy in America*, trans., George Lawrence (Harper Perennials, 1988), pp. 203–05.

45. Reagan roundtable, transcript, p. 18.

46. Reagan roundtable, transcript, p. 76.

47. Richard M. Nixon, *RN: Memoirs of a President* (Grosset and Dunlap, 1978), p. 768.

48. Reagan roundtable, transcript, pp. 101–02. For inferential evidence of selective targeting by the Reagan administration, see Robert Maranto, *Politics and Bureaucracy in the Modern Presidency: Careerists and Appointees in the Reagan Administration* (Greenwood, 1993), pp. 86–88.

49. Reagan roundtable, transcript, p. 11.

50. Efficiency Unit, U.K. Office of Public Service and Science, the Cabinet Office, *Career Management and Succession Planning Study*, (London: HMSO, 1993), p. 18.

51. NPR, *From Red Tape to Results*, p. 3.

52. NPR, *From Red Tape to Results*, p. 2.

53. Reagan roundtable, transcript, p. 116.

54. Donald Kettl, for example, asserts that "there is no governmental service that could not be delivered by nongovernmental organizations." Donald F. Kettl, *Reinventing Government? Appraising the National Performance Review*, CPM Report 94-2 (Brookings Center for Public Management, 1994), p. 31.

55. Donald F. Kettl, *Reinventing Government: A Fifth-Year Report Card*, CPM 98-1 (Brookings Center for Public Management, 1998), p. 7.

Chapter Two

1. See, for example, Alberta M. Sbragia, *Debt Wish: Entrepreneurial Cities, U.S. Federalism, and Economic Development* (University of Pittsburgh Press, 1996). Note, for example, the following passages: "Whereas the national government in European systems determined the level and purposes of subnational investment, American states would be able to determine their own investment policy" (p. 43). And, American city governments "provided services that city governments in other advanced countries did not" (p. 65).

2. In this regard, see Stephen Skowronek, *Building a New American State: The Expansion of National Administrative Capacities, 1877–1920* (Cambridge University Press, 1982).

3. This argument has been advanced by, among others, Terry Moe on the presidency and Joel Aberbach on the Congress. See Terry M. Moe, "The Politicized Presidency," in John E. Chubb and Paul E. Peterson, eds., *The New Direction in American Politics* (Brookings, 1985), and Joel D. Aberbach, "Sharing Isn't Easy: When Separate Institutions Clash," *Governance* 11 (April 1998): 137–52.

4. Fred I. Greenstein, *The Hidden-Hand Presidency: Eisenhower as Leader* (Basic Books, 1982).

5. Hugh Heclo, "OMB and the Presidency—the Problem of 'Neutral Competence,'" *The Public Interest* 39 (Winter 1975): 80–98.

6. Richard P. Nathan, *The Administrative Presidency* (John Wiley, 1983), p. 26.

7. Ibid., pp. 27 and 28–40, especially.

8. Ibid., pp. 8 and 53–55.

9. See especially Joel D. Aberbach, *Keeping a Watchful Eye* (Brookings, 1990), pp. 191–93.

10. See especially Roger B. Porter, *Presidential Decision Making: The Economic Policy Board* (Cambridge University Press, 1980).

11. Chester A. Newland, "The Politics of Civil Service Reform," in Patricia W. Ingraham and David H. Rosenbloom, eds., *The Promise and Paradox of Civil Service Reform* (University of Pittsburgh Press, 1992), p. 65.

12. Mark W. Huddleston, "To the Threshold of Reform: The Senior Executive Service and America's Search for a Higher Civil Service," in Ingraham and Rosenbloom, eds., *Promise and Paradox*, p. 165.

13. Transcript of April 19, 1971, meeting between Nixon and George Shultz published in *New York Times*, July 20, 1974, p. 14.

14. Kirke Harper, "The Senior Executive Service after One Decade," in Ingraham and Rosenbloom, *Promise and Paradox*, p. 273.

15. Mark Huddleston and William Boyer assert that the "Reagan administration undertook several measures to guarantee that career civil servants became responsive to executive 'political' direction." These included an increase in the number of noncareer appointments, exceeding the 10 percent limitation statutorily imposed on SES appointments, and an increase in the number of forced reassignments of SES career executives, including geographic transfers. In less than four years time (by May 1983), 40 percent of charter SES career executives had left the government. See Mark W. Huddleston and William W. Boyer, *The Higher Civil Service in the United States: Quest for Reform* (University of Pittsburgh Press, 1996), pp. 111–12. Patricia Ingraham also notes that the Senior Executive Service, with its provisions for improved political control, was quickly recognized as a valuable tool. Among those provisions was "the ability to place political members of the SES in non-policy-sensitive positions" and to move "career executives into insignificant positions." In addition, Ingraham claims, "the impact of political control of performance or merit bonuses under the new system was also important." Patricia W. Ingraham, "The Reform Game," in Ingraham and Rosenbloom, eds., *Promise and Paradox*, pp. 12–13. There is clear evidence that among SES career executives, bonuses were perceived as tinged with political favoritism. See Joel D. Aberbach and Bert A. Rockman, "Senior Executives in a Changing Political Environment," paper prepared for the Conference on the Future of Merit: Twenty Years after the Civil Service Reform Act, Woodrow Wilson Center, Washington, D.C., November 18, 1998.

16. By the second Reagan administration, for example, bonuses and other merit supplements had increased substantially over the first term. Part of this increase had to

do with the fact that Congress, which initially lowered the percentage of SES officials eligible for bonuses from the figure first mandated of 50 percent to a proportion as low as 20 percent when the law went into effect, raised the eligible percentage in 1984 to 35 percent and in 1987 abandoned the ceiling altogether. Harper, "Senior Executive Service," pp. 277–79.

17. Nathan, *Administrative Presidency*, pp. 74–76.

18. See, for example, Thomas J. Weko, *The Politicizing Presidency: The White House Personnel Office, 1948–1994* (University Press of Kansas, 1995), especially pp. 139–44.

19. For an emphasis on this general need in presidential transitions, see James P. Pfiffner, *The Strategic Presidency: Hitting the Ground Running* (The Dorsey Press, 1988).

20. Bert A. Rockman, "The Style and Organization of the Reagan Presidency," in Charles O. Jones, ed., *The Reagan Legacy: Promise and Performance* (Chatham House, 1988), pp. 3–29 (see especially pp. 23–26).

21. Like any administration, the Reagan presidency had difficulties with some appointees who were marching to the beat of a different drummer. Terrel Bell, the secretary of education during Reagan's first term; Everett Koop, the surgeon general; and, above all, Martin Feldstein, the second chair of the Council of Economic Advisers, were cases in point. In each case, the Reagan White House worked assiduously to limit the damage, and in the case of Feldstein, they worked hard to ridicule him.

22. For a general critique of Bush White House tactics in this regard, see Charles Tiefer, *The Semi-Sovereign Presidency: The Bush Administration Strategy for Governing without Congress* (Westview, 1994). See also Joel D. Aberbach, "The President and the Executive Branch," in Colin Campbell and Bert A. Rockman, eds., *The Bush Presidency: First Appraisals* (Chatham House, 1991), pp. 223–47.

23. David Mervin, *George Bush and the Guardianship Presidency* (Macmillan, 1996).

24. See Joel D. Aberbach, "The Federal Executive under Clinton," in Colin Campbell and Bert A. Rockman, eds., *The Clinton Presidency: First Appraisals* (Chatham House, 1996), pp. 163–87.

25. Ibid., p. 184.

26. See Joel D. Aberbach, "A Reinvented Government, or the Same Old Government?" in Colin Campbell and Bert A. Rockman, eds., *The Clinton Legacy* (Chatham House, 2000), pp. 118–39.

27. For example, see Maurice J. Ormsby, "The Provider-Purchaser Split: A Report from New Zealand," *Governance* 11 (July 1998): 357–87; Robert Gregory, "A New Zealand Tragedy: Problems of Political Responsibility," *Governance* 11 (April 1998): 231–40; John Halligan, "Private Sectorising the Australian Public Service," paper presented at the Conference on Public Policy without Administration at the Turn of the Century, Lady Margaret Hall, Oxford, U.K., July 10–11, 1998; and Colin Campbell, "Once the Input/Output/Outcome Triad Stops Rolling: Part 1-A Good Government Leaves a Bad Legacy," paper presented at the Conference on Public Policy without Administration at the Turn of the Century, Lady Margaret Hall, Oxford, U.K., July 10–11, 1998.

Chapter Three

1. See, for example, Rita Mae Kelly, "An Inclusive Democratic Polity, Representative Bureaucracies, and the New Public Management," *Public Administration Review* 58 (May/June 1998): 201–08. Kelly argues on page 204: "A large body of literature now exists demonstrating the difference for women of having women, and for minorities of having minorities, represent their descriptive group in legislatures and in public bureaucracies. . . . 'Being there' matters. If someone like oneself is not present, the likelihood of adequate substantive representation most likely will decline, and often decline sharply. When that happens, an inclusive democratic polity becomes less viable and less feasible."

2. Samuel Krislov and David H. Rosenbloom, *Representative Bureaucracy and the American Political System* (Praeger, 1981), pp. 21–22.

3. Ibid., p. 180.

4. See, for example, Andrew S. McFarland, *Common Cause: Lobbying in the Public Interest* (Chatham House, 1984).

5. Krislov and Rosenbloom, *Representative Bureaucracy*, p. 26.

6. Norton Long, "Power and Administration," *Public Administration Review* 9 (Autumn 1949): 257–64.

7. J. Donald Kingsley, *Representative Bureaucracy* (The Antioch Press, 1944).

8. Krislov and Rosenbloom, *Representative Bureaucracy*, p. 195.

9. Quoted in Robert D. Putnam, *The Comparative Study of Political Elites* (Prentice Hall, 1976), pp. 96–97.

10. Ibid., p. 96.

11. Ibid., p. 42.

12. Joel D. Aberbach, Robert D. Putnam, and Bert A. Rockman, *Bureaucrats and Politicians in Western Democracies* (Harvard University Press, 1981). The correlations are reported on page 160. The quotation is from page 162.

13. Krislov and Rosenbloom, *Representative Bureaucracy*, pp. 69–70.

14. For example, see citations in Kelly, "An Inclusive Democratic Polity," p. 204.

15. Milton C. Cummings Jr., M. Kent Jennings, and Franklin P. Kilpatrick, "Federal and Non-federal Employees: A Comparative Social-Occupational Analysis," *Public Administration Review* 27 (December 1967): 399.

16. Putnam, *Political Elites*, p. 33.

17. See Putnam, *Political Elites*, p. 209, on "Contemporary Trends in Communist Elites." Educational levels rose sharply among both national and local party and economic elites in almost every East European country in the two decades before Putnam's book was written (1976).

18. Carl J. Friedrich, "Public Policy and the Nature of Administrative Responsibility," in Carl J. Friedrich and E. S. Mason, eds., *Public Policy* (Harvard University Press, 1940), p. 3–24. The article is printed in abridged form in Francis E. Rourke, *Bureaucratic Power in National Politics*, 3d ed. (Little, Brown, 1978), pp. 399–409.

19. Herman Finer, "Administrative Responsibility in Democratic Government," *Public Administration Review* 1 (Summer 1941): 350. This article can also be found in abridged form in Rourke, *Bureaucratic Power*, 3d ed., pp. 410–21.

20. Francis E. Rourke, *Bureaucratic Power in National Politics*, 1st ed. (Little, Brown, 1965), p. xviii.

21. James Madison, "The Federalist No. 51," in Alexander Hamilton, John Jay, and James Madison, *The Federalist Papers* (The Modern Library, 1937), p. 337.

22. Aberbach, Putnam, and Rockman, *Bureaucrats and Politicians*, chapter 6, especially p. 195.

23. Volcker Commission, *Leadership for America: Rebuilding the Public Service* (D. C. Heath and Company, 1989), p. 59.

24. See, for example, the references to the "quiet crisis" in the preface to the Volcker Commission report, p. xiii–xiv. The commission was concerned about quality at all levels, but most particularly at senior administrative and professional levels of the federal government because of the import of these people for the leadership of the entire federal administrative apparatus.

25. Volcker Commission, *Leadership for America*, p. 2.

26. Paul A. Volcker to the editor, *The Key Reporter* 60, no. 3 (Spring 1995): 10.

27. This quotation is from the report of the commission's Task Force on Recruitment and Retention (Volcker Commission, *Leadership for America*, p. 139).

28. "The 'Best and Brightest': Can the Public Service Compete?" is included as an annex to the report of the Task Force on Recruitment and Retention of the Volcker Commission, p. 158.

29. For a brief discussion of the specialist/generalist controversy, see B. Guy Peters, *The Politics of Bureaucracy* (Longman, 1995), pp. 94–98. See also F. F. Ridley, *Specialists and Generalists: A Comparative Study of the Civil Service at Home and Abroad* (Routledge and Kegan Paul, 1968), cited in Peters.

30. Martin Trow, "Notes and Impressions on a Visit to Britain," January 31, 1985 (unpublished). Quoted in Walter Williams, *Washington, Westminster and Whitehall* (Cambridge University Press, 1988), p. 79.

Chapter Four

1. This quote can be found in a letter to the editor of Phi Beta Kappa's *The Key Reporter* 60, no. 3 (Spring 1995): 10.

2. See Donald F. Kettl, Patricia W. Ingraham, Ronald P. Sanders, and Constance Horner, *Civil Service Reform: Building a Government That Works* (Brookings, 1996), p. 89.

3. National Performance Review, *From Red Tape to Results: Creating a Government That Works Better and Costs Less* (Government Printing Office, 1993), pp. 2, 123.

4. Philip E. Crewson cites this fear of decline as well as the fact that "the percent of white males in the federal civil service has gradually declined from 50% in 1976 to 42%

in 1986." "A Comparative Analysis of Public and Private Sector Entrant Quality," *American Journal of Political Science* 39 (1995): 629. We should make clear that these fears and figures are cited by Crewson simply as part of a literature review, not as an expression of his own views.

5. See U.S. Bureau of the Census, *Statistical Abstract of the United States* (U.S. Government Printing Office, 1992), p. 16. Hispanics were 6.4 percent of the population in 1980 and between approximately 4.5 and 5.2 percent in 1970. For the derivation of the latter figures (the census did not include such data until 1980), see Frank Bean and Martha Tienda, *The Hispanic Population of the United States* (The Russell Sage Foundation, 1987).

6. Joel D. Aberbach, Robert D. Putnam, and Bert A. Rockman, *Bureaucrats and Politicians in Western Democracies* (Harvard University Press, 1981), p. 80.

7. The "edge" has remained roughly the same for political appointees—that is, they have more postgraduate training than the typical "peer"—but the ratio of political appointees with postgraduate training to peers with postgraduate training was the same in 1991–92 as in 1970.

8. Selectivity standards, the major criterion we use to classify the institutions in table 4-4, should mean that, on average, brighter students attended the schools we identify as prestigious institutions. (Presumably, they also received better training there.) Quality of graduate programs, the criterion we use to decide which institutions are "major state universities" is a reasonable, though clearly incomplete, indicator of quality of training for students who attended these schools, particularly their graduate programs. (These schools also tend to be quite selective in admissions, particularly at the graduate level.)

9. Joel D. Aberbach and Bert A. Rockman, "The Overlapping Worlds of American Federal Executives and Congressmen," *British Journal of Political Science* 7 (1977): 29. For data showing that the proportion of members of Congress who attended prestigious private universities was about the same in 1993 as it was in 1971, see Bert A. Rockman, "Change and Continuity among American Administrative and Political Elites," a paper prepared for the conference "The Recruitment of Elites," L'Observatoire du Changement Social en Europe, Poitiers, France, May 1994, table 4. The above is published in French as "Continuite et Changements: Les Elites Politiques et Administratives Americaines," in Ezra Suleiman and Henri Mendras, eds., *Le Recrutement des Elites en Europe*, (Editions La Decouverte, 1995), pp. 229–42.

10. See Thomas R. Dye, *Who's Running America?* (Prentice-Hall, 1979), pp. 171–73. Dye's study looked at a more rarefied set of government elites than was the case in our study, and he found a higher proportion of attendees at prestigious private institutions among his government group—44 percent of government elites in the domestic area (and 55 percent of the corporate elite). His definition of the government elite (pp. 53–54) specified "the President and Vice-President; secretaries, undersecretaries, and assistant secretaries of executive departments; White House presidential advisers;

congressional committee chairmen and ranking minority members; congressional majority and minority party leaders in the House and Senate; Supreme Court Justices; and members of the Federal Reserve Board and the Council of Economic Advisers." His corporate elite consisted of the presidents and directors of the corporations that controlled over half of the nation's corporate assets in 1970 (p. 12). Note that in Dye's study, as in ours, the government elite in the domestic area was much more likely than the corporate elite to have advanced degrees—71 percent versus 49 percent (p. 172).

11. We do not have exact figures for them. SES salaries in 1992 ranged between $90,000 and $112,000. Many of our executives also received the relatively small bonuses available to selected members of the SES.

12. This includes salary and bonuses, stock gains from the exercise of stock options, company-paid benefits, and payments under long-term compensation plans. See "What 800 Companies Paid Their Bosses," *Forbes* 147, no. 11 (May 27, 1991): 236–89.

13. But when one considers only those who attended graduate school (about half of the top corporate executives compared with 70 percent of political executives and over 90 percent of career executives), the top corporate executives were more likely to have attended prestigious private institutions.

14. See Aberbach, Putnam, and Rockman, *Bureaucrats and Politicians*, pp. 51–52, for a comparison of the types of university training received by elites in Britain, Germany, Italy, the Netherlands, and the United States.

15. See Joel D. Aberbach, Renate Mayntz, Hans-Ulrich Derlien, and Bert A. Rockman, "American and West German Federal Executives: Technocratic and Political Attitudes," *International Social Science Journal* 123 (1990): 6–7. Less than 20 percent of all top American federal executives in 1986–87, including political appointees, were lawyers, whereas 63 percent of top German executives sampled in 1986 were lawyers. The highest proportion of lawyers in the United States is found among political appointees, but even here the percentage is less than a quarter (23 percent).

16. Aberbach, Putnam, and Rockman, *Bureaucrats and Politicians*, pp. 67–68 (emphasis in original).

17. The exception is the Career I group in 1986–87. Our analysis indicates that many in this group were carefully selected by the Reagan administration, using the opportunities presented by the 1978 Civil Service Reform Act. See the discussion below and also see Joel D. Aberbach and Bert A. Rockman, "The Political Views of U.S. Senior Federal Executives, 1970–1992," *Journal of Politics* 57 (1995): 838–52.

18. The Nixon and Bush administrations were more likely to select executives with previous government service than the Reagan administration. The Reagan administration would likely look even more distinct if our study had been done in its first term.

19. Incidentally, top private sector executives average 56.34 years of age. They have a mean tenure in their current corporations of 22.64 years, a figure higher than that for any category of federal executive. Top corporate executives also average 8.1 years in their present positions, a figure close to double that for top career civil servants. These data

suggest that notions of rapid circulation in the corporate elite as compared with the government elite may be exaggerated.

20. For an analysis of SES's potential for facilitating control of career executives by political leaders, see Carolyn Ban, Edie Goldenberg, and Toni Marzotto, "Controlling the U.S. Federal Bureaucracy: Will SES Make a Difference?" pp. 205–20, in Gerald E. Caiden and Heinrich Siedentopf, eds., *Strategies for Administrative Reform* (D.C. Heath, 1982). On pp. 211–12 they note: "SES also attempts to facilitate executive mobility from agency to agency, as well as the hiring of new executives from outside the federal government. . . . The designers of SES hoped that by opening up positions to those who had not come up through the ranks of their agency or program, SES would lead to a broader, more government-wide perspective and would reduce the narrow allegiances to individual agency and program."

21. See Joel D. Aberbach, "The President and Executive Branch," in Colin Campbell and Bert A. Rockman, eds., *The Bush Presidency: First Appraisals* (Chatham House, 1991), pp. 223–47, and Aberbach and Rockman, " Political Views."

22. Fifty-one percent of top British civil servants surveyed in 1971 had served in more than one ministry. Aberbach, Putnam, and Rockman, *Bureaucrats and Politicians*, p. 71. A 1993 report on the top grades of the British administrative class shows that 65 percent of Grades 1–3, those at the top of the scale, had worked in more than one ministry. Thirty-five percent of Grades 4–7 had done the same. See Efficiency Unit, U.K. Office of Public Service and Science, the Cabinet Office, *Career Management and Succession Planning Study* (London: HMSO, 1993), p. 48.

23. Another 4 percent of the 1991–92 political appointees surveyed said they had worked for the Republicans in Congress immediately before their appointments.

24. The data in table 4-8 indicate how unique the Bush administration was in this respect. If one takes the mean years in the present agency as a percentage of the mean years of government service, the figures are as follows for the three administrations in our study: Nixon administration, 88 percent of government service in the present agency; Reagan administration, 71 percent of government service in the present agency; Bush administration, 41 percent of government service in the present agency.

25. See, for example, Hugh Heclo, *A Government of Strangers: Executive Politics in Washington* (Brookings, 1977), especially pp. 100–05, and Linda L. Fisher, "Fifty Years of Presidential Appointments," especially pp. 21–26, in Calvin Mackenzie, ed., *The In-and-Outers: Presidential Appointees and Transient Government in Washington* (The Johns Hopkins University Press, 1987).

26. Heclo, *A Government of Strangers*, pp. 102 and 103.

27. Ibid., p. 104.

28. In *A Government of Strangers*, Heclo (p. 102) notes that, in light of their tendency to serve in only one agency, "it is . . . difficult to see how the in-and-outers can be thought to supply anything like a general, government-wide capability for political leadership in the bureaucracy."

29. Volcker Commission, *Leadership for America: Rebuilding the Public Service* (D.C. Heath, 1989), p. 4.

30. Ibid., p. 3.

31. Ibid., pp. 3, 12, 13.

32. Kerry James Manning, "An Inquiry into the Importance of Morale to Individual and Collective Performance in the Senior Executive Service," (Ph.D. dissertation, submitted to the Department of Political Science, University of Pittsburgh, 1995). See especially chapter 6, pp. 199–207.

33. Parenthetically, Manning's analysis also fails to show a substantial relationship between individual job satisfaction and performance ratings, but this could easily be due to the limited variance in both measures in these data. (Supervisors tended to give SES executives extraordinarily high performance ratings.) See Manning, "Importance of Morale," chapter 4.

34. Crewson, "Public and Private Sector Entrant Quality," pp. 633–34.

35. Ibid., p. 630. The two studies cited are U.S. Office of Personnel Management, *Scientists and Engineers in Civilian Agencies: Studies of Quality-Related Factors* (OPM, 1991), and U.S. Office of Personnel Management, *Computer Specialists in Federal Agencies: Study of Quality-Related Factors* (OPM, 1990).

36. Crewson, "Public and Private Sector Entrant Quality," p. 631. The study cited is James K. Conant, "Universities and the Future of the Public Service," *Public Administration Quarterly* 13 (1989): 342–74.

37. Crewson, "Public and Private Sector Entrant Quality," pp. 635, 636.

38. Ibid., pp. 634–35.

39. An interesting argument by Derek Bok, based on a survey done in the early 1990s of Phi Beta Kappa members who graduated from college between 1970 and 1990, aims to show that there is a problem in government recruitment despite the fact that there are apparently about the same percentage (actually a slightly higher percentage) of Phi Beta Kappas from the 1980s employed by the federal government as Phi Beta Kappas from the 1970s. Bok says these data mask a problem because more Phi Beta Kappas from the 1970s were in the government at some point (10.5 percent) than the comparable numbers from the 1980s (7.5 percent). In short, more 1970s Phi Beta Kappas dropped out (or "in and out") than 1980s Phi Beta Kappas. Aside from the fact that one would expect more in-and-outers among the older and more established 1970s graduates in a survey done in the early 1990s, these results are a very thin reed on which to hang support for the notion that the government suffered a brain drain of serious proportions in the 1980s—although one would want to see a follow-up done at the turn of the century to see if Bok's fears have been realized. See Derek Bok, "A Survey of the Career Choices of Phi Beta Kappa Members," *The Key Reporter* 58 (Spring 1993): 11–12.

40. Within-group analysis did indicate one quality difference across sectors: whites scoring high on the AFQT are *more* likely to be found in the public sector. See Philip E. Crewson and James F. Guyot, "*Sartor Resartus:* A Comparative Analysis of Public and

Private Sector Entrant Quality Reanalyzed," *American Journal of Political Science* 41 (1997): 1057–65.

Chapter Five

1. This is reflected in the evidence that bureaucrats see themselves as policymakers as much as politicians do but differ in the style and nature of their policymaking roles. See Joel D. Aberbach, Robert D. Putnam, and Bert Rockman, *Bureaucrats and Politicians in Western Democracies* (Harvard University Press, 1981), especially pp. 84–114.

2. David R. Mayhew, *Congress: The Electoral Connection* (Yale University Press, 1974).

3. In *Interest Groups in Italian Politics* (Princeton University Press, 1964), Joseph LaPalombara described the Italian bureaucracy under the Christian Democrats in the 1950s more or less in these terms—favoring the clients of Christian Democracy and hindering its opponents.

4. See Charles E. Gilbert, "The Framework of Administrative Responsibility," *Journal of Politics* 21 (1959): 373–407.

5. Shirley Anne Warshaw, *The Domestic Presidency: Policy Making in the White House* (Boston: Allyn and Bacon, 1997), pp. 162–63.

6. Aberbach, Putnam, and Rockman, *Bureaucrats and Politicians*, chapters 4 and 8.

7. In fact, several scholars have noted that changes in the machinery of government (that is, administrative changes) tended to follow elections and the installation of new prime ministers in three parliamentary democracies based on the British Westminster system. As they put it: "For prime ministers, machinery of government questions have both policy and political content. The architecture of ministries is an opportunity to express priorities and to meet policy challenges with new organizational arrangements. Important initiatives can be given dedicated resources, while administrative obstacles are removed." Glyn Davis, Patrick Weller, Emma Craswell, and Susan Eggins, "What Drives Machinery of Government Change? Australia, Canada, and the United Kingdom, 1950–1977," *Public Administration* 77, 1 (1999): 7.

8. See Alexander Hamilton, James Madison, and John Jay, *The Federalist Papers*, no. 51 (Mentor Books, 1961), pp. 320–25, and Terry M. Moe, "The Politicized Presidency," in John E. Chubb and Paul E. Peterson, eds., *The New Direction in American Politics* (Brookings, 1990), pp. 235–69.

9. Differences of policy preferences need not always coincide strictly with party lines. Policy differences certainly may exist between presidents and congressional majorities of the same party. Even after Franklin Roosevelt's 1936 electoral landslide and lopsided Democratic majorities in both chambers of Congress, differences developed between the presidential administration and the Democratic Congress. Such situations are common. In his 1963 book, James MacGregor Burns talked about a four-party system in America, meaning a presidential branch of each party and, as Burns saw it, a more parochial congressional branch of each party (*The Deadlock of*

Democracy: Four-Party Politics in America [Prentice-Hall, 1963]). In *The Electoral Connection*, published in 1974, Mayhew noted that such differences were more likely to spring from the individualistic needs of congressional politicians (and one presumes presidents as well) to build political coalitions for reelection or for election to something else.

10. Gilbert, "Administrative Responsibility," pp. 373–407.

11. The term "iron triangle" implies a more immutable relationship than seems justified. The term originates with the late J. Lieper Freeman. See his *Political Process: Executive Bureau-Legislative Committee Relations*, rev. ed. (Random House, 1965). Roger H. Davidson refers to them as "cozy relationships" ("Senate Leaders: Janitors for an Untidy Chamber," in Lawrence C. Dodd and Bruce I. Oppenheimer, eds., *Congress Reconsidered*, 3d ed. [CQ Press, 1985], pp. 225–52.) One thing is clear: these relationships can be quite malleable. Changes in the legitimacy of interests, in the nature of congressional majorities, both partisan and otherwise, changes in larger policy environments, and, above all, some combination of all of these can change the basis of agency responsiveness. In this regard, see Frank R. Baumgartner and Bryan D. Jones, *Agendas and Instability in American Politics* (University of Chicago Press, 1993).

12. This version of the "iron triangle" logic was set forth by William Niskanen in his book, *Bureaucracy and Representative Government* (Aldine-Atherton, 1971).

13. See, for example, Samuel P. Huntington, "Political Modernization: America vs. Europe," *World Politics* 18 (1966): 378–414, and Richard E. Neustadt, *Presidential Power and the Modern Presidents: The Politics of Leadership from Roosevelt to Reagan* (The Free Press, 1990).

14. An expansive reading of the "take care" clause may be found in the U.S. Supreme Court's decision *In re Neagle*, 135 U.S. 1 (1890). This decision interpreted the term "laws" very broadly and offered numerous options to a president to enable him to take care that the laws of the nation are faithfully executed.

15. Norton Long, "Power and Administration," *Public Administration Review* 9 (Autumn 1949): 263. The corollary of this struggle is reflected in Herbert Simon's admonition that "administrative rationality depends on the establishment of uniform value premises in the decisional centers of organization," which, according to Long (p. 259), is infrequent in the American case for institutional reasons.

16. Examples include President Harry Truman's seizure of the steel mills during the Korean War and President Franklin D. Roosevelt's effort to pack the Supreme Court.

17. Charles O. Jones, "Congress and the Presidency," in Thomas E. Mann and Norman Ornstein, eds., *The New Congress* (American Enterprise Institute, 1981), pp. 223–49.

18. The southern strategy resulted, ironically, in the firing of at least two recalcitrant liberal Republican appointees: James Allen, the commissioner of education in the precabinet level Office of Education, and Leon Panetta, in the civil rights division of HEW. See chapter 6 for a fuller discussion of the problem Nixon faced in gaining bureaucrats' support for this strategy and the successful transformation of the bureaucracy carried out by the Reagan administration in these areas. Also see Joel D. Aberbach and Bert A.

Rockman, "Clashing Beliefs within the Executive Branch: The Nixon Administration Bureaucracy," *American Political Science Review* 70 (1976): 456–68, and Joel D. Aberbach and Bert A. Rockman, "The Political Views of U.S. Senior Executives, 1970–1992," *Journal of Politics* 57 (1995): 838–52.

19. Richard M. Nixon, *RN: The Memoirs of a President* (Grosset and Dunlap, 1978), p. 768. He specifically cited our data as the main source for his contention.

20. See Charles Tiefer, *The Semi-Sovereign Presidency: The Bush Administration's Strategy for Governing without Congress* (Westview Press, 1995).

21. See Joel D. Aberbach, "The Federal Executive under Clinton," in Colin Campbell and Bert A. Rockman, eds., *The Clinton Presidency: First Appraisals* (Chatham House Publishers, 1995), pp.163–87.

22. See Joel D. Aberbach, "A Reinvented Government, or the Same Old Government?" in Colin Campbell and Bert A. Rockman, eds., *The Clinton Legacy* (Chatham House, 2000), pp. 127–31, 137–39.

23. Interview subject #005, by authors, Washington, D.C., July 10, 1986. All interviewees were promised anonymity.

Chapter Six

1. The Nixon tapes and the Watergate hearings provide ample evidence in this regard. See especially, the Senate Select Committee on Presidential Campaign Activities, Executive Session Hearings on *Watergate and Related Activities, Federal "Political" Personnel Manual*, 93 Cong., 2 sess., 1974, exhibit 35 in book 19.

2. Richard M. Nixon, *RN: The Memoirs of Richard Nixon* (Grosset and Dunlap, 1978), p. 768.

3. Richard P. Nathan, *The Administrative Presidency* (John Wiley, 1983), p. 30.

4. James P. Pfiffner, "Establishing the Bush Presidency," *Public Administration Review* 50, no. 1 (January/February 1990): 69.

5. Volcker Commission, *Leadership for America: Rebuilding the Public Service*, report of the National Commission on the Public Service (D.C. Heath, 1989), p. xxiv.

6. See Charles Tiefer, *The Semi-Sovereign Presidency: The Bush Administration's Strategy for Governing without Congress* (Westview Press, 1994).

7. The career executives in 1970 are called supergrade career civil servants and are the equivalents of Career I civil servants in the other years.

8. Joel D. Aberbach and Bert A. Rockman, "Clashing Beliefs within the Executive Branch: The Nixon Administration Bureaucracy." *American Political Science Review* 70 (1976): 458, 466.

9. Joel D. Aberbach and Bert A. Rockman, "The Political Views of U.S. Senior Federal Executives, 1970–1992," *Journal of Politics* 57 (1995): 842–43.

10. For a statement of SES appointment procedures, see U.S. Office of Personnel Management, *Operations Handbook for the Senior Executive Service*, Federal Personnel Manual System, Supplement 920-1 (October 1989), especially subchapters S2 and S5.

11. Ibid., S5-5.

12. The correlations between job designation and party affiliation show relatively little variation across the three waves of our study (see table 6-1, note C).

13. Nathan, *Administrative Presidency*, p. 27.

14. Among the comparable career people (supergrades) in the social service agencies in the Nixon administration, only 11 percent were Republicans.

15. The following supplementary measures were included on both the 1986–87 and 1991–92 surveys (answers range along a four-point scale from "Agree" to "Disagree"):

1. Rectifying differences of income among the people is a proper task of government.

2. Many approaches to social and economic change have been used by government in modern societies. I am going to give you some options and ask you to circle the one you prefer the most.

—1. A major government role in directing social and political change, such as economic planning.

—2. A moderately active government role, such as government guidelines and incentives.

—3. A modified market approach with some government incentives.

—4. A basic market approach with the smallest possible role for government."

In the 1986–87 survey data, the average correlation coefficient between these three measures was .48 using Pearson's *r* and .60 using Gamma. The figures in 1991–92 were remarkably similar: .49 using Pearson's *r* and .60 using Gamma.

16. See Jack L. Walker Jr., *Mobilizing Interest Groups in America* (University of Michigan Press, 1991), especially chapters 2, 4, and 5.

17. For a partisan but excellent account of the use of OMB, particularly its Office of Information and Regulatory Affairs (OIRA), to control regulations, see Tiefer, *Semi-Sovereign Presidency*, especially chapters 2, 4 and 7.

18. See the subtle discussion of this aspect of the relationship between political appointees and career civil servants in Hugh Heclo, *A Government of Strangers: Executive Politics in Washington* (Brookings, 1977), especially pp. 182–90.

19. A career executive who participated in a round-table discussion, Brookings, May 28, 1992, transcript, pp. 24–25.

20. Former career executives were surveyed as well. U.S. Merit Systems Protection Board, *The Senior Executive Service: Views of Former Federal Executives*, 249-477-814/00777 (Government Printing Office, 1989).

21. Former civil servants in 1988 had high self-ratings, although not so high as our 1991–92 sample had. The lowest, although still very positive, self-rating in 1988 (as in the 1991–92 survey) was on management skills: 64 percent of the retired civil servants rated themselves and their colleagues as having good management skills.

22. See MSPB, *Views of Former Executives*, pp. 20–21. The comparable ratings in the Bush administration to those presented in the text were 28, 52, and 60 percent for the respective categories (see table 6-9).

23. Quoted in Nathan, *Administrative Presidency*, p. 30.

24. For a description of the Reagan administration recruitment and orientation strategy, see Michael Sanera, "Implementing the Mandate," part IV, in Stuart M. Butler, Michael Sanera, and W. Bruce Weinrod, eds., *Mandate for Leadership II: Continuing the Conservative Revolution* (Heritage Foundation, 1984).

25. Heclo, *Government of Strangers*, pp. 175–77, 224–25.

26. For a full account, see Joel D. Aberbach, Hans-Ulrich Derlien, and Bert A. Rockman, "Unity and Fragmentation: Themes in German and American Public Administration," in Hans-Ulrich Derlien, Uta Gerhardt, and Fritz W. Scharpf, eds., *Systemrationalität und Partialinteresse* (Baden-Baden, Germany: Nomos Verlagsgesellschaft, 1994), pp. 271–89 and especially pp. 284–85.

27. The 42 percent figure for the Americans breaks down into 4 percent who felt that the administration should be given unequivocal support and 38 percent who would keep any disagreements behind closed doors and ultimately do what their superiors wish.

28. For similar results in the United Kingdom, see Anthony Barker and Graham K. Wilson, "Whitehall's Disobedient Servants? Senior Officials' Potential Resistance to Ministers in British Government Departments," *British Journal of Political Science* 27 (1997): 223–46.

29. Joel D. Aberbach and Bert A. Rockman, "From Nixon's *Problem* to Reagan's *Achievement*: The Federal Executive Reexamined," in Larry Berman, ed., *Looking Back on the Reagan Presidency* (Johns Hopkins University Press, 1990), p. 179.

30. See James Q. Wilson, *Bureaucracy: What Government Agencies Do and Why They Do It* (Basic Books, 1989). Wilson marvels, despite the bewildering complications resulting from a system that both multiplies rules and expands opportunities for access, that it is still "possible to get drinkable water instantly, put through a telephone call in seconds, deliver a letter in a day, and obtain a passport in a week" (p. 378).

31. For an argument that it was precisely this separation between policy and administration, and therefore the use of civil servants as "intelligent tools," that was at the heart of the Reagan administration's management philosophy, see Bert A. Rockman, "Tightening the Reins: The Federal Executive and the Management Philosophy of the Reagan Presidency," *Presidential Studies Quarterly* 23 (Winter 1993): 103–14.

32. The literature on this subject is vast. The classic attack on the notion that politics and administration can be separated is by Paul Appleby in *Politics and Administration* (University of Alabama Press, 1949). For a summary and analysis of the debate, see Colin Campbell and B. Guy Peters, "The Politics/Administration Dichotomy: Death or Merely Change?" *Governance* 1 (1988): 79–100.

33. See Hans-Ulrich Derlien, "Repercussions of Government Change in the Career Civil Service in Germany: The Cases of 1969 and 1982," *Governance* 1 (1988): 50–78.

Chapter Seven

1. National Performance Review, *From Red Tape to Results: Creating a Government That Works Better and Costs Less* (Government Printing Office, 1993). The preface to the

report stresses that making the government work better and cost less are the "twin missions" of the NPR (p. i).

2. NPR, *From Red Tape to Results*, p. 2.

3. The quotation in the previous sentence is from Donald F. Kettl, *Reinventing Government: A Fifth-Year Report Card*, CPM 98-1 (Brookings Center for Public Management, 1998), p. 5. Also see John M. Kamensky, "Role of the 'Reinventing Government' Movement in Federal Management Reform," *Public Administration Review* 56, no. 3 (May/June 1996): 251.

4. NPR, *From Red Tape to Results*, p. 3.

5. Ibid., p. 83.

6. Ibid., p. 6.

7. The OECD web address is http://www.oecd.org/puma.

8. Christopher Hood, "De-Sir Humphreyfying the Westminster Model of Bureaucracy: A New Style of Governance?" *Governance* 3, no. 2 (April 1990): 207.

9. Malcolm Holmes and David Shand, "Management Reform: Some Practitioner Perspectives on the Past Ten Years," *Governance* 8, no. 4 (October 1995): 551–52.

10. Naomi Caiden, "A New Generation of Budget Reform," in B. Guy Peters and Donald J. Savoie, *Taking Stock: Assessing Public Sector Reforms* (McGill-Queens University Press, 1998), p. 252.

11. See Rupert Scholz, "Preface," in *Final Report of the Lean State Advisory Committee* (1997). Scholz chaired the committee, which reported to the German federal government. In it, he says: "The idea of the 'lean state,' or the need to 'streamline' the state, has now become the 'talk of the town.' Support for this aim is almost universal, although of course the exhausted state coffers, as well as a public-sector share which is too high, even in the face of a downward trend, have helped in many ways to heighten awareness and form opinions in this area" (p. 3).

12. B. Guy Peters, *The Future of Governing* (University of Kansas Press, 1996), pp. 1, 13. Also see, among others, Donald J. Savoie, "Globalization and Governance," in B. G. Peters and D. J. Savoie, eds., *Governance in a Changing Environment* (McGill/Queens University Press, 1995), and Kamensky, "Role of the 'Reinventing Government' Movement," p. 248.

13. Richard Rosecrance, "The Rise of the Virtual State," *Foreign Affairs* 75, no. 4 (July/August 1996): 60.

14. Donald F. Kettl, "The Global Revolution in Public Management: Driving Themes, Missing Links," *Journal of Policy Analysis and Management* 16, no. 3 (1997): 447. Italics in original.

15. Ibid., p. 447.

16. Ibid., p. 448.

17. Ibid., p. 449.

18. For an interesting perspective on the sources and coherence of New Public Management ideas in different countries, see Peter Aucoin, *New Public Management:*

Canada in Comparative Perspective (Institute for Research on Public Policy [IRPP], Ashgate, 1995).

19. James D. Carroll, "The Rhetoric of Reform and Political Reality in the National Performance Review," *Public Administration Review* 55, no. 3 (May/June 1995): 302.

20. Kettl, *Fifth-Year Report Card*, pp. 5–6.

21. NPR, *From Red Tape to Results*, p. 66.

22. Ibid., p. 77.

23. Ibid., p. 94.

24. Ibid., p. 102.

25. National Performance Review, *Common Sense Government* (September 1995), appendix C: New Recommendations by Agency, pp. 1–24.

26. Parenthetically, we should note that phase III of reinvention sought, in Kettl's words, "to move past downsizing" to an emphasis on "results," although unfortunately sometimes on "results [such as safe communities] that the federal government has little role in producing." See Kettl, *Fifth-Year Report Card*, pp. 5–6.

27. Donald F. Kettl, *Reinventing Government? Appraising the National Performance Review*, CPM 94-2 (Brookings Center for Public Management, August 19, 1994), pp. v–vi.

28. For example, see Warren E. Leary, "NASA Learns That Faster and Cheaper Isn't Always So," *New York Times*, September 15, 1998, pp. B9, B13. Leary describes NASA's failure in managing contracts for two satellites that were to be developed and launched within two years at a cost of $60 million each. Under the system devised to put NASA's "faster, better, cheaper" policy into practice, the contractors were given much leeway in achieving results, with a set of performance incentives and disincentives put in place to assure compliance and prevent cost overruns. The concept looked good on paper, but the lack of monitoring by NASA meant that the agency was not aware of many of the problems the contractors were having until it was too late.

29. Herbert Kaufman, *Red Tape: Its Origins, Uses, and Abuses* (Brookings, 1977), especially chapter 2.

30. James Q. Wilson, "Reinventing Public Administration," *PS: Political Science & Politics* 27, no. 4 (December 1994): 670.

31. Peter Aucoin, "Administrative Reform in Public Management: Paradigms, Principles, Paradoxes and Pendulums," *Governance*, vol. 3, no. 2 (April 1990): 132; see also, H. George Frederickson, "Comparing the Reinventing Government Movement with the New Public Administration," *Public Administration Review*, vol. 56, no. 3 (May/June 1996): 266.

32. Linda deLeon and Robert B. Denhardt, "The Political Theory of Reinvention," a paper prepared for the 1997 annual meeting of the American Political Science Association, Washington, D.C., August 27–31, 1997, pp. 8, 10.

33. Kamensky, "Role of the 'Reinventing Government' Movement," p. 252.

34. NPR, *From Red Tape to Results*, p. 3.

35. Ibid., pp. 72–76.

36. Wilson, "Reinventing Public Administration," p. 671.

37. Ronald C. Moe, "The 'Reinventing Government' Exercise: Misinterpreting the Problem, Misjudging the Consequences," *Public Administration Review* 54, no. 2 (May/June 1994): 119.

38. Frederickson, "Comparing Reinventing Government with New Public Management," p. 268.

39. Paul C. Light, *Thickening Government: Federal Hierarchy and the Diffusion of Accountability* (Brookings, 1995), and M. Bryna Sanger, review of *Thickening Government, Journal of Policy Analysis and Management* 15, no. 1 (Winter 1996): 126.

40. Volcker Commission, *Leadership for America: Rebuilding the Public Service*, the Report of the National Commission on the Public Service (D.C. Heath, 1989), pp. 16–19. The section is entitled "Make more room near the top for career executives."

41. Kettl, "Global Revolution," p. 457.

42. U.S. General Accounting Office, *The Government Performance and Results Act: 1997 Governmentwide Implementation Will Be Uneven*, GAO/GGD-97-109 (1997), p. 96.

43. National Performance Review, "Savings: Brief Explanation of Savings Estimates and How They Were Derived," NPR Savings 1997 (http://www.npr.gov/library/papers/bkgrd/expain.html), pp. 1-3.

44. Kettl, "Global Revolution," p. 456.

45. Kettl, *Appraising the NPR*, p. vi, and Carroll, "The Rhetoric of Reform," pp. 307, 309.

46. Frederickson, "Comparing Reinventing Government with New Public Administration," p. 269.

47. NPR, *From Red Tape to Results*, pp. 73–76.

48. Kettl, *Fifth-Year Report Card*, p. 5.

49. Frederick M. Kaiser and Virginia A. McMurtry, *Government Performance and Results Act: Implications for Congressional Oversight*, CRS Report for Congress 97-382-GOV (Congressional Research Service, Library of Congress, March 24, 1997), p. 1.

50. *Government Performance and Results Act*, sec. 4; amendment to chapter 11 of 31 *U.S. Code*, sec. 1115, Performance Plans (1993).

51. Kaiser and McMurtry, *Government Performance and Results Act*, p. 15.

52. Ibid., p. 5.

53. U.S. General Accounting Office, *Managing for Results: Agencies' Annual Performance Plans Can Help Address Strategic Planning Challenges*, GAO/GGD-98-44 (January 1998), and *Managing for Results: The Statutory Framework for Performance-Based Management and Accountability*, GAO/GGD/AIMD-98-52 (January 1998).

54. GAO, *Performance-Based Management and Accountability*, p. 19.

55. GAO, *Agencies' Annual Performance Plans*, pp. 3–4.

56. GAO, *Governmentwide Implementation Will Be Uneven*, pp. 5–6.

57. Congress did not accept the notion that it should establish goals for the agencies. However, Senator William Roth (R-Del.), a champion of the GPRA, believed otherwise. He penned the following "additional views" in the Senate Committee on Governmental Affairs

report on the act: "Under the legislation, federal agencies would be required to develop measurable goals for their programs. I believe we should go one step further, and also require that Congress itself play a direct role in the establishing of at least some of those goals. Congress creates and funds the programs, so it ought to give some indication as to what it expects them to accomplish. . . . Congress has an obligation to tell the American taxpayers what results we intend for the money we spend, and this requirement should be included in the legislation." See Senate Committee on Governmental Affairs, *Government Performance and Results Act*, S. Rept. 103-58, 103 Cong., 1 sess. (Government Printing Office), p. 57. Thanks to Robert D. Behn for bringing this quote to our attention and to Susan McGrath of the Brookings Institution Library for securing a copy of the committee report.

58. Office of the House Majority Leader, "Freedom Works: Clinton Administration Fails Accountability Review," November 1997 (http://freedom.house.gov/results/finalreport/release.asp), p. 1.

59. Anne Laurent, "The Results Act: Playing Chicken," *GovExec*, A Service of *Government Executive* magazine, January 1998 (http://www/govexec.com/features/0198mgmt.html), pp. 1, 2.

60. Kaiser and McMurtry, *Government Performance and Results Act*, p. 8.

61. Ibid., p. 13.

62. Ibid., p. 15.

63. GAO, *Government Performance and Results Act*, p. 6.

64. Ibid., p. 6.

65. Ibid., p. 7.

66. U. S. Office of Personnel Management (OPM), *The Fact Book, 1998 Edition: Federal Civilian Workforce Statistics,* Part 1: Employee Demographics, Trends of Federal Civilian Employment, 1982–1997. These data are also available on OPM's web page, created March 19, 1999 (www.opm.gov/feddata/factbook/1998).

67. Kettl, *Fifth-Year Report Card*, p. 18. The data run from the start of the administration until April 1998.

68. Ibid., p. 18; and Paul C. Light, *The True Size of Government* (Brookings, 1999), appendix A, pp. 196–97.

69. OPM, *Fact Book 1998*, "Executive Branch Employment by General Schedule (GS) and Related Grades: 1986–1997."

70. Light, *True Size of Government*, appendix A.

71. Kirke Harper, "The Senior Executive Service after One Decade," in Patricia W. Ingraham and David H. Rosenbloom, eds., *The Promise and Paradox of Civil Service Reform* (University of Pittsburgh Press, 1992), p. 270.

72. The average number of SES executives in the years from 1983 through 1988, the period for which we have exact data from OPM, was 6,921. These data on SES membership and those used in the balance of the paragraph were graciously provided to us by Charles Vaughn of OPM's Office of Executive Resources Management.

73. See OPM, *Fact Book 1998*, "Senior Executive Service Member Profile: 1990–1997." The years used to calculate the averages are those presented in the data

source. Note that the OPM data cover all members of SES, a more inclusive group than the relatively high-ranked, Washington-based domestic agency people in our samples.

74. U.S. Merit Systems Protection Board (MSPB), *The Changing Federal Workplace: Employee Perspectives* (March 1998), page 8, table 1.

75. Ibid., table 5, p. 29, for attitudes on downsizing, and p. 20 for the quotation.

76. MSPB, *Changing Federal Workplace,* pp. 27, 29.

77. U.S. Merit Systems Protection Board (MSPB), *Working for America: An Update* (July 1994), p. 32, figure 14.

78. Pew Research Center for the People and the Press, press release, "Washington Leaders Wary of Public Opinion" (http//:www.people-press.org/leadrpt.htm), p. 6.

79. Ibid., pp. 12 and 9, respectively.

80. Wilson, "Reinventing Public Administration," p. 672.

81. Jonathan Boston and June Pallot, "Linking Strategy and Performance: Developments in the New Zealand Public Sector," *Journal of Policy Analysis and Management* 16, no. 3 (1997): 386.

82. Donald F. Kettl, "Global Revolution," p. 459.

83. Ibid., p. 460.

84. James D. Carroll, "Rhetoric of Reform," p. 309.

Chapter Eight

1. See R. Shep Melnick, *Between the Lines: Interpreting Welfare Rights* (Brookings, 1994) with respect especially to the role of the courts in the expansive interpretation of rights and, thus, governmental obligations, especially at state and local levels.

2. This is well detailed in Richard Nathan, *The Administrative Presidency* (John Wiley, 1983).

3. As Chester Newland comments, "Carter campaigned against Washington in 1976 and promised to change it—committing himself to shake up the bureaucracy, including the civil service." Chester A. Newland, "The Politics of Civil Service Reform," in Patricia W. Ingraham and David H. Rosenbloom, eds., *The Promise and Paradox of Civil Service Reform* (University of Pittsburgh Press, 1992), p. 65.

4. "The [Carter] administration particularly stressed the need to simplify the process for firing nonperformers. . . . Two impressions were encouraged: that the federal government was full of nonperformers, and that the civil service system protected these employees" (Newland, "Civil Service Reform," p. 84).

5. The Volcker Commission, *Leadership for America: Rebuilding the Public Service,* the Report of the National Commission on the Public Service (D.C. Heath, 1989).

6. This is notably the case for the period of our study. There was a huge increase in university attendance, particularly in attendance at four-year public institutions, when our three samples of top federal executives were in college. Attendance jumped from just over 1 million at four-year public institutions in 1948, for example, to over 2.5 million in 1962 and to close to 3.5 million in 1967. Four-year private institutions also

increased in size, but at a much slower rate. Attendance at these institutions increased from 1.2 million in 1948 to a little less than 2 million in 1967. So public institution attendance more than tripled during this period while private institutions did not even double attendance. The result is a much larger pool, relatively speaking, of public institution graduates for the merit-conscious public sector to draw upon. Statistics are available from the authors. The source is U.S. Department of Education, National Center for Education Statistics, *Digest of Education Statistics* (various issues).

7. We coded the undergraduate institutions attended by the 1987 Forbes 800 top corporate executives (see chapter 4) in order to see if there was any drop-off in attendance at prestigious private institutions by top private-sector executives between the years 1987 and 1991. There is a drop-off from 41 percent in 1987 to 36 percent in 1991. When one considers that top corporate executives stay in their posts longer than top public-sector executives (thereby making for slower rates of change in yearly characteristics), it puts the drop-off among public-sector executives into perspective. There has most likely been a gradual democratizing of recruitment to top posts in both sectors as university enrollments have increased. This is an interesting area for future research.

8. U.S. Merit Systems Protection Board, Office of Policy and Evaluation, *The Senior Executive Service: Views of Former Federal Executives*, A report to the President and the Congress of the United States (Government Printing Office, 1989).

9. On the latter point especially, see the controversial essay by Terry M. Moe, "The Politicized Presidency," in John E. Chubb and Paul E. Peterson, eds., *The New Direction in American Politics* (Brookings, 1985), pp. 235–71.

10. Robert Maranto, "Political Ideology in the Higher Civil Service," a paper presented at the annual meeting of the Midwest Political Science Association, Chicago, April 1996, p. 12.

11. Mark Considine, "The Role and Significance of Strategic Core Reorganizations in the Australian Public Sector: Preliminary Findings," *International Journal of Public Sector Management* 6 (1993): 70. In another article, Considine noted that in both Australia and New Zealand, where extensive NPM reforms have been carried out, "the old civil service has now been largely demolished and . . . the new service is leaner but too narrow to function as anything more than an efficient instrument." Mark Considine, "Administrative Reform 'Down-Under': Recent Public Sector Change in Australia and New Zealand," *International Review of Administrative Sciences* 56 (1990): 183.

12. Paul C. Light, *The Tides of Reform: Making Government Work, 1945–1995* (Yale University Press, 1997), p. 51.

13. In the Canadian context, see Geoff Dinsdale, "The New Public Management and the Future Public Service: Push, Pull, Balance, and Beyond," *Canadian Public Administration* 40 (Summer 1998): 370–86.

14. William C. Plowden, "What Prospects for the Civil Service?" *Public Administration* 63 (Winter 1985): 408.

15. National Performance Review, *From Red Tape to Results: Creating a Government That Works Better and Costs Less* (Government Printing Office, 1993), p. 2.

16. In fact, the only piece of evidence that supports the notion that the loss of confidence is a consequence of administrative inadequacies is that when Americans are asked why they distrust government 80 percent say that it is because the government is inefficient and wastes money. This response is more likely the consequence of being primed by political rhetoric, news that focuses on waste, and talk show blather rather than being based on any actual experience. For these data, see Robert J. Blendon, John M. Benson, Richard Morin, Drew E. Altman, Mollyann Brodie, Mario Brossard, and Matt James, "Changing Attitudes in America," in Nye and others, p. 210. In fact, a recent survey shows that Americans rate civil servants more highly than the political institutions (see note 21). In surveying a variety of performance criteria in the United States, Derek Bok concludes, first, that "there is . . . little evidence to support the widespread impression that government inefficiency squanders huge amounts of money. . . ." and second, that "if large-scale waste exists, it probably results not so much from inefficient administration, as the public seems to believe, as from poorly designed programs." Derek Bok, "Measuring the Performance of Government" in Nye and others, pp. 62–63.

17. For a good summary of these findings, see Joseph S. Nye Jr., "Introduction: The Decline of Confidence in Government," in Nye and others, pp. 1–18. With regard to political polarization, see particularly David C. King, "The Polarization of American Parties and the Mistrust of Government," in Nye and others, and Richard E. Neustadt, "The Politics of Mistrust," in Nye and others, pp. 155–78, 179–201. With regard to the effects of democratization and loss of deferential attitudes, see Ronald Inglehart, "Postmaterialist Values and the Erosion of Institutional Authority," in Nye and others, pp. 217–36. With regard to economic anxieties, see Robert Z. Lawrence, "Is It Really the Economy, Stupid?" in Nye and others, pp. 111–32.

18. National Partnership for Reinventing Government, *Reinvention Express*, vol. 4, no. 5 (May 11, 1998), p. 1–2. The survey figures for data collected in late 1997 are 67 percent trusting federal workers and 16 percent trusting elected officials. In general, public confidence in government has risen substantially in a few years, from 21 percent in 1994 to 39 percent in 1997, although still far below the high figure of 76 percent in 1964. Nevertheless, once again the public rates the federal bureaucracy better than its political leaders. Of nineteen federal agencies assessed, for example, only one (not surprisingly, the Internal Revenue Service) was not rated favorably. At least six agencies had favorable ratings of 70 percent or higher. Finally, nearly 70 percent of the public had a favorable view of federal workers. And what is especially interesting is that even in 1981, 55 percent of the public held favorable opinions of federal workers (pp. 1, 2). In sum, there is little credible evidence that the public's negative view of government stems from a belief that administration is the source of its problems. Rather, performance in the domestic sphere and, to a lesser extent, judgments about the country's political leaders seem to drive these more general negative attitudes. The frustrations are more attributable to our politics than to the administration of government. The 1997 data are from "The Trust in Government Study," conducted by the Pew Research Center for the People and the Press. The 1981 findings are from a *Los Angeles Times* survey and reported in Pew Research

Center for the People and the Press, "Deconstructing Distrust: How Americans View Government," (www.people-press.org/trustrpt.htm).

19. Light, *Tides of Reform*, p. 180.

20. Kenneth J. Meier, "Bureaucracy and Democracy: The Case for More Bureaucracy and Less Democracy," *Public Administration Review* 57 (May/June 1997): 194.

21. As Derek Bok has put it, "Depending on one's conception of what an ideal society should be, different people can look at the same body of evidence and come away with radically different views of whether the nation has advanced or fallen back over the past thirty to forty years." Derek Bok, *The State of the Nation: Government and the Quest for a Better Society* (Harvard University Press, 1998), p. 9.

22. This, for example, is Paul Light's thesis. He argues that the tides of administrative reform have become more frequent and more contradictory and that the only thing predictable about them is the frequency of their rise and fall (Light, *Tides of Reform*, especially pp. 3–4 and p. 178).

23. Meier, "Bureaucracy and Democracy," p. 194.

24. Marver Bernstein, "The Presidency and Management Improvement," *Law and Contemporary Problems* 35 (Summer 1970): 515–16, as quoted in Light, *Tides of Reform*, p. 12.

25. Paul C. Light, *Thickening Government: Federal Hierarchy and the Diffusion of Accountability* (Brookings, 1995).

26. Terry Moe ("The Politicized Presidency," pp. 235–71) claims in a provocative essay that the president's main concern is exactly this.

27. A classic book in this regard is Victor A. Thompson, *Without Sympathy or Enthusiasm: The Problem of Administrative Compassion* (University of Alabama Press, 1975). See also Charles Goodsell, "Looking Once Again at Human Service Bureaucracy," *Journal of Politics* 43 (August 1981): 763–78, and Louis C. Gawthrop, "Democracy, Bureaucracy, and Hypocrisy Redux: A Search for Sympathy and Compassion," *Public Administration Review* 57 (May/June 1997): 205–10. Goodsell argues that bureaucrats are often caught between the limits of the law governing what they can do and what sympathetically they would like to do for their clients. A bureaucracy "without sympathy" conjures up Kafkaesque stereotypes, although the rules derive from externally originated laws. On the other hand, a bureaucracy with too much sympathy creates irregularity, lack of procedural standards, and therefore the likelihood of arbitrary and capricious decisionmaking, favoritism, and corruption. The balance is a difficult one to keep. Reinvention reforms suggesting that rules and procedures ought to be cut or deemphasized shift the balance precariously.

28. In a tragic incident in New Zealand known as "the Cave Creek tragedy," a viewing platform built under contract to the Department of Conservation collapsed, hurtling fourteen young people to their deaths and rendering another a tetraplegic. The extensive application of NPM reforms in New Zealand involving significant privatization, outsourcing, and performance contracting left a highly muddled system of accountability. The judge heading the subsequent commission of inquiry concluded that "the disaster

resulted from a 'pre-eminent' secondary cause of 'substantial systemic failure' . . . and that while a lack of money was not the cause of its [the viewing platform's] collapse, the platform had been 'conceived and built within a culture developed to do more with less.'" Ultimately, therefore, "the case of Cave Creek suggests that the [NPM] reforms have been less than completely successful in clarifying issues of political responsibility." See Robert Gregory, "Country Report—A New Zealand Tragedy: Problems of Political Responsibility," *Governance* 11 (April 1998): 232, 239.

29. The Pew Research Center for the People and the Press, *Deconstructing Distrust: How Americans View Government* (March 1998).

30. James Q. Wilson, *Bureaucracy: What Government Agencies Do and Why They Do It* (Basic Books, 1989), p. 342.

31. According to a survey by Louis Harris and Associates on April 15, 1998, (a day that lives in infamy year after year), "76 percent of Americans who have had direct contact with IRS employees said they were treated fairly." See Carol Marie Cropper, "Tangled Tale of the Oilman vs. the IRS—What a Senate Panel Wasn't Told at a Hearing," *New York Times*, August 2, 1998, sec. 3, p. 10.

32. Wilson, *Bureaucracy*, pp. 159–60.

33. Paul C. Light, *The True Size of Government* (Brookings, 1999).

Appendix

1. As in 1970, it was possible for several officials in the Career I sampling frame to hold positions of parallel rank within a single organizational unit. Following our procedure in 1970, in this case all of these officials were considered to be part of the sampling universe.

2. "There are two types of positions in the Senior Executive Service: career reserved and general. About half of the SES positions are designated in each category. Positions are designated career reserved when the need to ensure impartiality, or the public's confidence in the impartiality, of the Government requires that they be filled only by career employees (e.g., law enforcement and audit positions). [The general] category applies to all SES positions not designated as career reserved. General positions may be filled by career, noncareer, or limited appointment." See Senate Committee on Governmental Affairs, *United States Government Policy and Supporting Positions*, S-Rpt. 98-286, 98 Cong., 2 sess., December 31, 1984, appendix 3 (Senior Executive Service), p. 255.

3. Eighty-seven percent of the interviews were tape-recorded in 1970, 93 percent in 1986–87, and 90 percent in 1991–92. Interviewers took extensive notes when they could not tape.

Index

policy legacies, 168; Reagan Career II civil servants, 105

Directionless consensus, 12, 91

Diversity, 59–62, 85; Clinton goals, 39–40

Divided government: accountability and responsiveness, 11, 16, 90, 93–95; governmental control efforts, 95–96; ineffective, 177; management reform, 184–88; New Deal consensus, 29; NPR, 149; stability, 91

Downsizing, federal, 153–56

Educational attainment, 62–68, 85; of best and brightest, 68; Congress versus federal executive, 67; impact on federal executive, 65; quality of institutions attended, 65–68; quiet crisis, 164–65; specialized training, 67

Educational training, 71–72

Efficiency, 2; accountability and, 14; versus effectiveness, 17; political versus managerial, 160

Eisenhower, Dwight, 29

Employee empowerment, 140, 141; NPR goals for, 146

Family background of public servants, 79, 85

Federal executives, 24; age and tenure, 74; Bush administration, 38–39; careers, 72–78; Carter administration, 32–35; Clinton administration, 39–42; diversity, 59–62; educational attainment, 62–68; educational training, 71–72; family background, 79, 85; female, 61–62; future, 82–84, 85; interviewing, 190–93; morale of, 79–82, 86, 165–67; Nixon administration, 29–32; partisan complexion, 101–07; versus private executives, 66–71; Reagan administration, 35–38; recruits, 83–84; social status, 62–68; systemic problems versus personnel, 58–59. *See also* Civil

servants; Civil service; Political appointees

Federalist Papers (number *51*), 52

Federal "Political" Personnel Manual (Malek), 101, 128

Finer, Herman, 51

Ford, Gerald, 32–33

Frederickson, H. George, 147

Friedrich, Carl, 51

From Red Tape to Results (NPR), 22–23

General Accounting Office (GAO), 148; on agency goals, 151; on federal government measuring performance, 152; on GPRA, 150–51; on performance and budget, 152–53

Generalists versus specialists, 55–56

Germany, civil servants: and incoming administration, 131–32; preparation, 71

Gilbert, Charles, 92

Gore, Al, 15, 40, 58, 134

Gormley, William, 8

Government Performance and Results Act (GPRA) *1993*, 135; agency goal definition, 151; agency strategic planning, 152; budgeting, 148; dilemmas, 150–53; employee empowerment, 141, 146; program overlap, 151–52

Gray, Boyden, 38

Great Britain, civil servants: New Public Management, 136, 139, 174–75; performance agreements, 141; preparation, 71–72; responsiveness, 93; selection, 55–56

Great Society: New Deal legacy, 27; Reagan administration, 37–38

Guild systems, 73

Heclo, Hugh, 77, 126

Heritage Foundation, 96

Holmes, Malcolm, 137

Hood, Christopher, 137, 139